*and the Politics of
Race in the South*

DAVID DUKE

and the Politics of Race in the South

Edited by
John C. Kuzenski
Charles S. Bullock III
Ronald Keith Gaddie

Vanderbilt University Press
Nashville and London

Copyright © 1995 by Vanderbilt University Press
All Rights Reserved
First Edition 1995

95 96 97 98 99   5 4 3 2 1

This publication is made from recycled paper
and meets the minimum requirements of American National Standard
for Information Sciences—Permanence of Paper
for Printed Library Materials. ∞

Library of Congress Cataloging-in-Publication Data

David Duke and the politics of race in the South / edited by John C. Kuzenski,
Charles S. Bullock III, Ronald Keith Gaddie. -- 1st ed.
p.   cm.
Includes bibliographical references and index.
ISBN 0-8265-1266-6 (cloth : alk. paper)
1. Duke, David Ernest. 2. Louisiana--Politics and government--1951–
3. Louisiana--Race relations. I. Kuzenski, John C., 1964–   .
II. Bullock, Charles S. 1942–   . III. Gaddie, Ronald Keith.
F376.3.D84D38   1995
320.9763'09'049--dc20   95-20702
                                                                     CIP

Made in the United States of America

CONTENTS

List of Tables, Maps, and Figures   vii
Acknowledgments   ix
Introduction   xi

Part I: Backdrop to a Governor's Race

1 David Duke and the Nonpartisan Primary 3
   JOHN C. KUZENSKI

2 Messenger or Message?
   David Duke in the Louisiana Legislature 23
   KEITH BOECKELMAN, WILLIAM ARP III,
   AND BERNARD TERRADOT

3 David Duke and Social Science 35
   JOHN K. WILDGEN

Part II: David Duke and the Electorate

4 A Parish Profile of the David Duke Vote:
   Sociodemographic, Economic, and Voting
   Propensity Predictors 63
   STEPHEN J. CALDAS AND JOHN C. KILBURN

5 David Duke and the Electoral Politics of Racial Threat 88
   MICHAEL W. GILES AND MELANIE BUCKNER

6 The Candidacy of David Duke
   as a Stimulus to Minority Voting 99
   CHARLES S. BULLOCK III, RONALD KEITH GADDIE,
   AND JOHN C. KUZENSKI

Part III: The Aftermath

7	Race and the Republican Resurgence in the South: Success in Black and White? T. WAYNE PARENT	117
8	The Downfall of David Duke? Duke, Republicans, and the Structure of Elections in Louisiana RONALD F. KING, DOUGLAS D. ROSE, AND MATTHEW CROZAT	127
9	The White Knight Fades to Black: David Duke in the 1992 Presidential Campaign EUEL ELLIOTT AND GREGORY S. THIELEMANN	146
10	Epilogue	159
	Notes	165
	References	172
	List of Contributors	181
	Index	183

TABLES, MAPS, AND FIGURES

Tables

1.1	David Duke's Bids for Public Office	11
1.2	Party Competition in 1988 State Legislative Elections in Georgia and Louisiana	14
2.1	White Legislators' Support for Duke's Legislation	27
3.1	Regression of Duke's District 81 Vote on Dukakis's 1988 Presidential Vote	40
3.2	Regression of Duke District 81 on Clerk of Court and Sheriff Vote	42
3.3	Poll Results, September 1991	51
3.4	Logistic Regression Analysis of Edwards-Duke Preference	55
3.5	The Predicted Edwards / Duke Vote Shares	55
4.1	Duke Senate and Gubernatorial Primary and Runoff Elections	75
4.2	1991 Gubernatorial Primary: Economic and Demographic Profiles of Non-Duke and Duke Parishes	76
4.3	Standardized Regression Coefficients (Betas) of Effect of Independent Variables on Dependent Variables	77
4.4	1990 U.S. Senate Election: Economic and Demographic Profiles of Non-Duke and Duke Parishes	79
4.5	Duke Senate and Gubernatorial Primary and Runoff Elections: Zero-Order Correlation Coefficients	80
4.6	1991 Gubernatorial Runoff: Economic and Demographic Profiles of Non-Duke and Duke Parishes	81
5.1	Regression of White Mobilization for Duke and Bush on Black Registration and the Control Variables	94
5.2	Correlation Matrix among Dependent and Independent Variables	95

6.1	Registered Voter Turnout in Selected Elections in Louisiana, Georgia, and South Carolina	108
6.2	Models for Change in Black and White Turnout	112
8.1	October 1991 Gubernatorial Primary	132
8.2	March 1992 Presidential Primary	135
8.3	Exit Poll: How Voters in the 1992 Republican Presidential Primary Voted in the 1991 Gubernatorial Runoff	137
8.4	Exit Poll: How Voters in the November 1991 Gubernatorial Runoff Voted in the October Primary for Governor	139
9.1	David Duke's Performance in the 1992 Presidential Primary Season	153

Maps

3.1	Louisiana House District 81, Duke's Percentages in 1989	37
4.1	Cultural Regions of Louisiana	65
4.2	Voting Propensity	73
4.3	1991 Gubernatorial Runoff	74

Figures

3.1	Similarities in Duke and Dukakis Geography	40
3.2	Duke-Lee; Duke, Gegenheimer: Multiple Regression Model	41
3.3	Voting Patterns of New Orleans Legislators, 1989	46
3.4	Duke and Vitter: Different Geographies	48
3.5	Voting Patterns of New Orleans Legislators, 1992	49
3.6	Observed Groups and Predicted Probabilities	56

ACKNOWLEDGMENTS

◢

Scholars of southern politics form a comparatively small but extremely collegial group within the discipline of political science, and the editors would like to thank the authors who have contributed to this book for their fine work. The idea to compile this collection was engendered at the 1992 Southwestern Political Science Association meeting in Austin, Texas, from a panel that included a number of contributors. T. Wayne Parent was an excellent panel chair, and James Garand of Louisiana State University is to be thanked for his outstanding organization of the section under which our panel on David Duke sprang to life. Other chapters started out as papers—or ideas—from the Citadel Conference on Southern Politics, always a productive and collegial experience under the able direction of Robert Steed, Laurence Moreland, and Tod Baker.

Equally as important, the enthusiasm and efforts of Charles Backus, director, and Bard Young, editor, of Vanderbilt University Press provided an impetus to bring this work to its completion. Two referees commissioned by the Press offered invaluable comments on an earlier draft of the manuscript, and we are indebted to them, as well. Our respective institutions—Vanderbilt, Georgia, and Tulane—continued their proud traditions of supporting and encouraging compelling social science research. Early interest in the project was expressed by Margaret Dalrymple and by the staff of the Louisiana and Lower Mississippi Valley Collection of the Hill Memorial Library at Louisiana State University. John Kuzenski and Ronald Gaddie want to thank Professor Charles S. Bullock III for his years of thoughtful tutelage and friendship at the University of Georgia; we commonly hope, in our regular conversations with each other, to fulfill his expectations of and wishes for us in our own professional lives.

Finally, to our families, friends, confidantes, and colleagues, the editors of this volume would like to offer thanks and a special dedication for being such a vital part of our lives and works.

ACKNOWLEDGMENTS

∎

The authors would like to thank Wayne Parent, Thomas Langston, and the editors of this volume for their comments; the Murphy Institute of Political Economy and the Pew Foundation for their support; and Lee Shapiro, Director of Media Services for Voter Research and Surveys, for generously sharing his exit poll data with us.

INTRODUCTION

This volume presents some of the best current scholarship on David Duke and the resurgence of a more subtle, mainstream form of racism in contemporary southern politics. The efforts examine a variety of aspects about Duke and his politics, including his legislative activity in the Louisiana House of Representatives, the context of the Duke message, sources of electoral support, mobilization of a frustrated electorate, the "stealth Duke vote" (which went grossly underestimated at some times and similarly overestimated at others). These fine miniature portraits of different nuances of the Duke story blend into a larger, richer mosaic that goes beyond the "postgame commentary" or quasi-journalistic approach taken by a number of other available works on the subject. Our approach is the best way to understand completely the phenomenon at hand—which Duke did not, perhaps, create, but which in any case he skillfully exploited. This volume is divided into three parts, each focused on a distinct aspect of the Duke phenomenon but also carefully linked to the other parts in order to provide a logical exposition on the political rise and fall of the Grand Wizard of the Ku Klux Klan.

Part I, "Backdrop to a Governor's Race," focuses on the statewide ascent of Duke as a political force in Louisiana, and the types of mechanisms—institutional and otherwise—that made his rise possible. In chapter 1, "The Early Duke and Louisiana's Nonpartisan System," John C. Kuzenski provides background on Duke's past and Louisiana's unique system of open primary elections, referred to there as nonpartisan. Kuzenski argues that there is a link among the state's primary system, party identification, and Duke's meteoric rise to the status of serious candidate and offers a caveat to the dismissal "it can't happen here" that became common among non-Louisianians as they learned of Duke's success on the morning following the primary.

In chapter 2, "Messenger or Message? David Duke in the Louisiana Legislature," Keith Boeckelman, William Arp III and Bernard Terradot discuss David Duke from the institutional perspective of his three years in the Louisiana state legislature. Based on analyses of roll-call votes on legislation sponsored by Duke, as well as personal interviews with other legislators, they paint a picture of Duke as a cordial yet inherently disruptive member of the state House of Representatives who violated the norms of the institution. Opposition to his initiatives by other legislators (he passed one bill in three years) was closely related to the presence of large black populations in those members' districts. Legislators did not, the authors conclude, consider Duke "serious." Aside from his cordiality, he was widely perceived as a self-promoting attention-seeker who was not a reliable or effective colleague by traditional legislative measures.

In chapter 3, "David Duke and Social Science," John K. Wildgen addresses many of the problems professional pollsters and academics alike confront in trying to predict or explain the Duke vote. In the first gubernatorial primary in October 1991, Duke's candidacy was minimized by many observers as an "also-ran yahoo" type of campaign—not the first time in an election season that such a characterization had been made. When Duke entered the runoff against former Governor Edwin Edwards, many pollsters created devices to get at an alleged "hidden Duke vote," and thus pegged the race as too close to call. When Edwards won the runoff election by an overwhelming majority, Duke's candidacy once again confounded experts. Wildgen confronts two popular hypotheses that are used to excuse the previous failures of social science (and social scientists) to predict Duke's rise and fall: Duke was a product of the policies of the Reagan and Bush administrations, and Duke's strength was consistently underestimated by pollsters due to various forms of subterfuge (lying, unwillingness to respond, and so on) perpetrated by his followers—the so-called hidden Duke supporters. Correcting for the analytical errors of previous works, Wildgen argues that Duke's electoral success in 1989 derived from his pluck and skill, as well as the eccentricities of voters in his district in Metairie. The "hidden" Duke vote, however, is easily distilled from polling data using accepted statistical techniques; if pollsters had relied more on the tools of their trade, Wildgen argues, and less on ideology and obsession with the Duke persona, they would have more accurately predicted Duke's landslide loss to Edwards.

Part II of this work, "David Duke and the Electorate," analyzes the relationships between David Duke and various constituencies at the height of his popularity—the 1990 Senatorial and 1991 gubernatorial elections. In chapter 4, Stephen J. Caldas and John C. Kilburn provide "A Parish Profile of the David Duke Vote: Sociodemographic, Economic and Voting Propensity Predictors." This is a parish-level study of the Duke vote in three statewide elections, revealing that Republican candidate Duke derived much of his vote from what has traditionally been a very non-Republican base: less educated rural voters of lower socioeconomic status. In considering the significance of shifting party identification in the modern South, however, sociologists Caldas and Kilburn find that prior Republican voting propensity at the parish level is correlated with the level of support different parishes accorded Duke. Caldas and Kilburn's study is a fine, quantitatively compelling and theoretically interesting survey of the "nuts and bolts" of Duke's support, and it foreshadows the debate to come in part III—namely, did Duke's support come primarily from poorer, lower-status rural Democrats and independents, or did his voters consider themselves Republicans, engaging in a "white backlash" protest movement which the GOP has successfully used to encourage its growth in the post–Great Society South?

Michael W. Giles and Melanie Buckner, in chapter 5, examine the 1990 senatorial race in Louisiana, again at the parish level. "David Duke and the Electoral Politics of Racial Threat" focuses on Duke's ability to obtain white voter support. Although the findings are complementary with Caldas and Kilburn's, Giles and Buckner find that the "black threat" hypothesis, floated in a number of scholarly circles, contributed to Duke's success among whites. The likelihood of an outright Duke victory in this major statewide race, ironically, was nevertheless slim, because the numerous parishes from which Duke drew his strongest support were declining in population.

Charles S. Bullock III, Ronald Keith Gaddie, and John C. Kuzenski examine the impact of Duke's candidacy on bloc voter mobilization in chapter 6, "The Candidacy of David Duke as a Stimulus to Minority Voting." With a phenomenal turnout compared to most statewide primary or general elections, the 1991 Louisiana governor's runoff election attracted a remarkable 80 percent of registered voters to the polls. The perceived threat of Duke's election in 1991, the authors contend, resulted in a substantial mobilization of black voters, similar to that seen when black candidates appear on the ballot. Evidence of white countermobilization is present, but it does not necessarily represent backlash. Ironically, although one of Duke's stated goals was to "reduce the power of the liberal black caucus" in state affairs, his candidacy may have actually increased its pull. The new administration relied heavily on black support for its electoral success, and it provided the usual gratuities to key black political leaders as winning partners in the victorious election fight.

In part III, "The Aftermath," three contributions address the legacy of the David Duke phenomenon on the politics of Louisiana—with some important lessons about the region and the country, as well. These works trace the reasons for Duke's failure in the 1992 Republican presidential primary and place his rise and fall within the broader context of race and Republicanism in the South.

Chapter 7 uses the filter of party identification for the progression of its analysis. T. Wayne Parent's "Race and the Republican Resurgence in the South: Success in Black and White?" examines the broader disciplinary literature for clues to the existence of thematic racism in the Republican rise of the 1980s. Democrats found vindication in vanquished Republican governor Charles "Buddy" Roemer's assessment of Duke's runoff placement; Roemer contended that his loss to Duke was due, in part, to the power of racial messages and a "white code word" campaign approach in the successes of President Ronald Reagan. Parent concludes that although playing the race card contributed to the rise of the GOP in the South after 1964, the evidence of race as a sustaining force in the development of a regional two-party system is not clear. The future of a new, not always latent racism as a campaign tactic in modern southern politics "depends on whether it is nurtured by our political leadership."

In chapter 8, "The Downfall of David Duke? Duke, Republicans and the Structure of Elections in Louisiana," Ronald F. King, Douglas D. Rose and Matthew Crozat systematically examine the source of Duke's sizable vote in the 1991 gubernatorial election, contrasting it with his poor performance in the presidential Super Tuesday primary a scant four months later. Their analysis reveals that Duke's support in 1991 derived primarily from white Democrats. The use of the closed, partisan-preferential primary system in presidential elections was an impediment to voters who supported Duke. The authors demonstrate that pollsters and the mass media prematurely noted Duke's "loss" of support without considering the differences in the two electorates—and the two electoral systems. Duke did not lose support in March, they conclude, because he had none to lose—rather, he simply failed to make inroads with mainstream Republican voters. The contrast between chapters 7 and 8 will illuminate the nature of shifting political alliances and party strategies in the South, as well as the dangerous power of racism as an electoral tool for demagogues of either major party. The danger of such a tool is magnified when it is delivered by an admittedly polished messenger, and further so when it is dressed up to represent an allegedly mainstream and acceptable ideological movement.

As a conclusion, Euel Elliott and Gregory S. Thielemann examine the reasons behind the failure of David Duke's 1992 presidential bid. In chapter 9, "The White Knight Fades to Black: Duke in the 1992 Presidential Campaign," the authors contend that his candidacy collapsed because Duke was unable to establish the momentum necessary for the completion of a successful presidential campaign; furthermore, he was not able to raise sufficient funds to compete. The presence of presidential candidate and gadfly Patrick Buchanan played a substantial part, but the picture is more complex than laying of blame solely at Buchanan's feet (however much Buchanan wanted to take credit for Duke's political death). Of perhaps greater importance is that, at the time of the presidential campaign, Duke apparently failed to grasp the variation in the constituencies to which he was attempting to appeal. As he was not able to understand these variations, he could not adapt to the demands placed on him by the newer constituencies. Duke's failure to contest early primaries allowed Buchanan to seize the Louisianian's "natural constituency"—voters on the far right, frustrated by economic hard times—and become the Republicans' anti-Bush protest candidate.

The book closes with a brief epilogue that looks back over Duke's political life and casts a glance at his possible future. It considers his significance as both the remarkable, if ultimately ineffective, figure that he appeared to be and as the unremarkable, even typical, figure of racially motivated politics that made him unelectable and, at the same time, a staple of the American political scene.

PART I

Backdrop to a Governor's Race

1

David Duke and the Nonpartisan Primary

◤

John C. Kuzenski

Perhaps no other state in the United States has been blessed—or cursed—with the political notoriety that Louisiana has attained since its admission to the Union in 1812. Long before this current era of lottery fever, in which state governments desperately seek alternative revenue-generating devices, the notoriously corrupt Louisiana lottery of the early 1800s provided the early justification for many states to prohibit such gaming in their state constitutions. Rather than following the common-law tradition of the other forty-nine states, Louisiana's legal system is based on the Napoleonic Code, a form of statutory law dating back to some of the earliest French and Acadian communities that settled the state.

So, too, Louisiana has produced oddballs and demagogues, as well as a variety of otherwise extraordinary political figures of various ilks throughout its history. Confederate Attorney General Judah P. Benjamin, the only Jew to serve in high-level Confederate government, was by all historical measure one of the most brilliant and capable civilian leaders of that short-lived cause. The father of the Confederate Emancipation Proclamation (rejected by Jefferson Davis on the counsel of his other advisors), Benjamin is, however, one of the lesser known of Louisiana's political sons; brothers Huey and Earl Long probably strike a more familiar chord in the Bayou State observer.

Louisiana has, in the modern era, once again served as a breeding ground for such entities. Perhaps no other state politician in the country has captured the attention of party leaders, media, and individual citizens in the same manner as David Ernest Duke. As a student at Louisiana State University and a budding political activist in the 1970s, Duke quickly became well-known to south Louisiana locals for his vehement white supremacist stands, as well as his affiliation with local Ku Klux Klan and neo-Nazi organizations. During this era, when Duke was an occasional third-page story in the Baton Rouge *State-Times* and was unknown to the rest of the nation (save a fleeting early appearance on the *Donahue* television show to discuss "white power" movements), who could take him seriously? The profundity and irony of that question was not wholly to be felt until 1988. In the fall of that year, Duke declared himself a Republican primary candidate in a special election to fill the seat of the eighty-first Legislative District.

By that time, Louisiana had experienced slightly more than a decade with one of its most recent institutional oddities, the nonpartisan open primary. In 1975, the state legislature adopted the system at the behest of then-Governor Edwin W. Edwards.[1] Initially, Edwards and several incumbent Democratic legislators excitedly embraced the nonpartisan primary bill as a way to level the playing field between themselves and their Republican opposition. In the early 1970s, it became increasingly apparent that Democrats were facing two great battles during election season—one in the primary, against each other, and another in the general election, against a Republican candidate who enjoyed increasing support from white voters. Although the nonpartisan primary did not always work the way Edwards and the Louisiana Democratic party envisioned it (Kuzenski, 1994; Lamis, 1988), it survived a number of legislative challenges and remains the central feature of statewide election law.

This essay provides background information on David Duke and Louisiana's nonpartisan primary, both of which have been described as "odd products" of the Bayou State. A more-than-peripheral understanding of them may clarify important points brought up by the other contributions contained in this volume. There is a dearth of available literature on the interaction between Duke and the nonpartisan primary—that is to say, to what extent the primary system might have affected the Duke candidacy, and whether it is a phenomenon that is truly unique to Louisiana.

Duke the Person and the Politician

David Ernest Duke was born July 1, 1950, to U.S. Army Major David H. Duke and his wife, Maxine. He was the younger of two children, his sister, Dorothy, having been born five years earlier. Duke's early childhood was marked by the efforts of his father to "personally see to it that his daughter and son would be raised as he had been, with strict, conservative Christian values" (Zatarain, 1990: 60). Raised in suburban—and segregated—New Orleans, Duke attended a number of all-white schools. Still, in his early experiences with the race issue, according to Michael Zatarain (1990), he defended the civil rights movement and desegregationist positions in his academic papers and other assignments. Duke's first exposure to the more reactionary elements that he would later become notorious for defending appears to have been in 1964. While researching a school paper on integration, he learned of and later started attending meetings of the Citizens' Council (more commonly known as the White Citizen's Council), a white supremacist group formed a decade earlier in Mississippi. The founder of the Louisiana wing of the organization was Plaquemines Parish political boss Leander Perez, a noted anti-semite and anti-civil rights figure.

As a result of his experiences with the Citizens' Council, Duke worked for Barry Goldwater's presidential campaign, which was also under way that year; he began to spend significant amounts of time in the Council library, reading racist texts and absorbing the Council's segregationist attitudes. His increasing dedication to the Council was, in all likelihood, a reaction to a deteriorating situation at home; Dorothy and his father were increasingly alienated from and embittered toward each other, and Maxine began withdrawing from the family after losing her sister in an airplane crash. The Citizens' Council was a warm, receptive environment for the young David Duke:

In one year he had gone from a liberal, humanist viewpoint on race to a basic outlook that there are profound racial differences that affect the whole social fabric. Participation in the Goldwater campaign whet his appetite for current affairs and history. Over the next year, he would relate his newly found racial view to history, politics, and social policy. (Zatarain, 1990: 82)

Duke had joined a New Orleans chapter of the Knights of the Ku Klux Klan before leaving John F. Kennedy High School. After graduating from high school and holding a handful of menial jobs, Duke enrolled at Louisiana State University in 1968; by this time, he had also become more vehement in his racial views. He entered the Reserve Officers Training Corps at LSU (compulsory for male undergraduates at the time), which did little to moderate his increasingly militant views toward society and politics. Duke quickly gained notoriety in the turmoil of the late sixties as being one of the campus' most outspoken right-wingers. At the beginning of his sophomore year, having read American Nazi leader George Lincoln Rockwell's *White Power*, Duke began aligning himself with the National Socialist Liberation Front; his repeated vociferous appearances at LSU's Free Speech Alley and subsequent participation on a local radio talk show turned him into something of a notorious celebrity in and around Baton Rouge.

Thus was born the "public" David Duke in southern Louisiana. More in-depth Duke biographies (Bridges, 1994; Zatarain, 1990) recount in great detail the time between his racist "coming out party" in local media and his first attempt for elected office, in 1975. This essay is more concerned with understanding Duke as a politician, in particular as his decisions to run for office and his electoral chances may have been influenced by Louisiana's nonpartisan primary system. The question that engendered this approach has been presented to virtually every political commentator interviewed by Louisiana and national media on the Duke phenomenon: Could it happen anywhere, or is it a unique facet of Bayou State politics?

The Louisiana Nonpartisan Primary: Endorsements and Renegades

In a nonpartisan primary, candidates for elected office are placed on the same ballot, regardless of party affiliation (or lack of it), and voters choose the candidate of their preference from this single list of names. Regardless of whether a jurisdiction uses a majority or plurality election rule, one election can produce a victor. This system may significantly reduce the number of elections required to determine a winner. In a traditional primary system, the parties must hold their own contests, which may include a runoff to determine the party nominee.Only then do the canddidates face the nominee of the other party in the general election.² Although the nonpartisan process is streamlined, it presents a pitfall that does not exist in traditional systems; it does not guarantee both major parties representation in the runoff, which would be otherwise considered the general election.

In Louisiana, the majority-rule nonpartisan primary is the cornerstone of the state's election law. To win office, a candidate must either receive a simple majority of the vote against all other opponents in the first election, or must face the candidate with the next highest vote total in a runoff so as to produce a majority vote for one candidate.³ The origins of the shift to nonpartisan elections in Louisiana extend back to the 1971 gubernatorial campaign of Edwin W. Edwards. After fighting a bitter Democratic primary and runoff battle under the traditional majority-rule system, Edwards had been left financially and spiritually battered by the rigors of party infighting, and he eked out a general election win over Republican David C. Treen with only 57 percent of the vote.

Although according to conventional political wisdom, this is an appreciable margin of victory, it was certainly not viewed that way by the Louisiana Democratic party or Edwards himself; whereas 1.2 million people had voted in the Democratic primary, slightly more than ten thousand had participated in the Republican contest. After winning the GOP primary with 9,732 votes, Treen lost the general election with slightly less than half a million votes. Clearly, for Democratic party strategists, the draining of campaign resources that typified bitter interparty primary battles—to say nothing of the verbal battering that a primary winner and party nominee could suffer from the loser—was costing the party dearly in crossover votes in the general election (Kuzenski, 1994).

Upon assuming office, Edwards began pushing for the adoption of nonpartisan primary legislation. He told the Baton Rouge *State-Times* that such a system would save money and would cut out the "bitterness and hatred which Republicans have been able to do after our primaries, sitting back as scavengers" while Democrats fought among themselves for the honor of facing a lone GOP challenger (Lamis, 1988: 113).[4] The Republican, meanwhile, would marshal resources during the primary campaign while Democrats attacked each other unmercifully in the primary and runoff elections. Legislators resoundingly approved Edwards's plan, by a vote of 33–2 in the Senate and 92–10 in the House (Kazee, 1983). The bill, which became Act I of the 1975 state legislature, may have been viewed as much an "incumbent protection act" as a time and money saver; there is, in any case, little doubt that Louisiana Democrats thought of it as a way to level the playing field on which they and a small but growing Republican organization did battle.

The Louisiana Republican party immediately began preparing for that battle. The party's ranks were bolstered by a sudden influx of former Democratic voters and politicians, and while Democratic defections were nothing new to the South during this time (Lamis, 1988; Black and Black, 1987), Louisiana experienced a heightened effect. Concerning the increased rate of attrition in the Louisiana Democratic party's ranks after 1975, state Democratic chair James Brady (1990) confirmed a point of V. O. Key (1956) about the binding nature of the majority in one-party dominant systems. In an interview, he said:

> When that [nonpartisan primary] bill was introduced, we knew it would cause a large number of Democrats to become Republicans. . . . We've always had a Republican wing of the state Democratic Party, but they were so small and so weak. They knew if they switched, they wouldn't be able to . . . get anywhere in Louisiana politics. But with the adoption of that bill, yes, attrition came true.

At the same time, the leadership of the Louisiana GOP began experimenting with an endorsement procedure that was designed to propel a candidate of the party's choosing into a runoff under the nonpartisan system. The idea was simple: if the party selected one candidate for each office and used the devices at its disposal to dissuade other Republicans from challenging the designated party candidate, the solid and growing Republican bloc vote might be enough to insure at least a second-place finish (and thus a runoff position) to the anointed

Republican, thus avoiding a Democrat-versus-Democrat runoff election. If the party could capitalize on Democratic infighting, as it did in the 1971 gubernatorial contest, a Republican in the runoff would stand a decent chance of winning the office.

Formal preprimary candidate endorsement by a southern state party organization is rare. On the one hand, according to Charles Schroeder (1990), former Democratic party director of Georgia, there are general concerns that endorsement will alienate party voters who favor other candidates. On the other hand, a dilemma specifically for southern party organizations, there is the ever-present threat of a lawsuit or other judicial action arising under the Voting Rights Act. One intended target of the act was the Bourbon Democratic machine (old-line members of the antebellum southern "planter class") in many southern states, which attempted to circumvent earlier civil rights legislation (such as the Civil Rights Act and the fourteenth Amendment) by creating new devices to disfranchise black voters. Popular qualifications tests, such as character or literacy tests, are perhaps the best known of these tricks; the Arkansas "white primary" is a lesser known but equally nefarious one. Courts have been sensitive in the past to plaintiffs' arguments about the discriminatory nature of such devices, and the endorsement mechanism is generally perceived by Democratic leaders as one more practice that opens the door to a divisive and undesirable discrimination suit. As such, Schroeder maintains, the best defense against such a scenario is to avoid preprimary endorsements; after all, one cannot sue for relief from what does not exist.

Despite these concerns, the Louisiana Republican party moved ahead in formalizing the endorsement mechanism in their bylaws; the fact that southern *Democratic* party practices have traditionally invited the most scrutiny from the U.S. Department of Justice, because of the large number of black voters in that party, may have provided the Republicans with an advantage. As such, the potential benefit of endorsing a single candidate to represent the GOP in a given election greatly outweighed the relatively slim chance that black plaintiffs would care to challenge the practices of a party to which they did not belong. Between 1975 and 1985, the general perception among the leaders of both major parties in Louisiana was that the "resting buzzard" scenario had made a comeback under the nonpartisan primary system; whereas several Democrats battled each other on level ground and split the party faithful vote, a single Republican candidate, with a party endorsement, used the increasingly solid GOP bloc vote as a stepping-stone to the runoff election (Kuzenski, 1994). For many Republican candidates, such as David Treen, placement in the runoff and ultimate victory included a significant number of Democratic crossover and independent votes.

In 1985, the Louisiana Democratic State Central Committee (DSCC) codified its own endorsement process in an attempt to cut down on the number of Democrats running for key offices. It ran the risk of inviting a Voting Rights Act related lawsuit by doing so, but apparently the committee calculated that black Louisiana Democrats would recognize the beneficial effect to the party at large and would not challenge the practice as discriminatory de facto—a calculation that seems to have proven correct.[5] By providing fewer candidates from which the faithful could choose, it was hoped, the most viable or accomplished candidate (in the preprimary judgment of the endorsing body) would be better able to garner votes. As such, the chosen Democrat could enter a runoff with a commanding lead, if not win the office outright, on the first ballot.

Section 15(b) of the Louisiana Democratic party's constitution and bylaws provides that "no member of the DSCC shall use the name of the Committee in opposing a candidate who has been endorsed by the DSCC," yet there are few sanctions to control so-called renegade candidates who refuse to recognize the party's endorsement as sufficient reason to stay out of a particular race. This brings up another problem for the state party, which has been characterized as substantially less organized and disciplined than its Republican counterpart (Grosser, 1982). Theoretically, the party could move to ostracize renegade candidates, or withhold campaign funds or advisory expertise from their future bids for office; however, in an era of easily accessible campaign contributions and political consultants, these are not potentially deadly threats (Mahe and Kayden, 1985; Crotty, 1980). Although the Republican endorsement procedure is a similarly toothless tiger, the smaller, more organized, and more homogenous nature of the party has traditionally allowed it to make more successful appeals to abstract values such as "the good of the party" in controlling the actions of its members (Theodoulou, 1985; Grosser, 1982). As such, Louisiana

Democrats have had more of a problem with renegade candidates in a primary system where renegades are less easily controlled.

This pattern underwent a radical and profound change with the emergence of David Duke as a statewide political force. In 1975 and 1979, shortly after Louisiana's adoption of the nonpartisan primary, Duke ran for political office as a Democrat (see table 1.1). His race-baiting quasi-populism was not a particularly new phenomenon in the Louisiana Democratic party and, after more than a decade under the Voting Rights Act, the state party organization was changing in a way that made Duke more undesirable to Democratic identifiers. As such, and perhaps because the party organization and Duke's own primary opponents were accustomed to dealing with elements of a maverick fringe, his early bids for the state senate were easily dismissed.

Table 1.1
David Duke's Bids for Public Office

	Office	Party	Outcome
1975	16th Louisiana Senate	Democrat	def. by (D) incumbent
1979	10th Louisiana Senate	Democrat	def. by (D) incumbent
1988	President of U.S.	Indep. Populist	lost; no electoral votes
1989	81st Louisiana House	Republican	won
1990	U.S. Senate	Republican	def. by (D) incumbent
1991	Governor of Louisiana	Republican	def. by (R) incumbent
1992	President of U.S.	Republican	def. by (R) incumbent

Source: compiled by the author, with data from Zatarain (1990); Louisiana Office of the Secretary of State (Elections Division); and the Jefferson Parish (La.) Office of the Registrar of Voters.

After being rejected in his first two bids for public office, within four years of each other in different senate districts, Duke went into a nine-year hiatus from campaigns while he pursued his interests with the Ku Klux Klan and similar organizations. When he reemerged in 1988 to run for the presidency, it is likely that he realized that party affiliation would not have much impact on his fate. Duke's limited political support had seemingly always been centered around the person instead of the party, and as such, he enjoyed about the same amount of success in his bid for president as an independent populist as he did running for the state senate under the Democratic label.

Within one year after his publicity campaign for president, however, David Duke found an interesting accommodation in his newly proclaimed affiliation with the Louisiana Republican party. Race-issue stands had been central to the growth of the party in the South since the 1960s, whether veiled behind southerners' generally more conservative value systems or, in their more overt forms, as a backlash against the national Democratic party for its support of civil rights and voting rights legislation (Lamis, 1988; Black and Black, 1987). Considering the Democratic party's great popularity among newly enfranchised black voters, Duke—the perpetual opportunist—either saw or stumbled onto the opportunity to combine his traditional white racist support with a more mainstream brand of conservatism found in the right wing of the Grand Old Party.[6] While the former element of this coalition offered him loyal votes, the latter provided a legitimizing base from which Duke could enter into traditional two-party politics. The importance of having that base, in turn, was that "regular" Republicans could respond to Duke's disguised but still racially charged message without feeling as if they had joined the ranks of Louisiana antiregimists or abandoned the party.[7] The size and relative importance of these elements within the Duke coalition will be discussed briefly here, and more extensively by Stephen Caldas and John Kilburn in chapter 4 of this volume, but their combined electoral punch was profound.

The conditions within the state Republican party were ripe for exploitation—it was an expanding organization with a growing record of electoral victories within the state. It had little or no experience with disposing of renegade candidates, for, given its traditional cadre-like discipline of educated, wealthy, and upper-crust voters and candidates, party rules were followed as part of the gentleman's agreement that characterized its early development. With its devotion to conservative principles, which included racial issues, the Louisiana GOP experienced the two kinds of growth found in other southern states (Lamis, 1988; Black and Black, 1987). On the one hand, the emerging white southern middle class was attracted largely by economic concerns but also brought racial issues such as affirmative action programs and busing into its political world view. This class represented the visible growth in the Louisiana Republican party, and it was welcomed by the party leadership. On the other hand, there were apolitical people from poor, rural, less educated backgrounds for whom racial issues were more pronounced in their political thinking; some may have been Democrats through informal self-identification, while others thought little or nothing of politics and found no reason to participate in the electoral process (see chapter 4). This was the "stealth growth" in the party, unnoticed and largely innocuous in most elections, until David Duke came along and gave these people reason to activate their newfound political passions. While it is a point of contention among scholars as to what extent Duke's success is attributable to these different groups of "nouveau Republicans" (see chapters 7 and 8), there appears to be little doubt that both groups were factors in Duke's success.

The question remains as to how Duke's Republican identification may have helped him to fight the nonpartisan primary battle. His kind of Democratic supporters were, by the late eighties, his kind of Republican supporters, regardless of what their voter identification cards may have said.[8] They were more likely to be joined by other Republican sympathizers than by Democratic loyalists, if only the campaign message could be made more acceptable and mainstream; Duke, a charismatic man by all accounts, could also play off of and invoke the charismatic image of such modern Republican heroes as Ronald Reagan, despite the fact that they either did not endorse or flatly condemned his brand of conservatism. Because of the growth of black voting power in the Democratic party and the state party's closer alignment with national Democratic policies, the fire-and-brimstone renegade Democrat was quickly becoming an endangered species across the South and in Louisiana (Goldfield, 1990; Black and Black, 1987). Yet, how would a renegade Republican—a term heretofore unknown in Louisiana—fare under the nonpartisan primary system?

The Politician, the Party, and the Primary: Making Connections

In order to put the Duke-as-Republican phenomenon into proper context against the backdrop of Louisiana's nonpartisan primary, it is necessary to examine the effect nonpartisan elections may have had on party competition in general within the state. Table 1.2 provides a cursory examination of state legislative elections data, broken down by party, in Louisiana compared to Georgia, a partisan primary state, for the year 1988.[9]

Table 1.2
Party Competition in the 1988 State Legislative Elections in Georgia and Louisiana

	Georgia	Louisiana
(D) candidates, as percentage of all primary candidates	78%	72%
(R) candidates, as percentage of all primary candidates	22%	24%
(D) primary unopposed	56%	20%
(R) unopposed	11%	2%
percentage unopposed candidates, primary and general election	49%	22%
(D) unopposed, both elections, percentage of all races	43%	20%
(R) unopposed, both elections, percentage of all races	6%	2%
races requiring primary runoff election	7%	33%
average number of candidates (all parties) in primary	1.42	3.04
percentage republican in legislature (both chambers)	10%	15%

Source: compiled by the author, from data provided by the Louisiana Department of Elections, and Bullock (1988).

Although a host of intervening variables may affect the results of a larger study of the nonpartisan primary system, this compilation of data nevertheless produces some interesting observations. For example, the number of Republican candidacies for office in Louisiana does not vary dramatically from that of Georgia, nor does the number of Republican legislators, yet competition for seats in Louisiana seems much more heated. More than two-thirds of all primaries in Georgia feature uncontested candidates, whereas just over a fifth are unopposed in Louisiana. While this may not be attributable to the nonpartisan primary per se, the substantially higher percentage of contested races in the Bayou State makes it more fertile ground for dark-horse candidacies. The more candidates in a given race, the more fragmented the vote becomes; the more fragmented the vote, in turn, the easier it is for such candidates to win or place in a plurality vote, which is all that is required to move forward to the runoff—which, in Louisiana, is the general election.

The average number of candidates in all parties for Louisiana's legislative elections is more than twice that of Georgia's. Perhaps this is indicative of the power of coalition voting in nonpartisan races; more candidates in the race means a heightened importance for relatively small voting blocs, and in a self-fulfilling prophecy, more candidates thus enter the race to pit their blocs against those of all other comers. One may interpret these results in a best-case scenario for both parties. For Louisiana Democrats, the nonpartisan primary opens up the possibility of two members of the party facing each other in the general election—a win-win situation as far as the party is concerned. For Louisiana Republicans, the larger number of candidates in these races engendered by Democrats' traditional free-for-all approach to party discipline (Grosser, 1982) means that even the most modest of GOP candidacies can move to the general election if the party bloc vote remains solid (Kazee, 1983). This may explain why 71 percent of Louisiana Republican officials—and 46 percent of their Democratic counterparts—believed that the nonpartisan system would "provide a stimulus for the growth of the Louisiana Republican Party" in a study by Hadley (1985).

While Republican electoral fortunes are widely perceived to have benefitted from the nonpartisan system as a result of the vote-splitting phenomenon, it is similarly true that dark-horse candidates also appear to have gained. David Duke, an old-time dark horse and a new convert of the Republican faith, appears to have experienced an advantage on both counts. On the three occasions Duke has sought political office as a Republican in Louisiana—his Eighty-first Legislative District victory for a seat in the Louisiana House of Representatives in 1989, his narrow U.S. Senate loss to incumbent J. Bennett Johnston in 1990, and his tempestuous gubernatorial bid in 1991—he benefitted from two specific factors as a fringe candidate trying to make his way into the political mainstream. First, Duke had discovered the legitimizing benefits of belonging to a major party, the Republicans. In addition, his campaigns exploited the open and potentially explosive nature of Louisiana's nonpartisan primary system by bringing together a bloc of voters that could hold together for at least one election and place him in a runoff—one step away from the office.

Other chapters in this collection contain studies of the nature of Duke's coalition. In chapter 4, Caldas and Kilburn conclude that, at the parish level, Republican voting propensity is an important indicator of Duke's success in various parts of the state, whereas in chapter 7 Parent argues, from a slightly different but complementary tack, that racism within the Republican party attached many of these voters to the Duke bandwagon. In chapter 8, Rose, King, and Crozat offer powerful evidence that the key element in Duke's vote was not "regular" Republican support, but rather an influx of traditionally Democratic, conservative white votes. Using exclusively the lens of party identification, there is little doubt that Duke attracted large numbers of Democratic voters: Republicans in today's Louisiana cannot meet with Duke's level of success without them.[10]

What chapter 4 and chapter 7 do, respectively, is incorporate and recognize a broader spectrum of research on practical politics in the modern South. Many of Duke's Democratic crossover voters are such in party affiliation only. They are, by and large, the lower income, less-educated, more rural, and more reactionary conservative white voters who have long since abandoned their King Cotton Democratic voting days; their party loyalties, to the extent that such may exist, now firmly reside with the Republicans in national elections (Black and Black, 1992, 1987). That they may still vote Democratic in local elections is more often based on personal familiarity with the candidate or his or her ideological record than on the party he or she claims to represent. Except in black-majority districts, Louisiana produces few liberal public officials. Were it not for these locally popular Democrats, and perhaps the permissive crossover voting atmosphere of Louisiana's nonpartisan system, which effectively eliminates the need to vote a straight party ticket, such voters would feel more compelled to register as Republicans. As it is, conservative Democrats can pick and choose among candidates of both parties at will, save in presidential primaries.

Duke may have entered politics initially as a Democrat because he wanted to be on the winning team; as V. O. Key (1956) has pointed out, this tends to be the norm in one-party dominant systems. Because of the rich pool of experienced candidates within that party, Duke was an also-ran in Democratic bids for office, as more conventional and widely accepted candidates prevented a fragmentation of the vote. The Louisiana GOP of the late eighties, in contrast, offered Duke a unique blend of advantages. The party had enjoyed immense growth among southern voters in recent years, but it was nevertheless too young to have a stable of experienced candidates running for public office. As such, the Republican party provided David Duke with both a major party label and even political ground on which to compete with other Republicans for notoriety as a mainstream candidate.

In writing on Duke's candidacy for the U.S. Senate in 1990, Douglas Rose (1992: 192) comments that "non-Louisiana reactions seem most to stress that Duke would be labeled 'unacceptable' rather quickly in other locales. Perhaps." The author implies that somehow and somewhere else, those who take the "can't happen here" attitude toward the success of a candidate of Duke's background and political baggage may find themselves surprised by the viability of such a candidate in their own districts. While this is a noteworthy caveat in Rose's essay, he nevertheless misses a more compelling point: is it possible that Duke's successes *are* unique to Louisiana, not because of the presence or absence of any sort of labeling, but instead as a result of Louisiana's nonpartisan primary?

At least one exploration of the Duke phenomenon has explained it as a creation, by and large, of mass media (Bridges, 1994). Media paid little attention to Duke until he presented a serious challenge to J. Bennett Johnston in the 1990 Senate race; the amount of coverage Duke received during the 1991 gubernatorial race soared after he won a place in the runoff election. Few, if any, fringe candidates in other states have been the subject of such a media blitz, even after winning a spot in a traditional primary runoff. In other states, however, runoffs featuring traditional versus untraditional candidates overwhelmingly result in the victory of the former, who only then goes on to the final battle—the general election. In Louisiana's nonpartisan system, the first election is potentially the one for all the marbles. It was thus Duke's proximity to an actual victory that explains much of the attention with which he was showered, and in turn, the attitude in other states that it could not happen there. Perhaps, as Rose accurately qualifies that attitude, it could indeed happen; it is, nevertheless, a much safer utterance outside Louisiana than within as a result of the streamlined electoral process of the nonpartisan primary system.

What would the Duke legacy have been under traditional primary rules? Willis Hawley (1973) maintains, based on his study of municipal nonpartisan elections in the United States, that the pattern of party control of offices does not differ dramatically under a nonpartisan system than would be expected under a partisan one. It is uncomfortably speculative to assume that a Duke victory—and possibly even a spot in the general election—could have occurred under a traditional partisan (Republican) primary. While Duke captured an impressive 49.9 percent of all votes cast for a Republican candidate in the 1991 gubernatorial election, his total was bolstered by registered Democrats who would not have been able to vote in the Republican primary on election day—at least, not without switching parties and thus disqualifying themselves from voting for favored Democratic candidates in other races closer to home. Duke's failure in the 1992 Louisiana Republican presidential race—a traditional closed primary—seems to bear out this point (see chapters 8 and 9). The chances are thus too great that removal of Duke's Democratic supporters in a partisan primary would have significantly reduced his vote totals, perhaps even to the point where Charles ("Buddy") Roemer would have placed first among Republicans.

There also remains some debate surrounding the vote for Congressman Clyde Holloway, the Republican endorsee, who captured only 5 percent of the total vote and 8 percent of the Republican vote on election day. Had Louisiana operated a partisan primary system with a majority vote requirement, as do most southern states, many speculate that Holloway's vote could have split evenly between Duke and Roemer in a runoff. This would have provided Duke with the few extra votes needed to claim a position against Edwin Edwards in the general election. I am unconvinced by this argument on two counts. First, Duke's weighty Democratic crossover support would have been excluded from the initial vote. In addition, much of Holloway's vote outside of his congressional district appears to have come from the loyal Republican core that felt duty-bound to support the party's official nominee. Had Holloway not entered the first primary, or had he failed to make a partisan runoff primary, Roemer would have enjoyed the party's endorsement, captured most of the minuscule Holloway vote, and given the state Republican party the time it needed between a primary election and a runoff to marshal its anti-Duke forces on behalf of another Republican—Roemer—instead of Democrat Edwin Edwards.[11]

In stepping back from what could have been in the 1991 gubernatorial election, I return to the effect of Duke's Republican party affiliation as he faced a nonpartisan primary election. While Hawley's study (1973: 31) of eighty-eight nonpartisan cities concluded "that nonpartisanship enhances the electability of Republicans," the advantage was significantly less than had been hypothesized. Research on the Louisiana system indicates that while fewer state legislative seats have been challenged by Republicans since the adoption of the nonpartisan primary (Kazee, 1983), there has not been a significant statistical decrease in the likelihood of Republicans being elected (Theodoulou, 1985). In gubernatorial races, the number of Republicans running has increased since adoption of the nonpartisan primary, but usually there has been only one, anointed or endorsed to face a sea of Democrats.[12]

Republican party strategists seem to have learned and practiced for a number of years the rule proposed by Thomas Kazee (1983: 137) following an analysis of the 1979 David Treen–Louis Lambert gubernatorial election:

> Republican candidates are more likely to win in the first open election or advance to the runoff when their party remains unified and Democratic multiple candidacies fragment a decidedly Democratic electorate. . . . Conversely, Republican chances decrease significantly when more than one Republican enters the open election, or when Democrats unite behind a single candidate.

Operating on this assumption, Republican leaders have moved to solidify the inviolability of the endorsement mechanism among their candidates (Kuzenski, 1994). In order to capitalize on the party's growing popularity and make it successful even while in the minority, ironically, it invites greater numbers of the heretofore silent or apolitical fringe to run for office as Republicans and capitalize on the party's historically stable bloc vote.[13] The Republican bloc vote, in concert with the endorsement mechanism, is largely responsible for the appearance of two-party competition in Louisiana. Unfortunately for the state's Republican leadership, it may prove the party's undoing in the immediate future, as the mavericks who once cluttered Democratic ranks and split Democratic votes move in to get their share of the Republican fortune. The most appropriate analogy is that of a person who has few friends until he wins the lottery. As GOP fortunes increase, the party regulars may still adhere to the niceties and requirements of the endorsement mechanism; newfound companions like

David Duke, however, find no reason to follow the rules as long as they are able to crash the victory party with a coalition that includes voters who feel no particular allegiance to party elites or those elites' preferred candidates.

Duke's thinly veiled racist message, in its new and more acceptable mainstream wrapper, bound together such a coalition. It is perhaps most accurately described as a kind of "Republican proletariat"—an amalgam of fringe and conventional party supporters—conservative, working-class whites who primarily voted for either Duke the Imperial Wizard or Duke the ultraconservative Republican. Regardless of the Duke persona for which they voted, however, each vote moved him closer to overtaking Buddy Roemer on primary night and putting him in the runoff. In the end, the two candidates with the strongest coalition votes remained—Edwards on the strength of enhanced black turnout (which got even stronger in the runoff—see chapter 6), and Duke on the strength of his rebels.

Being one election away from the governorship at that point, Duke may have counted on the anti-Edwards vote to push him on to victory. In so doing, however, he may have underestimated the power of the anti-Duke vote when it came time for the electorate to take Duke seriously. The legitimacy of the Duke candidacy, nevertheless, was established in the minds of Louisiana's voters and in the national media by the fact that an unlikely candidate with no experience outside his local district had been largely successful, and that a former Ku Klux Klan leader and American Nazi was one step away from becoming Louisiana's chief executive.

Ultimately, the nonpartisan primary may have worked in concert with Republican party affiliation in Louisiana and the candidate's media status to enhance Duke's position as a viable contender, even if Kazee's and Theodoulou's individual studies are correct in finding that, as an independent variable, the system has little effect on GOP electoral fortunes. Perhaps Bullock and Johnson (1992) make an even clearer point along these lines in their discussion of a dual-primary (majority rule runoff) system. Such a system, they contend, is an easily understood device among voters which reduces the likelihood of a Condorcet winner, given the multiple electoral barriers that stand in the way of political dark horses. Although Louisiana uses a majority rule in its nonpartisan primary system, the removal of that extra barrier of a preelection partisan primary allows candidates who can incorporate fringe support into a broader alliance with major-party regulars to get noticeably—some might remark uncomfortably—close to victory. Under a nonpartisan plurality rule, David Duke would have been less than 32,000 first-primary votes from becoming the most notable Condorcet winner in recent southern political history.

CONCLUSION: NONPARTISAN ELECTIONS AND THE PERILS OF PLURALISM

Having distanced themselves from the implementation of the nonpartisan primary for roughly two decades, Louisiana politicians now better understand both causes and effects of the system. Ironically, as Hadley (1985) reports, what began as a Democratic initiative to protect Democratic seats and interests appealed by 1984 to only 46 percent of that party's leadership, whereas 86 percent of the Republican leadership believed the system should be kept. That survey was taken, however, years before David Duke entered the state's Republican ranks and brought with him from the Democratic front lines hordes of ideologically charged and politically alienated lower-class white voters. Although the old guard of the Louisiana Republican party thus tends to favor so-called mainstream conservative candidates, they have learned the dangers of expanding the party through open invitation—a lesson which has been historically reserved, since at least the 1960s, for southern Democrats. Brady (1990) comments on the new Republican dilemma:

I see a real problem coming about for them. [The nonpartisan primary] is allowing the extremes to make the runoff, like David Duke. . . . Republicans will have more problems with it than Democrats, as we've already seen. It allows single-issue "dark horse" candidates to get into a runoff and possibly prevail, [and]. . . . Louisiana is a very conservative state, leading back to 1948 and the rise of the Dixiecrats. That sends most of the state's radical fringe [the Republicans'] way. . . . Republicans are beginning to say—both to themselves and to some of us—"we're gonna start getting creamed with all the candidates coming in from the far right."[14]

In Louisiana, it is not as simple a problem for Republicans as "candidates coming in from the far right"; the situation is complicated by the inability of traditional GOP voters to rally against such candidates and instead elect one with broader appeal to represent their party in the general election. Their inability to do so is a result of the lack of time to put together an "anti-candidate X" strategy; this lack of time, in turn, is a direct result of Louisiana's nonpartisan system, which does not allow the party an opportunity to remedy its plight in private before presenting a united front to the voters of the state in the runoff election. Ben Bagert understood this fact when he withdrew from the 1990 Senate race and urged his fellow Republicans to vote for Johnston, the Democrat, over David Duke. Newly converted Republican scion and Governor Buddy Roemer was taught this lesson the hard way in 1992, when he endorsed nemesis Edwin Edwards over Duke in the runoff election.

Duke was extraordinarily successful in bringing more voters into the Republican fold. These voters, wearing a variety of party labels, were appreciated by the GOP when they supported traditional Republican moderate-to-conservative candidates as the lesser of two evils over a usually more liberal Democrat; indeed, as in most southern states, many initial Republican campaign meetings have started with the question of how to reach out to conservative Democrats and independents most effectively. In Duke, however, these voters found not the lesser of two evils, but a political messiah. In the Republican party, they found a certain number of generally mainstream Republican ideological allies who were willing to convert and swell the ranks of the faithful. And in the nonpartisan primary system, Duke found the final element to produce victory—an electoral system that featured more candidates, more frequently and profoundly fragmented returns, and an express route to winning the desired office by reducing the number of required victories.[15]

Someone may want to perform another survey of Louisiana party leadership's attitudes toward the nonpartisan primary and the strategies they implement to take advantage of it; this time around, they may also wish to spend a little extra time at Republican state headquarters in Baton Rouge. The situation since Hadley's revealing study of 1985 has become a bit more complicated for Republican elites, and complication, thy name is David Duke.

2

Messenger or Message?
David Duke in the Louisiana Legislature

◢

Keith Boeckelman
William Arp III
Bernard Terradot

Since the colonial era, racial issues have played a crucial role in American politics. Throughout most of American history an ethos that values equality, at least in the abstract, has conflicted with the reality of inequality, creating a moral dilemma for whites (Myrdal, 1964). The passage of civil rights legislation during the 1960s, including the Voting Rights Act, appeared to reconcile ideals and reality.

Instituting legal equality for blacks had at least two important consequences. First, the power of black voters and the number of black elected officials increased. Never far below the surface and, at times, violently erupting was a continuing, albeit shrinking, anti–civil rights strain among whites. Between 1989 and 1991 these two trends collided in the Louisiana legislature, as David Duke, the political epitome of white backlash, battled black legislators intent on stopping his racial agenda. Ultimately, Duke failed to enact his agenda despite the apparent popularity of some of his ideas.

Specifically, this chapter examines three possible explanations for Duke's failure as a legislator: (1) representation, which focuses on the electoral power of black constituencies; (2) coalition politics, which examines the extent to which black legislators united with their white counterparts in opposition to Duke and his legislative package; and (3) legislative norms, which focus on Duke's personal behavior in the legislature. By focusing on competing explanations, we seek at least partly to overcome the inherent limitation in case study research, that is, its lack of generalizability.

The research is significant for a number of reasons. Assessing why one state legislator's antiblack agenda failed also addresses the larger question of the power of blacks in political institutions. Specifically, the research pertains to the ability of black elected officials to provide policy representation twenty-five years after the Voting Rights Act. It also addresses whether black civil rights gains are likely to be reversed, and, if so, under what circumstances. Finally, it concerns the practical question of effective strategies for responding to the anti–civil rights backlash.

The following section provides background on Duke and his agenda. Next, the three competing explanations are examined using data from voting records, interviews with legislators, and various secondary sources. The final section suggests the conclusions that can be drawn from the findings.

Background

National attention began to focus on Duke in 1989, when he was elected to the Louisiana House of Representatives. He attracted further publicity with his relatively strong showing in two statewide races. As a candidate for the U.S. Senate in 1990, he received 44 percent of the vote against incumbent J. Bennett Johnston. In 1991 he scored slightly less than 40 percent of the vote in a runoff election for Louisiana governor.

Duke's notoriety rested, in large part, on his highly publicized past association with the Ku Klux Klan and with neo-Nazi organizations. Although he has publicly renounced his past, his agenda is explicitly antiblack. Literature from his 1991 campaign for governor of Louisiana, for example, warns of a state government "ultimately controlled by the Black Caucus/Liberal Coalition" (David Duke Campaign Committee, 1991). His policy views include a reversal of economic programs such as affirmative action and minority set-asides. He has also advocated more extreme positions such as an apartheid system for the state of Louisiana (*Times-Picayune*, 1991).

Duke's legislative agenda during his three years in the Louisiana

House of Representatives (1989–91) also focused primarily, although not exclusively, on racial issues. Four elements of his legislative package, which were considered racially motivated, included: (1) abolishing affirmative action programs; (2) increasing penalties for possession and sale of drugs in public housing projects; (3) cutting off welfare benefits to convicted drug offenders; (4) providing financial incentives for public assistance recipients to use contraceptives. Polls showing widespread opposition to affirmative action programs, especially among whites, suggest public support for at least part of his agenda (Gallup and Newport, 1991). As noted above, Duke failed to achieve success with his racial legislation. His only bill to become law during his three years in office was House Bill 1623 in 1991, which prohibited jurors from profiting from their jury service.

Representation and the Power of Black Constituencies

The first possible explanation for the failure of David Duke's racially motivated agenda stresses the power of black voters in influencing their legislators. State legislators with large black constituencies had shown high levels of support for issues of interest to blacks (Herring, 1991: 752). Louisiana has a substantial black population, and blacks make up about 27 percent of the state's registered voters (Louisiana Department of Registration and Elections 1991: 1). The analysis below examines the votes of white legislators to determine whether the racial composition of their constituencies affected their positions on David Duke's legislation. Black legislators are not included, because they unanimously opposed Duke's legislation.

Table 2.1 analyzes the votes of white legislators for the eight available recorded floor votes on David Duke's legislation. Five of the roll calls were final passage votes, and the other three dealt with procedural matters. The voting records of white legislators with more than 30 percent and more than 40 percent black registration in their districts were compared with those of all white legislators. Combs, Hibbing, and Welch (1984) have argued that a 40 percent black constituency is necessary in southern congressional districts to transfer them from conservative to liberal representation, but because only eight white Louisiana legislators represent districts that are more than

40 percent black, voting records of all members from districts more than 30 percent black in registration are also examined.

Evaluating votes at the final passage stage is somewhat problematic, sometimes owing to the context of the vote. In 1990, a Duke-sponsored anti–affirmative action bill (H.B. 1013) passed with 72 percent of the vote because of a temporary rift between black legislators and one of their frequent coalition partners, the Acadiana caucus, over a previous floor vote on a state lottery (Bridges, 1990). Also, it was common for David Duke's bills to pass overwhelmingly after amendments gutted the spirit of the legislation. Hostile amendments routinely reduced affirmative action bills to generic prohibitions of discrimination (H.B. 1483 and 1484). Bills providing financial incentives to public assistance recipients who used contraceptives (H.B. 1584) and cutting off welfare benefits for those convicted of drug crimes (H.B. 926) also were amended substantially.

For these reasons, the three available procedural votes were included in the analysis. For these votes the issues at stake were more clear cut, and the votes themselves were more closely divided. Two of the votes were to table anti–affirmative action bills (H.B. 1569 and the second vote on H.B. 77). The third was a request by Duke to hear an anti–affirmative action bill (H.B. 77) out of its normal order.

The above caveats aside, table 2.1 supports the contention that white legislators with a substantial black constituency are more inclined than their counterparts to oppose the Duke position. For each roll call, white legislators with a 30 percent or greater black constituency were more likely to vote against Duke than white legislators as a group. The eight white legislators with more than 40 percent black registration were also more likely to oppose the Duke position than the subset of all white legislators. Nevertheless, their voting behavior is not consistently different from the group with 30 percent black registration. In other words, white legislators with a 40 percent black constituency were not necessarily more likely to oppose Duke's bills than those with a 30 percent black constituency.

The results confirm the prediction that white legislators with a significant number of blacks in their districts (that is, greater than 30 percent) responded to black concerns. This responsiveness may be due to the desire to please an important constituency, or it may be that districts with a substantial number of blacks elect more liberal repre-

Table 2.1
White Legislators' Support for Duke's Legislation

	Bill number and year							
	1483[a] (1991)	1484[b] (1991)	1485[c] (1991)	1013[d] (1991)	926[e] (1991)	1569[f] (1991)	77[g] (1991)	77[h] (1991)
Percentage of white legislators voting against Duke position	5.4	10.5	7.4	14.2	2.4	44.4	37.3	49.3
Percentage of white legislators with 30% or above black constituency voting against Duke position	14.2	28.6	17.6	15.0	5.9	71.4	66.7	75.0
Percentage of white legislators with 40% or above black constituency voting against Duke position	33.3	12.3	12.5	28.6	16.7	75.0	57.1	66.7
Final vote (first number is Duke position)	70-13	77-22	75-9	66-26	80-16	40-44	42-39	37-48

[a] Originally cut off welfare benefits for those convicted of drug offenses. Amended to apply to anyone receiving government benefit or subsidy.
[b] Anti-affirmative action bill amended to require contraceptive counseling.
[c] Originally set up program for financial incentives for public assistance recipients. Amended to require contraceptive counseling.
[d] Prohibits affirmative action.
[e] Motion to table anti-affirmative action bill.
[f] Cuts off welfare benefits for those convicted of drug crimes. Amended so that it would not go into effect if federal funds are affected.
[g] Motion (by Duke) to hear anti-affirmative action bill out of its normal order.
[h] Motion to table anti-affirmative action bill.

sentatives. It would be a mistake, however, to conclude that black electoral representation was the decisive factor in stopping David Duke's agenda. As table 2.1 shows, many of the votes were not close. Also, the legislators' ability to alter Duke's bills before they reached the floor played a key role in the outcome.

Coalition Politics

An alternative explanation for David Duke's inability to enact his agenda focuses on coalition politics. Prior studies suggest that blacks are able to enhance their power by forming coalitions with other groups in the political system. Coalition partners in other contexts have included white liberals, labor organizations, and Jews (Smith, Rice, and Jones, 1987: 117-20). Browning, Rogers, and Tabb (1984: 168) contend that minority incorporation into the dominant coalitions of city government is essential for important policy changes.

Conversely, several scholars and political activists have challenged the extent to which coalitions are a viable strategy for black politicians. Carmichael and Hamilton (1968) argue that political coalitions between blacks and dominant/liberal whites do not benefit blacks. They contend that the political interests of the haves and the have-nots are fundamentally at odds and that coalitions based on appeals to conscience will fail. Political leaders such as Martin Luther King, Jr., essentially supported Carmichael and Hamilton's position that "coalitions with poor whites are the only viable option" (Henry, 1980: 223). Pinderhughes (1987: 259-61) challenges the underlying pluralist logic of coalition theory, arguing that blacks must negotiate from an essentially inferior position, and that racial issues are too broad and controversial to fit in a bargaining framework. Even with black leaders in positions of power, there is no certainty of substantive change in public policy, unless the character of decision making also changes. Finally, Smith, Rice, and Jones (1987, 115-20) argue that political coalitions may be unstable, and not always in blacks' best interests.

Much empirical coalition research has focused on urban political institutions, such as city councils. Few studies examine the impact of black representation on state legislatures and their policy outcomes. Campbell and Feagin (1975: 155-56), however, suggest that by the early 1970s, the presence of black legislators influenced the passage of open housing laws, and that "Southern blacks themselves have not found their struggle to attain political offices to be meaningless."

While the general applicability of coalition theory is open to debate, coalition building is a relevant strategy in the context of the Louisiana legislature. Herring (1990: 751) argues "Louisiana has a tradition, dating back to Huey Long, of including blacks in political coalitions." Also, in the Louisiana legislature, the caucuse rather than the political party is the key organizing principle. Because no single caucus constitutes a majority, coalitions are a fact of life. The Legislative Black Caucus, one of the best organized, has developed alliances with others (Bridges, 1990).

Interviews with legislators were used to assess the importance of coalition building in combating David Duke's racial initiatives. Six House members of the Louisiana Legislative Black Caucus who served with Duke were interviewed, as well as two white representatives whom the black legislators cited as allies in opposing David Duke's legislative package.

In interviewing black legislators, a questionnaire was utilized (see appendix). However, in interviews with political elites, it is important that the interviewer understand the interviewee's frame of reference, when shared meanings are problematic (Dexter, 1970). In other words, it is necessary to allow the interviewee to guide the direction of the interview. As Dexter argues, "a good many well-informed or influential people are unwilling to accept the assumptions with which the investigator starts; they insist on explaining to him how they view the situation, what the real problems are as they view the matter" (p. 20). Therefore, as the interviews progressed, and the interviewers became more knowledgeable, the nature of the questioning evolved. Because the final two interviews, with the white legislators, focused on clarifying issues raised in the previous conversations, the questionnaire was discarded.

All Legislative Black Caucus members agreed that Duke's presence in the legislature heightened the climate of racism and put them on the defensive. Interviewees cited instances in which social welfare programs benefiting black-majority legislative districts were subjected to greater scrutiny than similar programs targeted for predominantly white districts. Some also suggested that Duke was at least partially successful in turning back the clock on racial issues. As one black legislator put it, "some things taken for granted were reconsidered."

The caucus was unable to agree regarding Duke's impact on the legislature, which may reflect differences in emphasis rather than a genuine disagreement. About half of the members believed that Duke "polarized" the legislature. Others emphasized that his ineffectiveness as a legislator minimized his impact. According to one legislator, although Duke's presence was an "insult," he did not play an important role in the legislature because he was "more impressed with being a legislator than functioning as one."

Another indication that Duke was perceived as a threat was that stopping Duke formed part of the Legislative Black Caucus's agenda. Members disagreed on whether it was Duke personally or his legislation that was offensive. One member argued that the caucus unanimously opposed seating Duke, although other members disputed this claim.

Several members noted that David Duke's presence made day-to-day coalition building more difficult, because of heightened racial tensions in the legislature. According to one member, it became harder to "build coalitions to put fifty-three votes together." This member felt that Duke legitimized racism in the legislature, and that the publicity he received generated constituent pressure on some white members that weakened their support for the agenda of the Legislative Black Caucus. Another member argued that Duke's presence allowed his "closet supporters to come out of the woodwork," while a third claimed that it drove a wedge between black and white legislators and broke up friendships. Only one interviewee disputed the claim that Duke's presence made forming coalitions more difficult. Even this member, however, stated that the publicity Duke received left conservative members with "nowhere to hide" from constituent pressure on racial issues.

Despite the rifts that Duke's presence caused, black caucus members attempted to use coalitions to combat his agenda. Members approached other caucuses, especially regional ones, for commitments to stop his legislation. They also built coalitions with white legislators with large black constituencies, as the roll-call analysis in the previous section suggests. One member explicitly stressed the political power of black constituencies and downplayed the importance of moral and ideological reasons in leading white legislators to oppose Duke.

Legislative Norms

A third possible reason for Duke's failure to enact his agenda concerns legislative norms, the behavior that allows the institution to achieve its desired ends. In general, legislative norms seem to be weaker in state legislatures than in Congress. Still, prior research has documented the existence of certain widely shared standards of behavior in state legislatures, including norms against lying, disrespecting other members, giving priority to reelection and publicity over legislative work, talking about subjects on which the legislator is ill-informed, and dealing in personalities rather than substance (Wahlke et al., 1962; Hebert and McLemore, 1973: 507-8; Rosenthal, 1981: 124; Bernick and Wiggins, 1983: 196). Members who violate norms are often subject to sanctions such as obstruction of their own bills, and social ostracism (Wahlke et al., 1962: 144-45).

Despite its reputation for flamboyant politics, Louisiana has many of the basic norms found in other legislatures. For example, shortly after Duke entered the legislature, a fellow Republican justified his civil treatment of the freshman representative based on the norm of respect. In a letter to the New Orleans *Times-Picayune*, he wrote that, although he frequently disagreed with Duke, he had "no choice but to treat him with professional courtesy as I would any other legislator in the House" (St. Raymond, 1989).

The original questionnaire used when interviewing the Legislative Black Caucus members contained four questions related to the issue of legislative norms. According to caucus members, Duke most clearly violated norms concerning publicity seeking. The exposure sought was not tied to reelection to the legislature but rather to campaigns for higher office, particularly for governor. Members spoke of his constant "playing to the media" and his efforts to get his picture taken with other legislators. The media attention that Duke generated was viewed as diverting the spotlight from substantive issues, and having a negative impact on the legislative institution. According to one interviewee, Duke's presence made Louisiana and its legislature a "laughingstock." A black legislator who served on a committee with Duke reported that he disrupted meetings by acting like a celebrity for his many followers in attendance.

Duke was not viewed as a serious legislator. One colleague expressed disdain for Duke's ability to grasp nonracial issues, and believed that Duke lived on what he called Fantasy Island. Another legislator lamented Duke's tendency to present issues in racial rather than substantive terms, because he did not understand his own bills. Still another commented that Duke spent most of his time fighting "sacrificial battles" that he knew he could not win. The effect of Duke's behavior, interviewees felt, was to alienate middle-of-the-road legislators who might otherwise have given him the benefit of the doubt.

Black members did not necessarily perceive Duke to have violated the norms of courtesy or respect for other members. While some black legislators refused to talk to him on principle, more than one described their personal relationship with him as "cordial."

The white legislators also judged Duke to be ineffective because he violated norms, particularly the admonition not to be a show horse. One member expressed dismay over Duke's work habits and his publicity seeking in committee. Duke, this legislator claimed, rarely attended meetings, failed to pay attention when he was there, and talked or reacted "only when the cameras were on." According to another, "David was just there to use us" and showed a "callous disregard for the institution." This legislator also condemned Duke's understanding of the legislative bargaining process, commenting that he only heard from Duke when he wanted something, and that there was no quid pro quo in dealing with him. White legislators believed that Duke's ineptitude as a legislator, rather than coalition politics, accounted for his failure to further his legislative agenda. One called him a "paper tiger," while another commented that Duke "talks about problems but never solves them."

The comments above suggest that Duke violated the standards of behavior for representatives. Admittedly, the interviewees are a somewhat biased sample, being Duke opponents. Nevertheless, press accounts support the case that Duke's violation of legislative norms, particularly his obsession with publicity, led to his being ostracized and unable to pass his bills. According to a reporter covering the legislature, Duke "alienated his potential allies . . . with a swollen ego and grandstanding," and was publicly criticized by other legislators for his inability to think on his feet (Nauth, 1989).

Duke's considerable notoriety upon entering the legislature renders the connection between legislative norms and the defeat of his bills somewhat ambiguous. Clearly many members disliked him. As a Republican member anonymously commented to the press, "I don't want to be associated with that racist SOB. Just voting with him causes me anguish" (Nauth, 1989). Hostility toward Duke also affected the outcome of his legislation. As the Republican senator who also represented Duke's constituents argued, "His bills have somewhat of a red flag on them" (Nauth, 1989). Violation of legislative norms alone may not completely account for the hostility toward Duke and his legislation, however. Unlike a typical state legislative race, his bid for office received international publicity. Also, his antics outside the legislature, such as selling Nazi literature from his district office, may account for part of the animus toward him and the hostility toward his legislative program. Finally, David Duke's violation of legislative norms allowed him to achieve goals that may have been more important to him, such as raising money. Passing legislation was perhaps not a top priority.

Conclusion

David Duke's failure as a legislator could be accounted for in part by constituency representation, coalition politics, and legislative norms, but the findings are not conclusive.

Members with large black constituencies were more likely to oppose Duke's bills than those with fewer blacks, which may have altered the outcome on some votes. Duke's presence had a mixed effect on coalition building. While black legislators were ultimately able to build alliances to help weaken and defeat his bills, his presence hampered normal coalition-building efforts on issues of importance to black members. Other representatives ostracized Duke, at least in part because he violated legislative norms.

David Duke's uniqueness as America's most famous state legislator may exaggerate his importance. Because of the international attention his campaign received, in a sense he violated legislative norms even before he was elected. Despite the publicity, his impact on the legislature was minimal, in terms of his failure both to pass legislation and to earn other members' respect. Interviewees felt that he was more significant in the public consciousness than in the legislature itself, and they criticized the media for building up Duke beyond his real importance. In a similar vein, one interviewee argued that this study should have focused on more respected and "important" legislators. This perspective on David Duke suggests that a more low-profile messenger might have had more success with the same message. Nevertheless, black legislators and their allies have weapons of their own to use in the continuing struggle over civil rights policy.

APPENDIX

Questionnaire Used in Interviews with Legislative Black Caucus Members

1. What was David Duke's impact on the Louisiana legislature? How do you personally feel about his role in the legislature? What does he do (or what bills does he sponsor) that you find most threatening?
2. To what extent is "stopping Duke" part of the agenda of the Legislative Black Caucus?
3. Do you think there are legislators who "secretly" support Duke and/or his agenda?
4. Do you have allies outside the Legislative Black Caucus who will support your efforts to "stop" Duke?
5. Can you think of any Duke bills that you would support if he were not the sponsor?
6. Do you serve on any committees with David Duke? How effective is he in committee? How is he treated?
7. Do you treat David Duke differently than other legislators?
8. Do other legislators treat him in a different way (e.g. as an outcast, etc.)? Is he talked about during debate?
9. Does the publicity he receives bother you? How does this affect the process?
10. To what extent do you think that David Duke's presence in the legislature has intensified the climate of racism for black officials?

3
David Duke and Social Science

John K. Wildgen

David Duke is no longer Louisiana's biggest political problem. But he is the biggest scientific problem faced by the state's political scientists and their allied colleagues. Although Duke did not succeed in bringing Louisiana politics into crisis, many academic observers of Duke have, perhaps because Duke put them ideologically off balance, snarled themselves in methodological problems that open social science's treatment of controversial personalities and ideas to public skepticism. Two unconnected theories about Duke are symptomatic of this breakdown. One is the theory that Duke was the product of twelve years of Reagan-Bush rule. The second is the theory of a hidden Duke vote—a bloc of voters whose views are opaque to the techniques of polling and statistics. The first theory, advanced by a historian, requires us to forget how to tell time and exaggerates the role of exogenous political forces in explaining the Duke phenomenon. The second theory, advanced by a political scientist, requires us to forget how to compute, and exaggerates the role of Louisiana's endogenous racism.

Both theories fail to take into account the complicated multivariate milieu that spawned Duke's sudden rise to global notoriety and his equally sudden plunge into obscurity. The Duke phenomenon had three facets: the local Duke, the legislative Duke, and the gubernatorial Duke. Each of these personas fared worse in successive encounters with the Louisiana electorate, but many observers of Duke, while eager to take credit for his demise, are unwilling to bury him, so within social science he is an "undead" phenomenon.

I will take up some issues that point to a David Duke who got into office by the narrowest of margins, who had a lackluster, copycat role in Louisiana's legislature, and who bamboozled pollsters who should have known better. The kinds of evidence used to weave this tale—aggregate election returns, legislative roll-calls votes, and polling data—show how to get a fix on a political phenomenon like Duke and put him in social and historical perspective, as the voters of Louisiana did well before many scholars.

David Duke And Parish Politics

David Duke's narrowly won 1989 prize, Louisiana Legislative District 81, was a socially and economically heterogeneous constituency typical of neither the city of New Orleans just to its east nor the dormitory suburbs just to its west. District 81 is a combination of two buffer zones that separate Jefferson Parish from Orleans Parish. In the northern half of the district the most distinctive area is the community of Bucktown. This corner of Jefferson Parish has a blue-collar tone brought about largely by Bucktown's one-time dependence on fishing, as well as its thriving seafood restaurant business. A sizeable commercial vessel marina there takes good advantage of the harbor formed by the 17th Street drainage canal. The canal, the western bank of which is the Orleans–Jefferson Parish boundary, is owned by Orleans Parish. This anomaly in jurisdiction has made the canal an occasional source of contention between the two frequently feuding parishes.

The Bucktown canal bank of a decade or so ago was inhabited by squatter fisherfolk who built rickety docks and houses on what was once an urban wasteland. In the late 1970s, pressure mounted to clear the squatters' dwellings and install a modern marina. Community activists defended the squatter population, calling them "water people." Bucktown's residents enjoyed a brief notoriety as anthropological treasures with a unique culture. Notoriety suited the fishing people of the neighborhood, who understood that a marina meant an important cultural change—paying rent for boat slips.

By the late 1980s improvements to the canal could not be put off. The squatter dwellings were razed. Now concrete bulkheads and pilings replaced the forest of rotting wooden structures that once docked the distinctive fantail transomed Lafitte skiffs still favored by fishing

Map 3.1
Louisiana House District 81
Duke percents in 1989

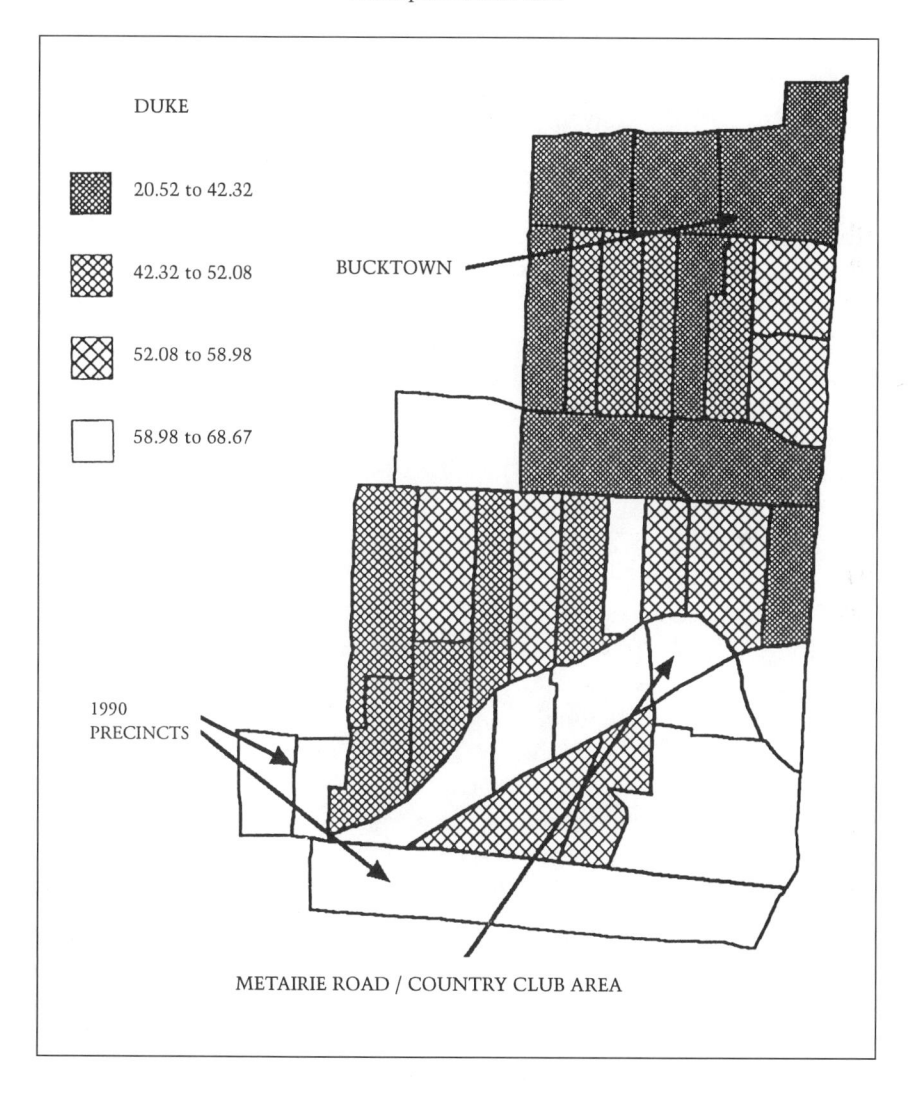

DUKE

20.52 to 42.32

42.32 to 52.08

52.08 to 58.98

58.98 to 68.67

BUCKTOWN

1990 PRECINCTS

METAIRIE ROAD / COUNTRY CLUB AREA

people on Lake Pontchartrain. Bucktown is still full of "water people," though, including some fishers who work in the seafood restaurants that draw thousands to Bucktown on the weekends, and even a few up-scale sailmakers who cater to the nearby yachting marinas.

But adjacent to quaint Bucktown are more conventional middle-class concentrations. Running south of Bucktown toward Veterans Boulevard is a long string of apartment complexes that attract single people, as well as new families who can use both public and parochial schools in the vicinity. To the immediate west is a large expanse of medium-income single-family dwellings and some expensive villas fronting the levee that borders Lake Pontchartrain's twenty-four- by forty-mile expanse. Still, it is Bucktown—no bigger than a precinct or two—that gives the northern half of District 81 its working-class atmosphere.

The district is bisected east-west by Veterans Boulevard and the parallel Interstate 10. South of Veterans Boulevard, the New Orleans area's largest retail strip, is another kind of District 81. This area is dominated by the meandering Metairie Road. Much of this two-lane arterial is shaded by oaks and bordered by old and expensive houses. From time to time, small shopping areas intrude, but there are no regional-scale malls. Toward the south are some elegant homes and the exclusive Metairie Country Club. This area is home to a kind of Republican who is enthusiastic about neither someone "in trade" like the homebuilder and mainstream Republican John Treen nor a neo-Nazi like David Duke.

The differences between the two parts of the district are not to be exaggerated. There has been some gentrification of Bucktown over the years, and there are some down-at-the-heels neighborhoods near Metairie Road. But the Bucktown area is still a place where there are more pickup trucks than on average, and Metairie Road has more Volvos. Notably absent from District 81, at least as constituted at the time of David Duke's election, were blacks. Only a scattering lived in the district at the time of Duke's election.

District 81, then, is not what one would conventionally think of as a nursery for political extremism or neo-Nazi movements. While not in any sense a model of America at large, it has the elements of grit and polish, affluence and frugality, class and kitsch that any American would recognize. There is no way to guess that District 81—or any area like it—would send David Duke to the Louisiana House of Representatives.

Very few people in Jefferson Parish in 1989 were, in fact, aware that David Duke was seeking a House seat until *Times-Picayune* columnist James Gill brought it to notice in a blistering editorial. Gill is the journalist Jeffersonians love to hate. A rumpled, portly Briton, Gill makes no attempt to conceal his condescension toward and contempt for American suburbanites. Moreover, his Papist-baiting, English-Protestant views on religion grate on the French-Catholic traditions of the region. Naturally, Jefferson Parish politicians like popular sheriff Harry Lee revel in being attacked by Gill, because his displeasure is seen as worth thousands of votes. Indeed, Lee takes every chance he can to antagonize the *Times-Picayune* because press antagonism so easily converts into votes.

Duke took a cue from Lee and skillfully exploited the media by insulting and hectoring reporters with manners that eventually would cause even ABC's Sam Donaldson discomfort in Duke's *Prime Time Live* television appearance. So, by the eve of his state house election, Duke had drawn in not only local newspapers and television, but also global media. Jefferson Parish's chief election officer, the clerk of court, had to arrange broadcast facilities for correspondents from national networks, Europe, Japan, the former Soviet Republics, and Australia. As the runoff with John Treen drew near, Presidents Bush and Reagan flooded local radio with anti-Duke messages—and even one pro-Treen message. No by-election in recent memory for the lower house of a minor state (nine electoral votes) has ever gotten so much national and global attention.

How Duke managed to defeat mainstream Republican John Treen, brother of Louisiana's only post-Reconstruction Republican governor, requires some scientific detective work. The contrast between Duke's strong showing in the Bucktown area and his failure to carry several upscale precincts along Metairie Road suggests that his support divided along class lines. Further evidence consistent with this notion is the rough correlation between support for Duke in 1989 and support for Michael Dukakis in the 1988 presidential contest shown in figure 3.1 and table 3.1.

These data, however, cannot be taken literally because of problems inherent in aggregate data known collectively as the ecological fallacy.

Figure 3.1
Similarities in Duke and Dukakis Geography

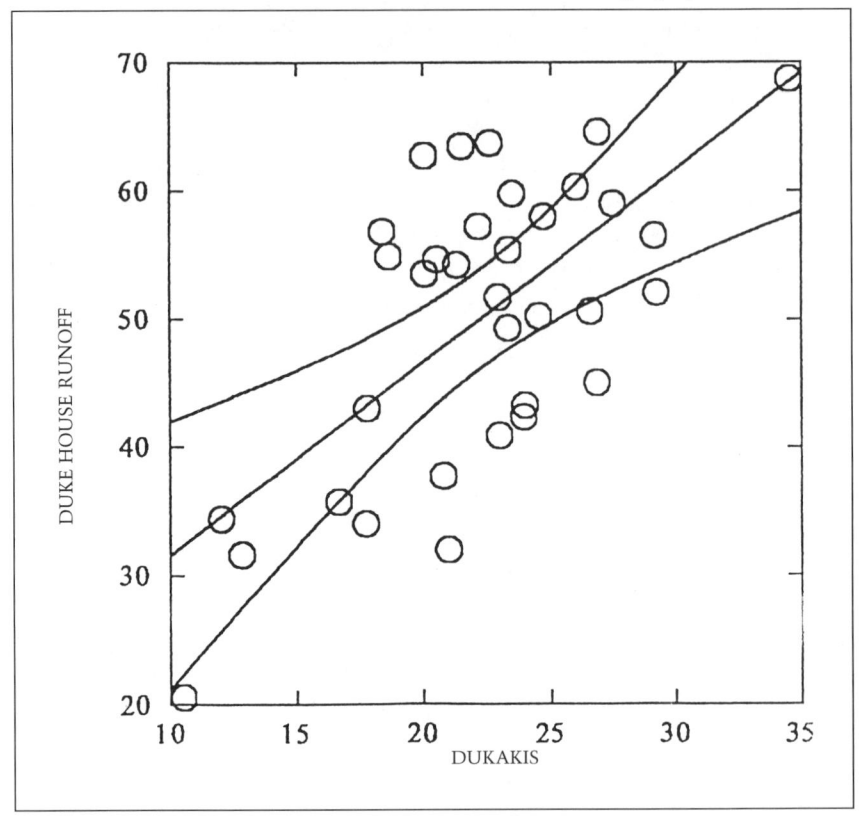

Table 3.1
Regression of Duke's District 81 Vote on Dukakis's 1988 Presidential Vote
(Common Precincts)

Dep. Var. = DUKERP; $N = 34$;   Multiple $R = 0.654$;   Squared Multiple $R = 0.428$
Adjusted Squared Multiple $R = 0.410$;   Standard Error Of Estimate = 8.800

Variable	Coefficient	Std. Error	Std. Coef.	T	P(2 Tail)
CONSTANT	16.495	6.989	0.000	2.360	0.025
DUKAKIS	1.506	0.308	0.654	4.895	0.000

ANALYSIS OF VARIANCE

Source	Sum-of-Squares	DF	Mean-Square	F-ratio	p*
REGRESSION	1855.253	1	1855.253	23.958	0.000
RESIDUAL	2477.957	32	77.436		

* Data do not meet random sampling assumptions.

Duke's precinct-level voting patterns create statistical anomalies. Figure 3.2 is a graphic presentation of a multiple regression of Duke's vote on those for Sheriff Harry Lee and Clerk of Court Jon Gegenheimer. The gridded plane models the positive relationship between the Duke and Lee (Democratic) vote and the negative relationship between the Duke and Gegenheimer (Republican) vote. The vertical lines intersecting the plane show the data points and their distance from the plane (that is, residuals).

There are no two more contrasting politicians in Jefferson Parish than Lee and Gegenheimer. Lee is probably second only to Duke in notoriety. In the late 1980s he announced that he was stepping up surveillance of blacks driving, in what Lee characterized as "rinky-dink" cars, through white neighborhoods. Lee can get away with a public an-

Figure 3.2
Duke-Lee; Duke-Gegenheimer
Multiple Regression Model

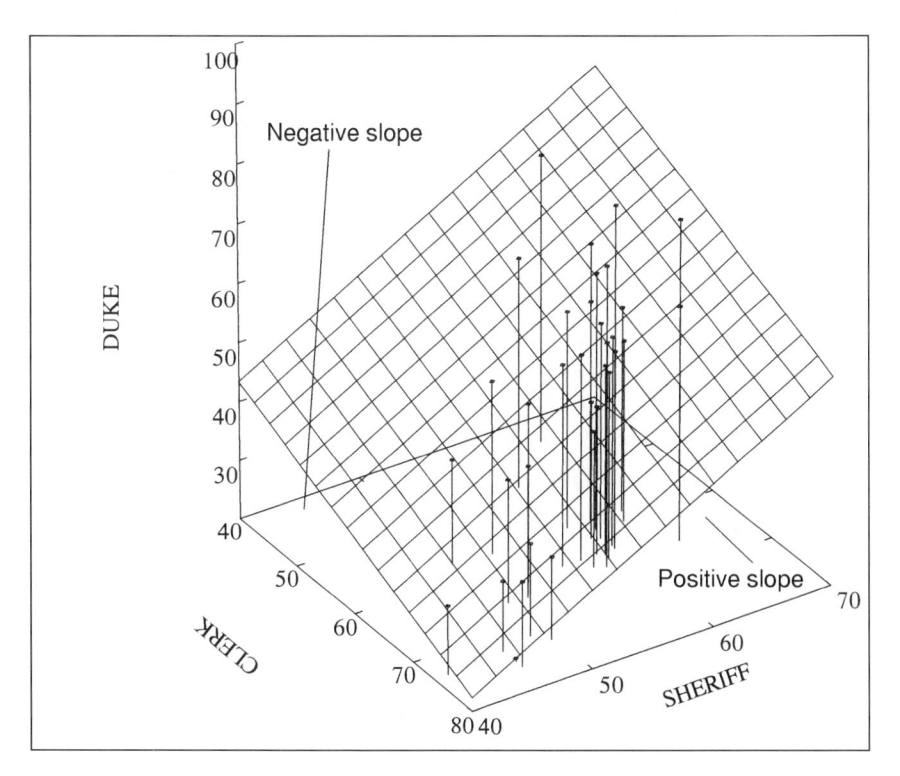

Table 3.2
Regression of Duke District 81 on Clerk of Court and Sheriff Vote
(Common Precincts)

Dep. Var. = DUKERP; $N = 34$; Multiple $R = 0.911$; Squared Multiple $R = 0.829$; Adjusted Squared Multiple $R = .818$; Standard Error of Estimate = 4.886

Variable	Coefficient	Std. Error	Std. Coef.	T	P(2 Tail)
CONSTANT	20.357	20.064	0.000	1.015	0.318
CLERKPCT	-0.527	0.172	-0.336	-3.067	0.004
SHERPCT	1.102	0.190	0.635	5.805	0.000

ANALYSIS OF VARIANCE

Source	Sum-Of-Squares	Df	Mean-Square	F-Ratio	P*
REGRESSION	3593.082	2	1796.541	75.248	0.000
RESIDUAL	740.128	31	23.875		

* Data do not meet random sampling assumptions.
CLERKPCT = % Vote for Gegenheimer; SHERPCT = % Vote for Lee.

nouncement of race-based selective enforcement due to his background and flamboyant personality. He is a successful Chinese restaurateur who turned to politics, is a heaveyset man, and prefers to dress in cowboy-style clothing, complete with boots and ten-gallon hat. Despite his chronic insensitivity to black feelings, in elections he regularly carries homogeneous black precincts by overwhelming majorities. This is largely because his opposition has been limited to Republicans of Italian-American extraction.

Most Louisiana Republican incumbents are Democratic defectors. Gegenheimer is an unusual southern Republican in that he became one before being elected to office. When questioned about his long-term Republicanism he once quipped, "In college I experimented with being a liberal, but I did not inhale." Gegenheimer, by contrast with Lee, has a reedy build, favors blazers and slacks, and conveys an image rather like Jimmy Stewart playing a small-college dean. His geographical basis of support tracks that of national and state-level Republicans, though he has some personal areas of support, especially among Hispanics, and has won (unusual for a Republican) the endorsement of some parochial black leaders.

The importance of these two politicians to the understanding of Duke lies in the way their records put Duke into statistical and political context. The relatively small size of the residuals the multiple-regression model of Duke's District 81 results on Lee and Gegenheimer's support in the area (figure 3.2) corresponds to an R of 0.911, with Duke's vote being positively correlated with Democrat Lee's and negatively correlated with Republican Gegenheimer's. Statistically, Duke fits well within Jefferson Parish voting patterns but not Republican patterns (see chapter 8). His support correlates positively with that of the race-card playing sheriff, and negatively with that of the clerk of court, whose campaigns have made no racial appeals. These data do not prove that Duke gets Lee votes and loses Gegenheimer votes one-for-one. What they indicate is that Duke's vote is easily explicable in the context of long-term geographical patterns of Jefferson Parish voting. There is nothing sui generis about Duke—nor anything attributable to Reagan-Bush policies. Instead, much of Duke's appeal lies simply in his outrageousness. Voting for Duke is a way locals can thumb their noses at politically correct national and local opinion leaders.

These kinds of data do not make intuitive sense, and they seem to baffle some of Duke's observers, who find it awkward to explain why presumptively Democratic voters support a racist candidate more so than do presumptively Republican voters in Louisiana more receptive to racial appeals. For example, historian Lawrence N. Powell (1992) writes of the voters of District 81: "[T]heir newfound readiness to embrace a symbol of racial extremism was only partly due to Republican racial policies. Republican economic policies that have helped shift wealth and opportunity upward played an important part in preparing the ground for Duke's racist insurgency."

This passage is confusing because it stretches credulity, as would any symptom of methodological meltdown. While certainly there was some "readiness to embrace a symbol of racial extremism" in certain District 81 precincts, there is no reason to call it newfound. Willingness to embrace a symbol of racial extremism is a chronic condition in parts of Jefferson Parish. Eleven years earlier, in 1979, Duke had picked up the same geographical base of support. Twenty-one years earlier (1968), George Wallace had done the same (Powell, 1992). Why, with so much precedent, was there apparent surprise at Duke's emergence? Duke had been cultivating this area for years and had finally learned how to campaign in District 81 by simply knocking on doors and soliciting votes. It seems that an ignored factor in Duke's rise was that he had mastered some of the craft of campaigning. In other words, Duke is not just a dependent variable blown about by external forces; he is partially a product of his own pluck.

There are two reasons for attributing Duke's success more to himself than to Reagan and Bush. First, it is a simpler explanation. Second, it corresponds to the fact that there were at least two decades of local electoral precedent for Duke's 1989 pattern. And although any citizen or scholar could have reservations about Reaganomics and the Bush administration variant, there is no evidence that either "played an important part in preparing the ground for Duke's racist insurgency." The ground was already plowed and seeded by Wallace, Lee, and Duke himself.

Duke is too important a phenomenon to be instrumentalized as a tool for Reagan and Bush bashing. Why then argue that Duke's appeal, statistically and geographically tied to a long tradition of race-oriented voting, was created by Reaganomics? Moreover, why was the claimed turn to the radical right in Bucktown so quickly achieved? That is, why are we expected to believe that voters turned from Dukakis, whose patterns of voter support Powell left out of his analysis, to Duke in a matter of a few weeks? It is not plausible to argue that the fact of Bush's election created an instantaneous critical realignment in Bucktown. But Powell is not the only scientist baffled by Duke.

Duke in Baton Rouge

Duke's narrow victory over John Treen was followed by a brief legislative career that served largely as a comma between two unsuccessful campaigns, a 1990 run against Louisiana's senior U.S. Senator, J. Bennett Johnston, and a 1991 run against Governor Charles ("Buddy") Roemer and former governor Edwin Edwards. Duke's sojourn in the Louisiana legislature, a body generally held in low esteem, was in many respects a period in which the body as a collectivity comported itself well. In campaigns, Duke's presence brings out the worst in people; he actually brought out the best in the legislature. How this came about is hard to narrate because often we find that while generalities come easily, there is a devil in the details. For

Duke, the legislature provided a devil in the generalities. Duke's strength was found in areas of Republican weakness, but he still went to Baton Rouge as a Republican and tried to act like one.

Louisiana Republicans are fairly cohesive as legislators, but not in the sense one normally associates with political parties. Rather, they are bound together by ties that can be partisan, ideological, regional, and personal. They are more cohesive than Democrats, but not as cohesive as the Legislative Black Caucus. There is a lot of blurring in Louisiana legislative behavior. It is the kind of place that reminds observers of fractal mathematics. There is, however, one simplifying factor: it is greatly affected by gubernatorial leadership style. Duke's appearances in the legislature were closely covered by the press, and he continued to attract intense attention, even though not all of it was wanted. For example, Republican state committeewoman Beth Rickey hounded Duke by confronting him with the fact that his home-based bookstore featured copies of *Mein Kampf*. For reasons that are inexplicable, Duke, who was usually a master of sang-froid under pressure, was chronically caught off balance by Rickey and continued to defend his book-stocking choices long after people had stopped caring. Less noticed was his overall behavior as a legislator. As a matter of fact, Duke actually tried to act like a Republican, at least by aping Republican regulars on important roll-call votes.

It is difficult and tedious to try to characterize the meaning of roll-call votes in any legislature, but it is easy to track the membership of voting cliques with conventional statistical techniques. For example, we can use principal component axes derived from selected roll call votes to "map" Duke relative to his colleagues. In effect, the statistics of grouping are easier than analysis of the political basis for group cohesion.

Statistically, Duke was a Republican in the House. The evidence for this comes from the small database of important Louisiana legislature roll-call votes published after each session by the *Times-Picayune*. The *Times-Picayune* lists fifteen or so key votes for thirty or so regional incumbents in the 105-member House.

Analyses of these data consistently indicate three groups in the House: blacks, white Democrats, and Republicans. Usually a three-axis principal-components solution explains most of the variance in roll-call votes—though it takes great mastery of the House to interpret the axes. Indeed, even a statistical summary of the House is far from simple; in the following figures, individual legislators have been statistically mapped and then linked with a minimum spanning tree to aid visual interpretation.

This kind of statistical visualization, perhaps unfamiliar at first, is an extension of an old idea: the notion of describing politicians in terms of a left-right continuum invented by the French during the rev-

Figure 3.3
Voting Patterns of New Orleans Legislators
1989 Regular Session

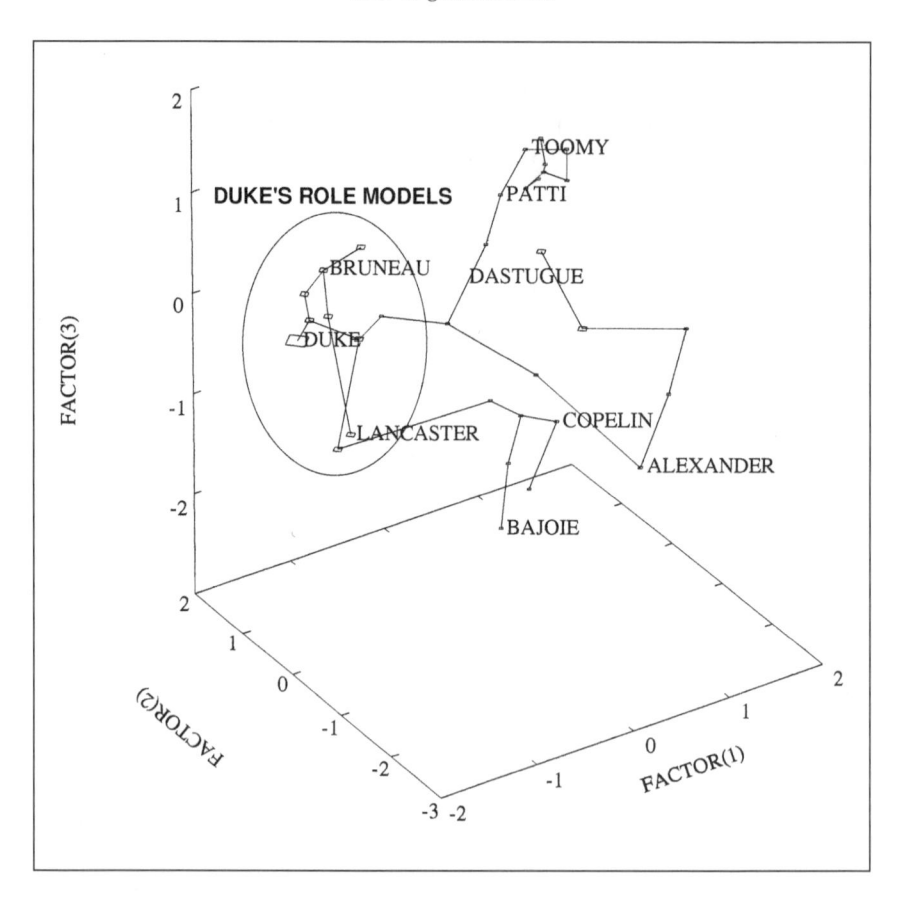

olution. Using a single left-right metaphor we can place politicians on line. In two dimensions, say, left-right and interventionist-isolationist, we could locate candidates on a square surface like a map, with individual politicians located both west-east (left-right) and north-south. In three dimensions we could map politicians in cube. The following figures tell us a lot about a politician by locating him or her in a neighborhood of similar politicians.

A summary of a principal-components analysis of key votes for New Orleans area legislators in 1989, Duke's freshman session, shows Duke's behavior relative to that of other legislators in terms of roll-call votes on important issues (figure 3.3). In the array of representatives in this figure, Duke is marked by the large circle. He is located near Republicans such as Jim Donelon, Skip Hand, and Peppi Bruneau (medium-sized circles). One can get an idea of Duke's general location by noting the tight cluster of politicians toward the top of this figure. This bundle of almost identically behaving legislators is composed of black House members. Duke appears to be a copycat Republican. His own bills, designed to "reform" welfare and control substance abuse in housing projects, were tabled, died in committee, or were killed by the Senate. As time passed, Duke became more isolated statistically from Republicans. It is risky to draw too much from his isolation since, save for blacks in the legislature, the late 1980s and early 1990s were not a period of rigid party roll-call voting blocs due to the party-switching of Governor Roemer.

Even with reservations about roll-call vote analysis and principal-components analysis, Duke generally tracked mainstream Republican behavior on issues recognized as being important. This is an argument not that Duke was actually a moderate, but rather that Duke did not know anything about legislation, did not care about it, and simply took easy cues from hardened professionals such as Peppi Bruneau, Louisiana's master of gerrymandering. Duke's Republican colleagues did not take him seriously as a legislator.

In 1991, Duke was succeeded in office by David Vitter. Although very conservative, Vitter is a marked contrast to Duke. Vitter graduated from Harvard, received an M.A. at Oxford while a Rhodes Scholar, and went on to take a law degree at Tulane. Vitter's geographical support does not track with that of Duke and Lee (figure 3.4). Vitter drew his best support from the Gegenheimer precincts.

By 1992, it was possible to map Vitter's legislative behavior. Vitter is in many respects a statistical replacement for Duke in that he occupies the same neighborhood of legislators (figure 3.5). The Republicans (large circles) are on the right. Vitter (largest circle) voted almost identically with some fellow Republicans, which is why the circle representing him appears with several concentric circles. Unlike Duke, Vitter is a seriously committed legislator with a widely understood agenda: disapproval of four-time governor Edwin Edwards. Vitter is no public race-baiter, but rather the kind of Republican one might expect to find in a place like District 81. This adds to the evidence that Duke as a legislator was a bad fit. Duke had no Republican

Figure 3.4
Duke and Vitter: Different Georgraphies

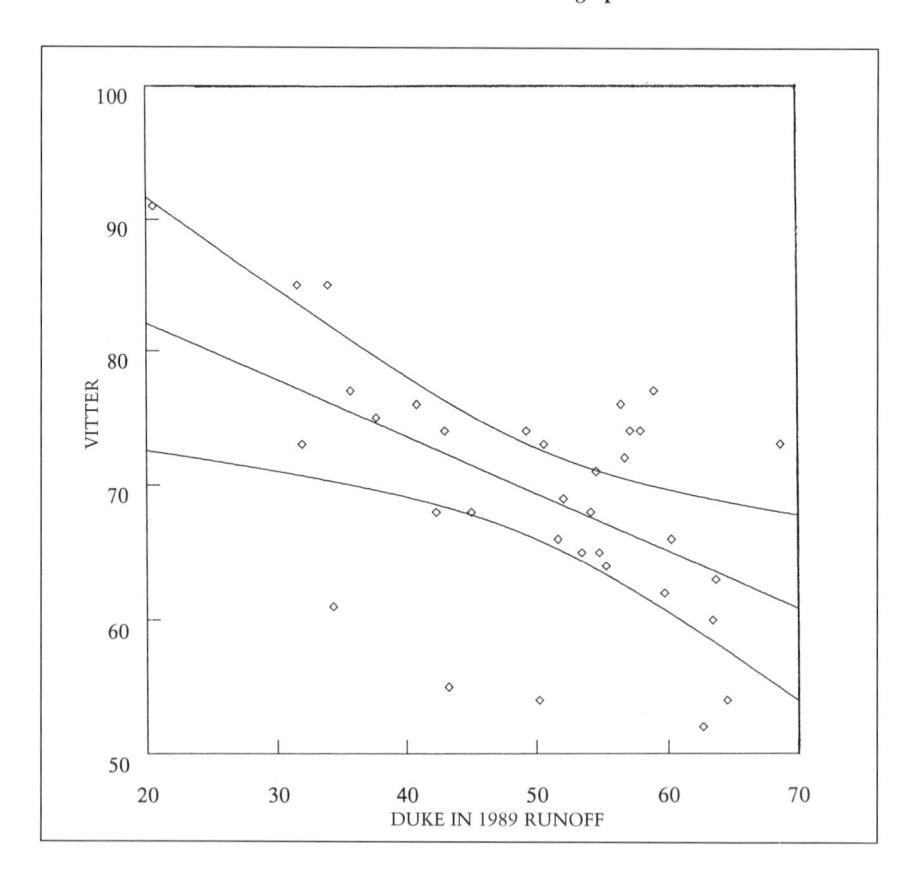

credentials and no Republican instincts. Duke knew this, and so he continued to try for higher office.

The Hidden Edwards Vote and the Landslide That Was Too Close to Call

While Duke was a superfluity in the Louisiana House of Representatives, he certainly was a factor in Louisiana campaigning. Even before settling into the House, Duke had set his sights on the Senate as a stepping-stone to the presidency, for he was deadly serious about

Figure 3.5
Voting Patterns of New Orleans Legislators
1992 Regular Session

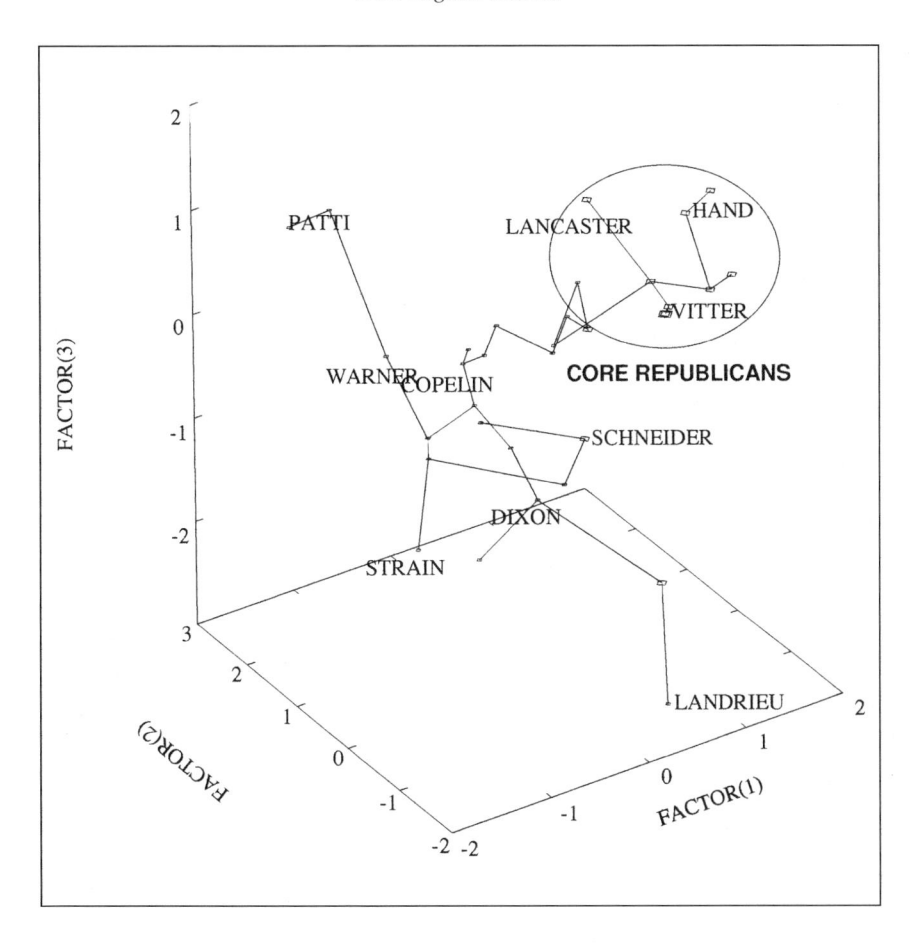

becoming president. So, in 1990, Duke decided to challenge incumbent Democrat J. Bennett Johnston and the official Republican candidate, Ben Bagert.

Johnston was a generally popular senator who had taken office in 1972 after losing the 1971 gubernatorial contest to Edwin Edwards. Eighteen years in office had him well placed in the Senate, but he sometimes incurred the displeasure of the White House. This cost him, it was widely supposed, some lucrative government contracts for Louisiana. Johnston was also, in the view of Duke supporters, "soft on race." But Johnston was by no means what one would have thought of as a vulnerable candidate.

It was, rather, Duke's perception of himself as unstoppable that induced him to run.[1] Bagert's campaign never made any progress with the voters and he dropped out in mid-campaign, leaving the race to Johnston, Duke, and two minor candidates. Duke's showing in the Senate race caught a number of pollsters by surprise. He managed to get a respectable 44 percent of the vote, making him in the views of some a very credible candidate for Governor. Consequently, he came under even closer scrutiny. By 1991 it was impossible to discuss Louisiana politics without reference to Duke.

There were, even without Duke, reasons for noticing Louisiana's gubernatorial race. Three-time governor Edwin Edwards (1971, 1975, 1983) was staging a fourth-term comeback effort against incumbent Buddy Roemer. Roemer, son of a longtime Edwards aide, was one of Louisiana's long string of reformist governors. In fact, Edwin Edwards himself had been a reformer in 1971, but years in office had given him opportunities for a combination of sexual dalliances and financial shenanigans that he found irresistible. The state's voters, too, often found Edwards irresistible, and his impact on the state has been second in this century only to Huey Long.

Incumbent Buddy Roemer's behavior in office had been eccentric even by Louisiana standards. Notably, he had made too public the pain of his divorce, had switched parties from Democrat to Republican, had taken aides on "retreats" at countryside resorts, had unleashed his overly eager appointees (called "Romeristas") on state bureaucracies, and had taken to greeting important visitors to his New Age decorated office while wearing jeans and assorted copper amulets. Any one or two of these things might have endeared him to the electorate since no one doubted his personal integrity. But the cumulative burden of eccentricity, party-switching, bureaucratic disruption, and unconventional manners made him vulnerable. Moreover, in Duke and Edwards he had serious opposition because each possessed wide name recognition, notoriety, a political base, and money.

Edwards, who had come in second to Roemer in the 1987 race, had matured into a politician capable of shouldering the burden of perceptions of corruption with remarkable ease. Between 1983 and 1987 he was indicted twice for (basically) selling licenses to construct and operate superfluous hospitals. The statutes under which he was tried—including federal anti-racketeering law, or RICO—were complex, and the legal processes occupied much of his third term. But Edwards was lucky in two ways. He was tried in predominantly black New Orleans by a Republican U.S. Attorney. Although he escaped conviction, there was widespread suspicion that he was guilty of wrongdoing—though not the wrongdoing with which he was charged. This cost him re-election in 1987.

As the primary approached, the polls in September 1991 indicated a Roemer-Edwards runoff (see table 3.3).

Pollsters, however, had been burned by Duke's unexpected show-

Table 3.3
Poll Results, September 1991

	TV Station Consortium	Verne Kennedy	Penn & Schoen	University of New Orleans
Roemer	26%	33%	32%	35%
Edwards	25	31	28	30
Duke	10	15	16	12
Holloway	9	8	8	8
Undecided / Refused	28	13	16	15

Source: Adapted from "Governor's Race Survey October, 1991" UNO Poll, University of New Orleans.

ing in the senate race and began covering their flanks. One explanation for the frustration and embarrassment pollsters felt was the "hidden Duke vote." Susan Howell, director of the University of New Orleans Poll, commented in her October 1991 press release that her estimates, revised to take into account the "hidden Duke vote," placed "Duke very close to Edwards in the total electorate. If black turnout is much lower than white turnout, the result could be a Roemer-Duke runoff" (Howell, 1991). When the primary results were in, Howell had two hidden votes to explain, those of Duke and of Edwards. Roemer had been squeezed out, and Louisiana faced an Edwards-Duke runoff. This was the nightmare scenario Louisiana's pessimists feared: a choice between a racist and a man indicted on racketeering charges. Indeed, thousands of Louisiana's car bumpers sported the sticker, "Vote For The Crook. It's Important."

The contest was also a nightmare for some pollsters. Even though Edwards seemed to have the lead, University of New Orleans pollsters labeled the outcome "too close to call" five days before the balloting started. As it turned out, the results were a landslide too close to call. An election-eve *Times-Picayune* story captured the skittish mood pollsters were in:

EDWARDS LEADS DUKE IN 3 POLLS
DUKE VOTE HARD TO TALLY
Thursday November 14, 1991
By: Tyler Bridges, Staff writer

Edwin Edwards is leading David Duke in three opinion polls released Wednesday, but the hazards of measuring Duke's support leave the pollsters unwilling to forecast an Edwards victory in Saturday's election for governor. Duke consistently has registered less support in voter surveys than he draws on election day, and pollsters have struggled to account for the "hidden" Duke vote. It is attributed to an unwillingness among some of his backers to acknowledge their support for someone with his extremist background.

The polls were the first independent surveys released in a week in the hotly contested campaign. In the surveys: Susan Howell of the University of New Orleans showed Edwards leading 55 percent to 45 percent. Mason-Dixon Opinion Research showed Edwards leading 49 percent to 42 percent, with 9 percent undecided, in a poll for WDSU-TV. Ed Renwick of Loyola University showed Edwards ahead 54 percent to 46 percent, in a poll for WWL-TV. Edwards said the hard-fought election is difficult to forecast. Nevertheless, he said, "I feel very comfortable. The election is pretty much in the bag." But Duke discounted the poll results. "I think this election is going to be decided by a whisker," he said. "I think we're ahead at this point." The Howell and

Renwick polls were completed before the potentially damaging defection of a member of Duke's inner circle of advisers, who quit the campaign Monday. He said he had concluded Duke is not the born-again Christian he claims to be.

The Mason-Dixon poll was conducted Monday and Tuesday. Howell arrived at the 55-45 figure after attempting to account for Duke's hidden vote in several ways. Voters who rated Duke more honest, inspiring and caring than Edwards were considered Duke voters, even if they said they favored Edwards. All undecided white voters also were considered to be Duke voters by Howell. In the Oct. 19 primary, most of the undecided white voters in pre-race polling wound up in Duke's column. Duke was a leader of the Ku Klux Klan in 1973-80 and then formed the National Association for the Advancement of White People, a white supremacist group he headed until 1990, a year after his election to the state House as a Republican from Metairie. Howell refigured Edwards' total by assigning all undecided black voters to him. Simply asking people whom they favored - the traditional polling technique -showed Edwards with 52 percent, Duke with 26 percent and 22 percent undecided. Howell also said she wasn't sure how accurately her poll accounts for the hidden Duke vote. She said more than 20 percent of the people who were called hung up and thus are not included in the survey.

These people, whom she described as alienated and cynical, are more likely to be Duke voters, she said. Her poll also assumes an equal turnout rate of black and white voters. White voters traditionally turn out in larger numbers, but black voters are considered highly motivated in this election. "There are scenarios that create a Duke victory, but they require radical surgery on the figures," Howell said. Her poll of 701 registered voters, conducted Nov. 6-10, has a margin of error of 3.6 percentage points. The Mason-Dixon results indicate Edwards has gained slightly since a Mason-Dixon poll in late October that showed him ahead 45 percent to 42 percent with 12 percent undecided. Edwards' gain has occurred among white voters, Mason-Dixon said. The Mason-Dixon poll showed that Edwards has a higher favorable rating than Duke, 44 to 31 percent, and that Duke has a higher negative rating than Edwards, 55 to 40 percent. The Mason-Dixon poll sampled 816 voters statewide and has a margin of error of 3.5 percentage points.

Renwick also sought to account for the hidden Duke vote in arriving at the 54-46 breakdown. Before the adjustment, his figures showed Edwards with 48 percent, Duke with 28 percent, "neither" at 12 percent and undecided at 12 percent. Adding in the 4 percent of voters in the neither or undecided column who said they were leaning to Edwards boosted him to 52 percent. "Renwick's always wrong," Duke said. The poll of 750 voters was taken Nov. 5-9 and has a margin of error of 3.5 percentage points.

Why did some pollsters miscall these elections? It may be that some had bad samples. In the case of Howell, whose data are public record, there are two complementary answers. First, University of New Orleans pollsters had a contempt for voters even exceeding that of most politicians. Recalling how Duke had taken 44 percent of the vote in the senate race, while her respondents indicated a 30 percent plurality, Howell (1991) opined:

Another way to estimate the hidden Duke vote is to ask respondents whom they voted for in the 1990 Senate election, assuming that those who were deceptive once will be deceptive again. Only 30% of those voting in 1990 said they had voted for Duke, yet he received 44% in the election. Thus, his support increased by a factor of 1.5. If we apply the same rule to our 1991 governor's race preferences (excluding the Undecideds) we obtain the following estimates:

        Duke's percentage among all voters: 21%
        Duke's percentage among white voters: 28%.

Certainly there is a mendacity factor in polls, and Howell's allowance for it put Duke uncomfortably close to Edwards. But mendacity is not measurable simply by taking the difference between sampled marginal frequencies and election results. Discrepancies in polls come from far more than respondents' lack of candor. One of the great advantages of surveys is that, when cleverly designed and carefully analyzed, they give a better prediction of the respondent's behavior than he or she can. A good poll is a blend of social psychology and social statistics.

Howell's poll is a good example—up to a point. She recognized that the crucial predictive variables in this election were race and candidate perception questions—such as whether the candidate is "inspiring" or "honest." A simple logistic-regression analysis of these variables used to predict the probability of voting for Duke in the Edwards-Duke runoff provides evidence of an Edwards runaway, a "hidden" Edwards vote. The strategy used to generate this poll-based prediction was elementary. The respondents were divided into two groups: those who stated their voting intention and those who did not. By taking those who stated their preference it was easy to build a logistic model by regressing their preference on race, Edwards's honesty, and Duke's charisma. Subsequently the parameter estimates were applied to the other (less candid) part of the sample to predict statistically their choices. From there, it was a matter of tabulating predicted preferences to estimate the Duke and Edwards pluralities. A related approach, multiple discriminant analysis, fortuitously provides results closer to the actual outcome, but logistic regression is the preferred technique here. Regardless of method, the Edwards landslide is the common prediction.

Table 3.4 shows the logistic parameter estimates and associated standard errors. Figure 3.6 shows the distribution of estimated probabilities, and table 3.5 shows the logistic regression based predictions

Table 3.4
Logistic Regression Analysis of Edwards-Duke Preference in 1991 Runoff

—Variables in the Equation—

Variable	B	S.E.	Wald	df	Sig	R	Exp(B)
DUINSPIR	1.1486	.1151	99.5321	1	.0000	.3766	3.1537
EDHONEST	-1.0873	.1523	50.9584	1	.0000	-.2668	.3371
RACE	2.9128	.8284	12.3640	1	.0004	.1228	18.4079
Constant	-4.0913	.9262	19.5119	1	.0000		

DUINSPIR = Respondents who find Duke inspiring
EDHONEST = Respondents who find Edwards Honest

Source: Statistics compiled by author; data courtesy of the University of New Orleans Poll.

Table 3.5
The Predicted Edwards/Duke Vote Shares

Value Label	Value	Frequency	Percentage
Edwards	0	467	67%
Duke	1	232	33%
	Total	699	100%

Figure 3.6
Observed Groups and Predicted Probabilities

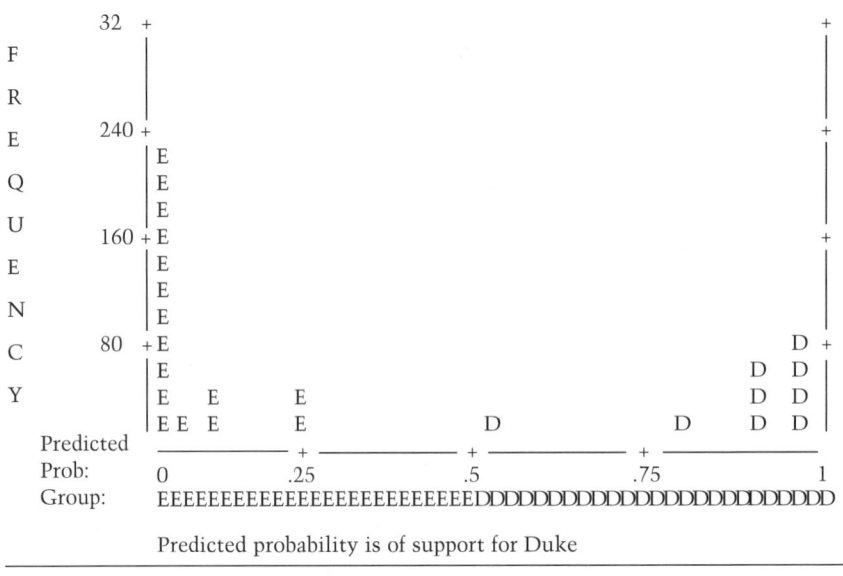

```
              32 +                                                              +
F                |
R                |
E             240 +                                                             +
Q                | E
U                | E
              160 + E                                                           +
E                | E
                 | E
N                | E
C              80 + E                                                      D +
                 | E                                                   D  D  |
Y                | E    E     E                                        D  D  |
                 | E E  E     E          D                D            D  D  |
   Predicted     ─────────────────+──────────────+──────────────+──────────────
   Prob:         0              .25            .5            .75             1
   Group:        EEEEEEEEEEEEEEEEEEEEEEEEEEEEEDDDDDDDDDDDDDDDDDDDDDDDDDDDDDD
```

Predicted probability is of support for Duke

Source: Computed by author.

for Howell's sample, including those who claimed they were undecided.

There are several lessons to be drawn from these findings. First, while the logistic regression model is not really sophisticated, but based only on some political science truisms, it is still rugged enough to allow pollsters to have called the election with great confidence.[2] This landslide was not too close to call. Moreover, as the histogram shows, there were rather sharp distinctions between Edwards and Duke voters. The voters piled up at each side of the histogram in the bimodal pattern typical of a polarized electorate. This is consistent with what was known on the street: Duke and Edwards were not after the same voters. This was no Downsian contest. Third, the notion of the "hidden Duke vote" is not supportable on the basis of these data. We would have to argue that a "hidden Edwards vote" was bigger. Duke voters are easy to find, unless you assume that everyone is lying to pollsters. The rate of successful logistic classification of respondents whose vote was known is above 90 percent. When the model parameters derived from these data were applied to the undecideds, the predictions fit reality acceptably well for prognostication purposes in the case of this lopsided contest.

Why did pollsters not take advantage of this? How did the hidden Edwards vote trump the hidden Duke vote? Howell's belief, expressed to the *Times-Picayune,* that the "alienated and cynical, are more likely to be Duke voters," provides a clue. Lumping the alienated and cynical into the Duke column provided the basis for the hidden Edwards vote. It may be that nonrespondents to surveys are alienated and cynical, but the appeal of Edwards' supporters to "vote for the crook" was an explicit appeal to alienated and cynical voters. Given the choices available there was scant reason to expect many affiliated idealists within the electorate. It did not occur to enough observers that many Louisiana voters, understandably alienated and cynical, regarded voting for a crook as morally indistinguishable from voting for a racist. So, history has been as cruel to the hidden Duke vote as it has been to other chimeras on the fringe of political science: Barry Goldwater's claim in 1964 of millions of conservatives in the political woodwork, or Spiro Agnew's silent majority.

Conclusion

In this essay we have looked at three forms of data: aggregate election returns, roll-call votes, and polling data. Roll call votes tell us the most about Duke as an elected official, but they are the most ignored of all data, even though the easiest to analyze, in that they are not subject to the ecological fallacy (which has been ignored in most studies of Duke) nor to the "hidden Duke vote," which has infected many studies of Duke. What the roll call votes indicate is an absence of original thinking and behavior on Duke's part. He is a *faux* Republican.

Aggregate data do show, however, that the geographical pattern of race-based voting is chronic in pockets of Jefferson Parish. This is inconsistent with Lawrence Powell's thesis that there is a connection (on the basis of these data) between Reagan-Bush trickle-down economics and Duke. It is consistent with notions that racial appeals have a continuing appeal to some Louisiana voters—an appeal of long standing and that could be used again.

Survey data emerge as the most problematic. Pollsters have taken a drubbing in public opinion in the past few years. Many did poorly not only in the Louisiana battles over Duke, but also on a national scale in the Bush-Clinton contest. This may be due in part to the pollsters' rush to gather data. It does not take a lot more time to build and test statistical models of voting behavior, given that both theoretical and statistical models have improved remarkably since the 1960s.

In the case of Duke, however, the notion of the hidden Duke vote was seductive politically and professionally. Most scientists would instinctively reject the notion that they could not penetrate voter intentions and would devise various work-arounds such as logistic regression, a powerful technique that nonpollsters can use successfully. Duke, however, enraged many of those who studied him. Indeed, he put not only the press but also social scientists off-balance, and the two groups fell over each other in contests to denounce him and his supporters. Journalists and academics could both attack Duke, but attacking his supporters was the preserve solely of social scientists wielding polls and computer models.

Historians like Powell actually lost track of time and failed to include important aggregate data from the 1998 presidential election. Some political scientists lost track of data and modeling techniques, in that it became an article of faith with them that respondents were lying. This was easy to believe, the logic goes, since many of the respondents had to be racists; from there it was easy to conclude that racists naturally lied to pollsters and were going to vote for Duke.

What might have occurred to some pollsters was the nature of Duke's opposition. Certainly one can suspect that respondents might find it hard to admit, on grounds of social acceptability, that they are supporting a racist like Duke. But it is arguably just as likely that social acceptability would disincline respondents to admit they were supporting a "crook" like Edwards. This dilemma is the explanation for the hidden Edwards vote that created the landslide too close to call.

Thus, in this atmosphere of misspecified mendacity, the process of scientific observation became, *ad initio*, not a search for the unknown—the role of statistics—but a guessing game. In short, the presumption of respondent duplicity (even though it was the wrong kind of duplicity) made science impossible. With science impossible due to a database of falsehood, no scientist could be held responsible for being wrong in parameters as long as he or she was right in his or her politics.

Where does this leave us in terms of David Duke, whose star was eclipsed? Six points need to be made about his rise to notoriety.

1. Chronic racism

Duke defies any single simple explanation such as the trickle-down effect or a hidden vote. What is undeniable is that Duke came from an area with a record of serious and frequent flirtation with racist candidates. There are other areas in Louisiana just as addicted, but in Louisiana racism is not enough to carry the day. Duke has one narrow electoral victory in an isolated area to his credit. In larger constituencies he cannot win.

2. Campaign skills

Duke had mastered, with a lot of practice, the door-to-door, flesh-pressing campaigning so essential in south Louisiana. This kind of campaigning works in other parts of the country, as well, and it is not unique to Louisiana. But, in local races a candidate's most important tool is a stout pair of shoes. None of Duke's 1989 opponents, including the aloof John Treen, could match Duke's street-smart campaigning.

3. The press

Duke came into the arena a year after Bush succeeded Reagan. He was easy to hate, not just for his hostility to blacks, but also for his unaccountable anti-Semitism, in a state were Jews are rare and, in politics at least, assimilated. No candidate could buy the exposure Duke got. For some, voting for Duke must have amounted to the thrill of thumbing one's nose at the national and international press. While Duke is not witty like Edwin Edwards, or moving like Buddy Roemer, he is an outgrowth of Louisiana's political culture—a culture that places a high value on being outrageous. The press was an unwilling Duke ally.

4. Personal Magnetism

We have to consider Duke himself. It is indisputable that he has some sort of magnetic effect on crowds. It is not just that he is mediagenic. Rather, he has an ability to gather attention and hold it. He is impervious to heckling. He also has an ability to reduce his platform to a set of simple propositions. In turn, he can reduce simple propositions to sound bites.

5. Issues

Duke inevitably brings up discussions of "symbolic racism." This is an inchoate concept that while useful for labeling almost any idea racist, has dubious scientific value. Duke, not entirely unintentionally, made his racism clear by burlesquing the slogans and personalities of the civil rights movement; his thinly disguised imitations of Jesse Jackson and his paper organization, the National Association for the Advancement of White People, were at least partially done tongue-in-cheek. Duke's "equal rights for all" slogan was his most effective device. His pokes at reverse racism were never directly answered since no white politician, not Bush, and certainly not Clinton, wanted to leap to the defense of the racial spoils system Duke was lampooning. Probably Duke's greatest satisfaction was seeing (though perhaps not causing) the Democrats to move towards the center in the campaign of 1992.

6. The Future

People love their nightmares. If they did not we would lack a lot of our narrative and fantasy culture. Gone would be the Hades of Greco-Roman times, Dante's *Inferno,* and Mary Shelley's Frankenstein myth.

Subcultures, too, have their favorite nightmares and sorcerers. In political science, it is David Duke's political cadaver that haunts the land. For some time to come every Louisiana politician to the right of Edwin Edwards will be compared to Duke—some perhaps fairly so. But Duke was ultimately defeated by Louisiana voters, and repeatedly so. His biggest victory has been over social scientists.

PART II

David Duke and the Electorate

4
A Parish Profile of the David Duke Vote: Sociodemographic, Economic, and Voting Propensity Predictors

◢

Stephen J. Caldas
John C. Kilburn

Maverick Republican and former Ku Klux Klan Grand Wizard David Duke has, in recent years, shown significant electoral support in the state of Louisiana. He first surprised many with a better than expected showing in his 1990 attempt to unseat Louisiana's three-term incumbent U.S. Senator J. Bennett Johnston, receiving 43.5 percent of the vote. In the 1991 nonpartisan gubernatorial primary election less than one year later, Duke finished a close second to former Democratic three-time Governor Edwin Edwards, beating out the moderate-Republican Governor Charles ("Buddy") Roemer, and state party endorsed conservative-Republican U.S. Representative Clyde Holloway. Though Edwards easily defeated Duke in the gubernatorial runoff with over 60 percent of the vote, Duke still managed to garner 55 percent of the white vote.

Duke's campaign focused on recurrent themes of restructuring programs of the welfare state, eliminating affirmative action programs, and reducing the number of illegitimate births. However, the media, public interest groups, and many concerned citizens focused much of their attention on Duke's past ties with white supremacist and neo-Nazi groups.

Who voted for this self-proclaimed Republican who became something of a political pariah to his own party? Utilizing parish-level data, this chapter attempts to answer this question by entering sociodemographic, economic, and voting propensity variables into a regression model. We present a comprehensive profile of parishes that supported Duke in the three elections. Though Duke received little support in his 1992 bid for the Republican presidential nomination, we find that Republican voting propensity was the primary predictor of his electoral support.

Parish-Level Analysis

Mason-Dixon Opinion Research of Columbia, Maryland, conducted a poll immediately before the 1990 Louisiana U.S. senatorial election which showed Johnston with 53 percent, Duke with 26 percent, and Ben Bagert with 8 percent of the vote (Bridges, 1990). These predictions and others were woefully off base, suggesting that a survey may not be the appropriate method for determining voters' preferences in an election that featured David Duke. Clearly, Duke received the votes of many Louisianians who were not publicly willing to declare their support for him.

There is, however, a statistical radar net below which his supporters cannot fly. Many sociologists and political scientists agree that with proper model specification and appropriate statistical and methodological checks, the use of aggregate-level data to infer individual behavior is justifiable (Gove and Hughes, 1980; Hanushek, Jackson, and Kain, 1974). In fact, challenging Robinson's (1950) renowned claim to the contrary, Kramer (1983) pointed out that aggregate-level data analysis is more likely to yield valid inferences about individual behavior than analysis based on individual-level data. The Michigan model of normal vote analysis (Campbell, Converse, Miller, and Stokes, 1960) suggests that certain influences measured at the aggregate level—such as sociodemographic, economic, and ideological disposition—are important in determining electoral outcomes. Employing a sociological perspective, this chapter looks at characteristics of the parishes which supported the former Ku Klux Klan leader. We find that aggregate sociodemographic, economic, and voting propensity parish-level data are powerful predictors of individual-level voting behavior. Our findings are partially corroborated by a precinct-level analysis conducted on results from the 1991 Louisiana gubernatorial runoff (Parent, Caldas, Kilburn, and Petrakis, 1992). Our research indicates that the combination of these variables can explain as much as 88 percent of the Duke vote.

LOUISIANA POLITICAL CULTURE

Since Huey P. Long's political reign in the 1920s and early 1930s, Louisiana officials elected in statewide elections, as well as their public policies, have been strongly influenced by Liberal-Populist demands (Williams, 1969). Louisianians have traditionally pitted economically conservative Bourbons against the more liberal Populists in elections. Only four fiscally conservative *neo*-Bourbons have held the office of governor since Huey Long.

Louisiana elections have also typically been clashes between North Louisiana (northern and Florida parishes) and South Louisiana (Acadiana, and Orleans parish) ideologies. Map 4.1 highlights these four major subregions of Louisiana.

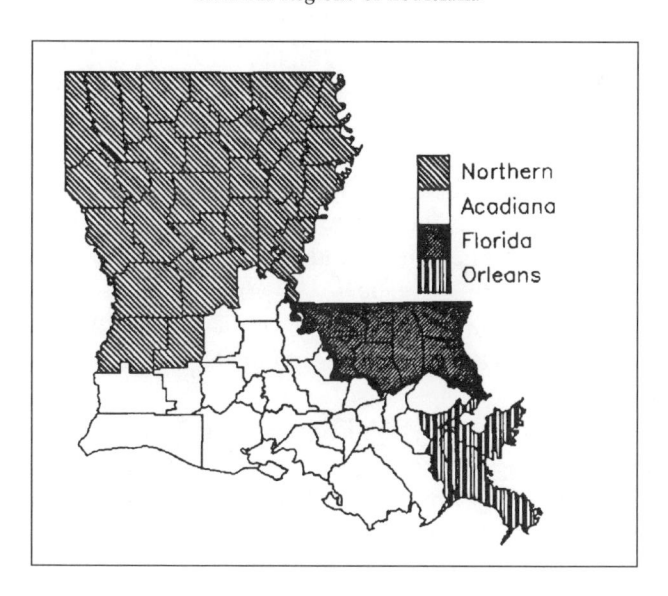

Map 4.1
Cultural Regions of Louisiana

The Acadiana-black coalition has voted loyally Democratic, electing governor Edwin Edwards to four terms, President Jimmy Carter in 1976, U.S. Senator John Breaux in 1986 and 1992, and made the state "too close to call" until election day in the 1988 presidential contest. This coalition helped Bill Clinton win Louisiana in the 1992 presidential election. It has been observed that the poor whites of North Louisiana have occasionally joined the Cajun-black coalition against the wealthy in elections specifically dealing with bread and butter economic issues (Landry and Parker, 1982).

However, poor North Louisiana whites have adopted David Duke, rather than Bennett Johnston or Edwin Edwards, as the champion of their interests. It may in part be because of Duke's ties to an organization that has traditionally been anti-Catholic as well as anti-black, which explains why the Cajun-black coalition held together in opposition to Duke in the 1990 U.S. senatorial and 1991 gubernatorial elections. Significantly, the Acadiana and metro New Orleans parishes of South Louisiana are predominantly Catholic, whereas the parishes of North Louisiana are predominantly Baptist.

David Duke: A Populist?

In Louisiana, the poor North Louisiana whites, and not blacks or Acadians, increasingly perceive of themselves as the politically alienated: David Duke, and not Bennett Johnston or Edwin Edwards, was perceived as the standard bearer of their cause. Moreover, Duke's Louisiana constituency is a representative microcosm of a larger, nationwide segment of the electorate who find Duke's message, if not Duke himself, attractive. The populist speaks for the disfranchised, and, as in the days of Reconstruction and Huey Long, poor whites are once again looking to those leaders who will represent their interests. When asked about this during the gubernatorial campaign on statewide public television, Duke responded, "Yes, I consider myself a populist."

Nie, Verba, and Petrocik (1976) suggest that parties and candidates try to present themselves as centrists, while defining the opposition as extremists. Duke claimed that the mainstream of Louisiana's voters agreed with his platform, whereas Johnston's Senate voting record was not representative of the will of the people. Duke went so far as to claim that Johnston's voting record was more liberal than Ted Kennedy's, although this claim was never substantiated. Though a Democrat, Johnston was also a North Louisiana Protestant. By contrast, there was no need for Duke to exaggerate the truth regarding the liberalism of his Catholic, Democratic South Louisiana gubernatorial challenger Edwin Edwards. A notorious gambler and twice indicted (though both times acquitted), Edwards was perceived as a threat by the typical North Louisiana Duke supporter. As a result, the gubernatorial runoff polarized voters to an even greater extent than the 1990 U.S. Senate race, or the 1991 gubernatorial primary (Caldas, 1992).

Duke appealed to an increasingly alienated constituency, both in Louisiana and across the nation. He publicly empathized with his supporters by insisting that it was he who had been banned from certain establishments and not allowed to tell his side of the story. Duke also claimed that he was being discriminated against and that his supporters had been threatened and ostracized (Cooper, 1990). Legitimacy was added to this fiery message in 1990 when Johnston refused Duke's challenge to debate, and later in 1992 when several state Republican party machines refused to enter Duke's name on their 1992 Presidential primary ballots.

Aggregate-Level Determinants of Voting Behavior

Race

David Duke's strong showing in both the senatorial and gubernatorial elections underscores the fact that race continues to dominate politics in Louisiana and the nation. His popularity in statewide elections in combination with his election to the state legislature in 1989 has been interpreted as a manifestation of latent racist attitudes in Louisiana (Moreland and Parent, 1991). Moreover, according to Moreland and Parent, "The politics of the South continued to offer no apparent avenues for poor Southern whites to voice their concerns. In the eyes of the poor white Southerner, the national Democratic party had increasingly taken the 'side' of blacks, while Republicans remained the party of the rich" (p. 12).

In his book *The Two-Party South*, Alexander Lamis (1988) observed that native southerners started to turn against the Democratic party due to the civil rights stances of the organization. While this may also hold true for the more typically "southern" culture of North Louisiana, David Landry and Joseph Parker (1982) noted a Latin tradition of tolerance in which racism was "rarely as intense or, one might argue, was never as institutionalized in Southern Louisiana as it was in other parts of the South" (p. 2). Landry and Parker also pointed out that the French (Acadiana) parishes had a higher percentage of blacks registered to vote prior to the 1965 Voting Rights Act than in any other area of the South. Nor did the Ku Klux Klan find much support in South Louisiana, primarily because the Klan is anti-Catholic as well as anti-black. Thus, one would predict less support for Duke in southern as opposed to northern Louisiana.

Duke's past and present ties to the Ku Klux Klan and neo-Nazi groups and his founding of the National Association for the Advancement of White People suggest that race is a significant predictor of voting support. Indeed, Duke received a majority of the white vote in the runoff elections for senator and governor. Thus, our model controls for the percentage of the parish population which is black.

Education

In their study of southerners, Black and Black (1987) found that education is the variable most closely associated with attitudes of racial and religious bigotry. In Duke's 1989 election for state representative, precincts with large numbers of college graduates favored Duke's opponent, the more centrist Republican John Treen (Powell, 1990). Further, data from an April 1990 U.S Senate race poll of Orleans and Jefferson parishes showed education as the best predictor of candidate preference (Howell, 1990): as the educational level of white voters increased, Duke's support decreased, whereas Johnston and Bagert's support increased. Caldas (1992) found that percentage of a parish's population with a college degree was strongly and negatively related to the Duke vote in the 1990 U.S. Senate election, as well as in the 1991 gubernatorial primary and runoff elections. For these reasons, and because college graduates make up an increasing proportion of the electorate (Dalton, 1988), we include the percentage of parish population with a college degree as the measure of education.

Income Change, Poverty, and Income Distribution

Louisiana's unusual economic circumstances could explain electoral support for a candidate like Duke, according to Paul R. Abramson, who notes that "Louisiana is a special case in that even with the rebound of oil prices, it has really had a much tougher go during [1988 and 1989] than most states" (in Raber and Alpert, 1990). Kramer (1971) found that economic fluctuations did affect voting outcomes. Many politicians across the nation have recently faced closer than expected elections due to nationwide anti-incumbent sentiment. Protest is a product of an environment in which expectations and opportunities differ significantly. It is not necessarily the most needy, but rather those who *believe* that they are not receiving their "entitlements," who are likely protest voters. Davies (1962) and Gurr (1970) are leading proponents of the claim that relative economic deprivation leads to protests. The media has often linked economic hard times in Louisiana with support for Duke. Could it be that parishes showing slower economic growth would be more likely to vote for a protest candidate like Duke? Parent, Jillson and Weber (1987) found that change in per capita income was a significant predictor of election outcomes. In order to capture the effect of change in income on voting behavior, and thus test the notion that relative economic deprivation had an impact on the Duke vote, we have included percentage change in median parish household income from 1979 to 1989 as a predictor variable in the study.

James Wright (1976) reported that alienated persons are more likely to have lower social status and to participate less in the electoral process. Interestingly, however, no significant political science literature addresses the voting behavior of those in poverty, independent of poverty's association with race. This deficiency in research notwithstanding, poverty is not exclusive to minorities, especially in Louisiana. Caldas (1992) demonstrated a link between white poverty and the Duke vote in the gubernatorial runoff: controlling for other factors, as white poverty increased, so did parish-level support for Duke. Given that welfare reform was the centerpiece of Duke's campaigns, and that his public appeal was to the working poor, we feel it is also necessary to include poverty as a predictor variable in the study. This allows us not only to remove the confounding effect that poverty may have on other variables in the model, but also to determine its unique effect on the Duke vote.

Although it is true that those in poverty do tend to be more politically alienated, a single measure of poverty does not capture the differing degrees of economic need. Further, the poverty line, which is arbitrarily established by the federal government, could be as much as 50 percent below the actual poverty boundary in America (Wilson, 1991). Are those voters in income brackets marginally above the poverty level, who do not qualify for certain government entitlements, more likely to vote for a candidate like Duke? Given Louisiana's notoriously regressive tax structure, which burdens lower income voters disproportionately, one would predict more resentment among those who perceive that they are helping to fund government programs from which they do not benefit. In order to examine this possibility, we compare the proportion of households in selected income brackets in those parishes where more than 50 percent of the vote was cast for Duke, with the income distribution in the rest of the state's parishes for both the U.S. Senate and gubernatorial elections.

Urbanization

Riley Baker (1982) asserts that urbanization has led to a growing emphasis on interdependence that leads to increasing acceptance of government programs which redistribute financial resources. Given Duke's strong antigovernment spending message, this would suggest that the less urbanized an area, the more likely voters are to support Duke. In order to examine this possibility, we have included a measure of urbanization in this study.

Republican Voting Propensity

When inconsistent individual attitudes are aggregated into socially meaningful groups based on characteristics like class and gender, it is possible to speak of group beliefs (Feld and Grofman, 1988). Converse (1964) also demonstrated that, while very few people identified themselves as ideologues, almost half of the respondents claimed to vote according to group interests. Powell (1990) showed that Duke's partisan support in his successful bid for the state legislature was the Reagan-Democrat working class. The Democratic party has held a long reign in Louisiana since the end of Reconstruction. The Republican party began to show strength in the South at the time that the Democrats became associated with the civil rights movement (Bass and DeVries, 1976). Yet have those alienated poor whites who typically voted Democrat been casting their votes for Republicans, and consequently, was David Duke's support mobilized from parishes that voted for the Conservative-Republican candidates in recent statewide elections? In order to address the latter question, we have included a predictor variable that is a measure of a parish's propensity to vote Republican.

Data and Methods

The data used in this study come from the U. S. Census Bureau Louisiana Household Characteristics (1990) and the 1990 U.S. Census Bureau data tape STF–3A. The voting records used were reported by the Associated Press in Louisiana newspapers (November 5, 1986; November 9, 1988; October 8, 1990) and were also obtained from the Office of the Louisiana Secretary of State. All data were collected at the parish level; Louisiana has sixty-four parishes.

Focusing on the parish as the level of analysis is appropriate for several reasons. The parish (county) may be the local governmental subdivision that most accurately captures the notion of "community" and hence serves as a socially meaningful group for which aggregated data are available (Caldas, 1991). The county encompasses all other forms of local government within its boundaries and regulates law enforcement, zoning, distribution of welfare, and a multitude of other functions (Berkley and Fox, 1978; Ross, Bluestone, and Hines, 1979). In Louisiana, where school district boundaries are coterminous with parish boundaries, the sense of parish as an integrated community is further heightened (Caldas and Pounder, 1990). Thus, perhaps especially in Louisiana, the parish reflects a particularly well integrated social microcosm of shared norms and values.

Parent, Jillson, and Weber (1987) have demonstrated that aggregated sociodemographic and economic factors do indeed affect electoral outcomes at the state level of analysis. Given that measures at the county level are more likely to be reflective of its individual members than state-level measures, the current approach is likely to overcome much of the aggregation bias associated with larger units of analysis.

Variable Selection

The variables listed below, chosen for this study's analysis, are all aggregated to the parish level.

Dependent Variables

(1) Percentage of Duke Senate vote (Duke90S)—The number of votes cast for Duke in the 1990 Louisiana Senate election divided by total votes cast, and multiplied by 100.

(2) Percentage of Duke gubernatorial primary vote (Duke91P)—The number of votes cast for Duke in the 1991 Louisiana gubernatorial primary election divided by total votes cast, and multiplied by 100.

(3) Percentage of Duke gubernatorial runoff vote (Duke91R)—The number of votes cast for Duke in the 1991 Louisiana gubernatorial runoff election divided by total votes cast, and multiplied by 100.

Independent Variables

(1) Percentage of high school graduates in 1990 (HSGRAD90)

(2) Percentage of college graduates in 1990 (COLGRD90)

(3) Percentage of blacks (PCTBLACK) - The percentage of the parish population that was black in 1990.

(4) Median household income in 1989 (MEDINC89)

(5) Percentage of income change, 1979–1989 (PCTINCHG)—(Median household income 1989—Median household income 1979) / Median household income 1979 and multiplied by 100.

(6) Percentage of population in poverty in 1989 (PCTPOVTY)

(7) Percentage Urban (PCTURBAN)—Percentage of population living in an urban area in 1990.

(8) Distribution of 1989 households by following annual income levels:
  a. Less than $10,000 (INCLES10)
  b. $10,000–$14,999 (INC10–14)
  c. $15,000–$24,999 (INC15–24)
  d. $25,000–$34,999 (INC25–34)
  e. $35,000–$49,999 (INC35–49)
  f. $50,000–$74,999 (INC50–74)
  g. $75,000 or more (INCGR75)

(9) Republican voting propensity of parish (REPUBLIC)—Percentage of the vote in the 1986 U.S. Senate election for Republican candidate Henson Moore added to percentage of the vote in the 1988 presidential election for Republican candidate George Bush, then divided by two.

Research Design

Given that our principal task was to predict the percentage of the Duke vote in the three statewide elections, and that the Duke-dependent variables are measured on a continuous interval-level scale, ordinary least squares multiple regression was employed. However, since the N (number of parishes) is relatively small (sixty-four), and a minimum of ten subjects per predictor variable are typically required in a regression analysis (DiLeonardi and Curtis, 1988), a limited number of variables could be included in our regression models. For this reason, in order to profile and analyze those parishes voting for Duke in as great a depth as possible, we supplemented our regression analysis with an alternative mode of inquiry in order to include all relevant variables. We did T-test comparisons of the means of a range of variables between Duke and non-Duke parishes in the U.S. Senate, gubernatorial primary, and gubernatorial runoff elections (tables 4.1, 4.2, and 4.3).

Map 4.2
Voting Propensity

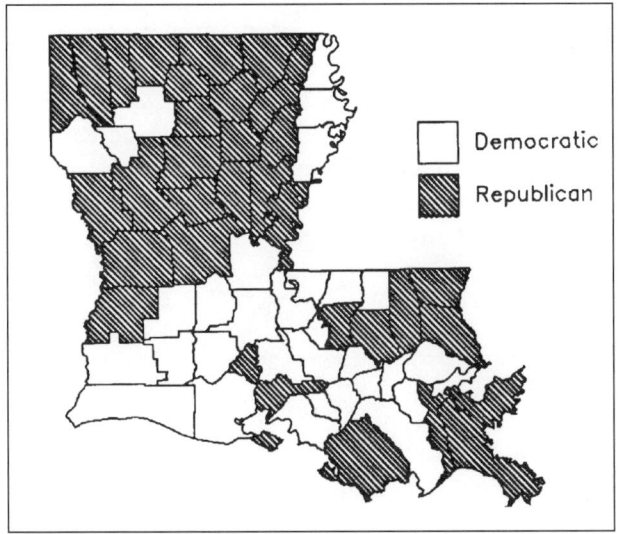

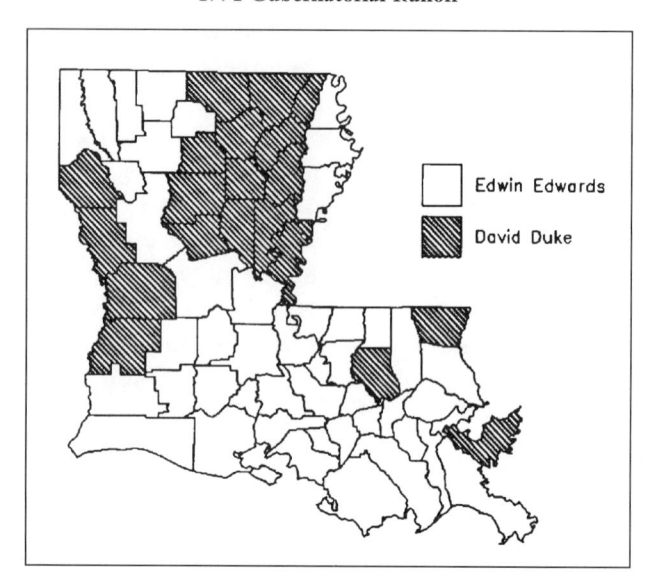

Map 4.3
1991 Gubernatorial Runoff

The Duke parishes were those twenty-four parishes in the U.S. Senate election and nineteen parishes in the gubernatorial runoff where more than 50 percent of the vote was cast for David Duke. In the gubernatorial primary, where there were 12 candidates, the Duke parishes are the 31 parishes where Duke received a plurality of the vote. Map 4.2 highlights those parishes with a propensity to vote Republican, and map 4.3 highlights those parishes that voted for Duke in the gubernatorial runoff.

Results

Duke Parishes

Tables 4.1, 4.2, and 4.3 compare the means of key demographic, economic, and voting propensity variables of the Duke and non-Duke parishes in all three statewide contests. T-test values are generated to determine statistically significant differences.

The characteristics of parishes voting for Duke in the U.S. Senate race, the gubernatorial primary, and the gubernatorial runoff elections are remarkably similar. The important distinction among the three elections is that in the runoff, the differences between the means of each variable are greater and are more likely to be statistically significant. In other words, there was a greater polarization between Duke and non-Duke parishes in the gubernatorial runoff between Duke and

Table 4.1
Duke Senate and Gubernatorial Primary and Runoff Elections
(N=64)

Variable	Mean	Standard Deviation
DUKE90S (Percent Duke Senate Vote)	46.8	8.40
DUKE91P (Percent Duke Gubernatorial Primary)	35.7	8.12
DUKE91R (Percent Duke Runoff)	44.6	9.82
COLGRD90 (Percent College Graduates)	11.25	4.79
HSGRAD90 (Percent High School Graduates)	62.15	7.86
MEDINC89 (Median Household Income, 1989)	19,573	4,704
PCTBLACK (Percent Black)	30.45	14.10
PCTINCHG (Percent Income Change, 1979–89)	45.25	15.19
PCTPOVTY (Percent Living in Poverty)	27.07	8.07
PCTURBAN (Percent Living in Urban Areas)	42.38	28.34
REPUBLIC (Republican Voting Propensity)	49.66	9.11

Table 4.2
1991 Gubernatorial Primary
Economic and Demographic Profiles of Non-Duke and Duke Parishes:
T-test Comparisons

Variable	MEAN Non-Duke Parishes (N=33)	SD	MEAN Duke Parishes (N=31)	SD	T-Value
1. Percent Duke Primary Vote, 1991	29.99	4.59	41.78	6.46	-8.46***
2. Percent College Graduates	11.84	5.95	10.62	3.10	1.04
3. Median Household Income, 1989	19,515	5,016	19,635	4,420	-0.10
4. Percent 1989 Household Income Distribution:					
a. less than $10,000	29.75	8.15	27.95	6.80	0.96
b. $10,000–14,999	11.83	1.81	12.54	1.84	-1.56
c. $15,000–24,999	18.93	1.83	19.95	2.29	-1.97
d. $25,000–34,999	13.72	2.14	14.70	1.90	-1.95
e. $35,000–49,999	13.26	3.45	13.38	3.36	-0.13
f. $50,000–74,999	8.68	3.55	8.15	2.98	0.65
g. more than $75,000	3.82	1.96	3.34	1.23	1.18
5. Percent Black	36.58	15.12	23.92	9.39	4.05***
6. Percent Income Change, 1979–89	40.75	12.83	50.05	16.21	-2.55*
7. Percent Living in Poverty	28.66	9.06	25.37	6.59	1.65
8. Percent Living in Urban Areas	42.69	29.82	42.02	27.16	0.09
9. Republican Voting Propensity	44.47	8.87	55.08	5.61	-5.70***

*p≤ .05   **p≤ .01   ***p≤ .001

Edwards. Thus, the comparison between the Duke and non-Duke parishes in the runoff provides the best profile of a Duke parish. For this reason we focus on the parishes voting for Duke in the gubernatorial runoff in our profile of a typical Duke parish (table 4.3). These parishes are a better representation of Duke's true support. Accordingly, in the following section, the "Duke vote" and "Duke parishes" refer exclusively to the results of the gubernatorial runoff.

PROFILE OF A DUKE PARISH

Not surprisingly, Duke parishes have a statistically significant

Table 4.3
Standardized Regression Coefficients (Betas) of Effect of Independent Variables on Dependent Variables
(Duke Senate, Gubernatorial Primary, and Runoff Elections)
(T-values in parentheses)

Independent Variables	Senate	Gubernatorial Primary	Runoff
Percent Poverty (PCTPOVTY)	.113 (1.22)	.090 (0.97)	.182** (2.76)
Percent Black (PCTBLACK)	-.367*** (-3.51)	-.256* (-2.45)	-.366*** (-4.91)
Percent Income Change (PCTINCHG)	.209** (2.74)	.258** (3.39)	.325*** (5.99)
College Graduates (COLGRD80)	-.503*** (-6.52)	-.596*** (-7.75)	-.517*** (-9.41)
Republican Voting Propensity (REPUBLIC)	.613*** (6.76)	.617*** (6.81)	.630*** (9.74)
Intercept =	26.96	15.58	15.02
Adjusted R^2 =	.7668***	.7681***	.8817***
N =	64	64	64

* $p \leq .05$ ** $p \leq .01$ *** $p \leq .001$

smaller proportion of blacks than do non-Duke parishes (23 percent versus 33 percent). They also have a smaller proportion of college graduates, a difference which approaches statistical significance (p=.06). Duke parishes are significantly less urban than non-Duke parishes (33 percent versus 47 percent), lending support to the notion that Duke's antigovernment spending message was better received in more rural areas. The differences in the Republican voting propensity variable show that the average Duke parish was also much more likely to vote Republican in the 1986 Senate and 1988 presidential elections than the average non-Duke parish.

The 1989 average household income is lower in Duke parishes than in non-Duke parishes ($18,303 versus $20,107), a difference that comes close to statistical significance (p=.10). Even so, average percent income change was statistically greater in Duke parishes than in non-Duke parishes, refuting the notion that economic stagnation accounts for Duke's popularity.

A close inspection of the percentage of the population in selected income brackets for Duke and non-Duke parishes discloses an interesting pattern. A statistically greater proportion of the population of Duke parishes have household incomes within the working poor and lower-middle income brackets. that is between $10,000 and $14,999, and between $15,000 and $24,999. However, beginning with the $35,000–$49,999 income bracket, the proportion of households of Duke parishes is smaller than the proportion of non-Duke parishes. Moreover, the discrepancy becomes greater and more statistically significant with each bracket through the highest income bracket, $75,000 or more($t=2.63$, $p \leq .05$).

This pattern of income distribution in Duke and non-Duke parishes indicates that there is a disproportionate percentage of households in the upper-middle and upper income brackets of non-Duke parishes. In contrast, Duke parishes have a disproportionate percentage of households in the working poor to working-class income brackets. If casting a vote for Duke signifies a desire to check the rise of black efficacy, then these findings are consistent with Grabb's (1979) conclusions that working-class individuals "are more willing than middle class individuals to limit the rise of outgroup members" (p. 45).

Bivariate and Multivariate Relationships

The strength of Duke's appeal is demonstrated by his average total parish vote in the 1990 U.S. Senate and the 1991 gubernatorial primary and runoff elections. Table 4.4 provides the means and standard deviations for all variables; these parish percentages were 46.8 percent, 35.7 percent, and 44.6 percent, respectively.

The zero-order correlation coefficients in table 4.5 offer insights into the bivariate relationships between the Duke vote and central sociodemographic, economic, and voting propensity variables. All zero-order correlations of .24 and higher are statistically significant ($p \leq .05$).

There is a relatively unambiguous pattern of correlations between the Duke vote in each election and the independent variables. The statistically significant correlations are in the same direction for each election, with the exception of percentage of income change. It is worth noting that with only two exceptions (percentages of college graduates and black population), the magnitude of the significant bivariate correlations are strongest for the runoff election. As would be expected, there is a relatively strong negative relationship between the Duke vote and percentage black ($r=-49$ in runoff). The other significant negative correlations with the Duke vote are percent college graduates ($r=-.30$ in runoff) and percent urban ($r=-.39$ in runoff). The positive zero-order correlation between Republican voting propensity

Table 4.4
1990 U.S. Senate Election
Economic and Demographic Profiles of Non-Duke and Duke Parishes
T-test Comparisons

Variable	MEAN Non-Duke Parishes (N=40)	SD	MEAN Duke Parishes (N=24)	SD	T-VALUE
1. Percent Duke Senate Vote, 1990	41.71	5.26	55.22	5.03	-10.12***
2. Percent College Graduates	11.47	5.20	10.89	4.09	0.47
3. Median Household Income, 1989	20,073	4,641	18,739	4,787	1.10
4. Percent 1989 Household Income Distribution:					
a. less than $10,000	28.37	7.45	29.73	7.72	-0.69
b. $10,000–14,999	11.85	1.87	12.72	1.70	-1.86
c. $15,000–24,999	19.22	2.42	19.77	1.45	-1.14
d. $25,000–34,999	14.1	2.13	14.23	2.00	-0.09
e. $35,000–49,999	16.67	3.50	12.74	3.17	1.06
f. $50,000–74,999	8.95	3.21	7.55	3.26	1.67
g. more than $75,000	3.77	1.51	3.28	1.85	1.14
5. Percent Black	34.27	14.74	24.08	10.42	2.97**
6. Percent Income Change, 1979–89	40.63	14.74	52.97	12.82	-3.40**
7. Percent Living in Poverty	27.28	8.45	26.72	7.55	0.27
8. Percent Living in Urban Areas	46.85	28.99	1.74	24.23	1.99*
9. Republican Voting Propensity	46.55	8.82	57.03	4.34	-6.35***

* $p \leq .05$ ** $p \leq .01$ *** $p \leq .001$

Table 4.5
Duke Senate and Gubernatorial Primary and Runoff Elections
Zero-Order Correlation Coefficients (N=64)

Variables	X2	X3	X4	X5	X6	X7	X8	X9	X10	X11
X1-DUKE90S (Duke Senate)	.94***	.92***	-.29*	-.24*	.02	-.54***	-.14	.01	-.32**	.63***
X2-DUKE91P (Duke Gub. Primary)		.94***	-.36**	-.18	.13	-.45***	.42***	-.12	-.35**	.58***
X3-DUKE91R (Duke Gub. Runoff)			-.30*	-.12	-.16	-.49***	.49***	-.13	-.39**	.67***
X4-COLGRD90 (College Graduates)				.72***	.39**	.07	.16	-.27*	.55***	.38**
X5-HSGRD90 (High School Graduates)					.72***	-.22	.19	-.70***	.52***	.41***
X6-MEDINC89 (Median Household Income)						-.42***	-.10	-.88***	.50***	.15
X7-PCTBLACK (Percent Black)							.12	.67***	-.03	-.39**
X8-PCTINCHG (Percent Income Change 1979–89)								-.03	-.27*	.47***
X9-PCTPOVTY (Percent Poverty)									-.32**	-.31*
X10 PCTURB90 (Percent Urban)										.17
X11 REPUBLIC (Republican Voting Propensity)										

* $p \leq .05$ ** $p \leq .01$ *** $p \leq .001$

and the Duke vote is the strongest bivariate relationship with all three elections (r=.67 in runoff). The bivariate relationship between the Duke vote and poverty is statistically insignificant for all three elections.

The multivariate model for the three elections in table 4.6 reveals a similar pattern of relationships as the bivariate correlation matrix. That is, the direction of each standardized correlation coefficient is the same in each election. Moreover, all three models are strong pre-

Table 4.6
1991 Gubernatorial Runoff
Economic and Demographic Profiles of Non-Duke and Duke Parishes:
T-test Comparisons

Variable	MEAN Non-Duke Parishes (N=45)	SD	MEAN Duke Parishes (N=19)	SD	T-Value
1. Percent Duke Runoff Vote, 1991	39.40	5.90	56.78	5.37	-11.04***
2. Percent College Graduates	11.80	5.41	9.95	2.53	1.86
3. Median Household Income, 1989	20,107	5,145	18,308	3,218	1.69
4. Percent 1989 Household Income Distribution:					
a. less than $10,000	28.69	8.07	29.34	6.22	-0.32
b. $10,000–14,999	11.75	1.82	13.17	1.52	-2.97**
c. $15,000–24,999	18.92	1.77	20.63	2.41	-3.17**
d. $25,000–34,999	14.20	2.14	14.19	1.96	0.00
e. $35,000–49,999	13.65	3.62	12.52	2.65	.23
f. $50,000–74,999	8.94	3.48	7.20	2.37	2.00*
g. greater than $75,000	3.85	1.84	2.97	0.04	2.63*
5. Percent Black	33.48	14.34	23.28	10.77	2.78**
6. Percent Income Change, 1979–89	40.00	12.90	57.71	12.97	-5.01***
7. Percent Living in Poverty	27.52	8.71	26.00	6.39	0.69
8. Percent Living in Urban Areas	46.85	28.99	36.35	27.73	1.32
9. Republican Voting Propensity	45.31	7.70	56.92	6.24	-6.25***

*p≤ .05   **p≤ .01   ***p≤ .001

dictors of which parishes voted for Duke. Both the senatorial and gubernatorial primary models explain about 77 percent of the variance of the Duke vote. The strongest model, however, is the gubernatorial runoff, which explains 88 percent of the variance of the Duke vote.

In light of the findings of the Duke and non-Duke parish comparisons in tables 4.1, 4.2, and 4.3, the bivariate correlation coefficients (see table 4.5), and the three regression models (see table 4.6), we can conclude that the gubernatorial runoff had the greatest polarizing effect on the Louisiana electorate. Thus, given the remarkable similarity in the coefficients of each regression model, we will examine in more detail the signification of the individual regression coefficients in the runoff model.

Because multiple regression allows us the examine an independent variable's unique effect on a dependent variable while controlling for the effects of all other independent variables, we can interpret more precisely the effect of the model's central variables. Thus, whereas the bivariate relationship between poverty and the Duke vote is insignificant and even negative for two elections, such is not the case in the multivariate regression model for the runoff. Here, the effect of poverty is significant and positive: as the percentage of households in poverty increases, so does the percentage of Duke's runoff vote. It is only when percentage black is entered into the model (evident in stepwise regression results not shown) that the true nature of the relationship between poverty and the Duke vote emerges. The unique effect of the percentage black, on the other hand, is an even stronger though negative predictor of the Duke vote in the runoff election (ß=-.366, p≤.001).

The true relationship between poverty and the Duke runoff vote is initially masked by the high correlation between percent black and poverty ($r=.67$). In other words, the effects of black and white poverty cancel each other out. Controlling for percent black effectively removes the confounding influence of black poverty. Consequently, the emergence of poverty as a significant predictor indicates the positive influence of white poverty on the Duke vote.

In order to control for the changing economic conditions between parishes and the effect that this could have on voters' propensity to vote for David Duke, percentage income change is included in the three regression equations. Surprisingly, its effect is positive and significant: the greater the percentage increase in income, the higher the percentage voting for Duke in all three elections. Thus, Duke's support does not seem to be the result of negative changes in a parish's economic fortunes over the course of the past decade. We consider this a significant finding, as there was much speculation to the contrary by many analysts in the media.

Given the high bivariate correlation between the percentage of high school and college graduates ($r=.72$), it was deemed necessary to include only one of these measures of education in the regression equation. We included the percentage of college graduates. The standard deviation indicates that there was more variation among parishes in terms of college graduates as compared to high school graduates. Second, the percentage of college graduates correlated more highly with the percentage of Duke vote in each election. The magnitude of the bivariate correlation was twice as high with the percentage of Duke vote in the primary, and more than twice the magnitude for high school graduates with the percentage of Duke vote in the runoff. Finally, Powell (1990) has already demonstrated that percentage of college graduates at the precinct level was the more highly correlated of the two education variables with the percentage of Duke vote in his 1989 election to the Louisiana state legislature. For our purposes, the percentage of college graduates is the more discriminating of the two measures of education.

As can be seen, the percentage of college graduates is a strong negative predictor of the Duke vote in all three elections. Indeed, it is the second best predictor, even stronger in effect than percentage of blacks. This finding lends support to Lipset's (1981) contention that better educated voters are less likely to be alienated and thus susceptible to overly simplistic themes like Duke's. Moreover, for all of the speculation that Duke appealed across the entire spectrum of white voters, this study's results suggest that his appeal was disproportionately high in parishes with rural, poor, less educated whites, a finding corroborated by Caldas (1992).

As significant a predictor as education is of the Duke vote, the best predictor in each election by a substantial margin is a parish's propensity to vote Republican. This is striking, especially in the gubernatorial primary, where Duke faced opposition from a moderate and a conservative Republican. One would expect a considerable dilution in the strength of this regression coefficient in an election where the Republican vote was split three ways. However, using precinct-level data, Parent, Caldas, Kilburn, and Petrakis (1992) demonstrated that, in the gubernatorial runoff, Duke's support was part of the pattern of normal Republican voting down the ticket.

In sum, the combination of the five sociodemographic, economic and voting propensity variables account for a large portion of the Duke vote in all three statewide elections, and we have a better idea of what kinds of parishes voted for David Duke. Moreover, the statistical profile of the elections are remarkably similar, suggesting that regardless of what kind of or how many voters constituted the opposition, the characteristics and strength of Duke's support did not change appreciably. Duke not only received a large share of the vote that went to the Republican candidates in the U.S. Senate and presidential races of the mid- to late 1980s, but he also held on to these voters in his own three statewide elections. Moreover, he did this even when the opposition candidates were themselves Republicans who were endorsed by both the state and national Republican parties. Taken as a whole, all of this suggests that Duke's support represents a block that is strong and entrenched and that votes consistently. In short, the typical Duke parish consists of disproportionately poor and working-class, non–college educated whites, who have been supporting Republican candidates.

The pre-election polls of individual responses were poor predictors of who actually voted for Duke. Contrary to Robinson's (1950) classic assertion, this finding lends further credence to the notion that aggregate-level data analysis can indeed yield inferences that are more valid about individual behavior than analyses based on individual data. These parish-level results were corroborated indirectly by a precinct-level analysis of the 1991 Louisiana gubernatorial runoff, which correlated the Republican vote with the Duke vote (Parent, Caldas, Kilburn, and Petrakis, 1992). The precinct-level analysis revealed a correlation of $r=.70$ between the percentage of the electorate voting for the four other Republican candidates for statewide office and the percentage voting for Duke. These results substantiate the notion that Duke's support comes in large part from those voting a straight Republican ticket. Additionally, the findings from these two studies further validate Firebaugh's (1978) contention that "the ecological fallacy is itself a near fallacy" (p. 570).

Summary and Conclusion

Sociodemographic, economic, and voting propensity variables are powerful predictors of who voted for David Duke in the 1990 U.S. Senate election and in the 1991 gubernatorial primary and runoff elections. The findings suggest that the legacy of racial politics in Louisiana is far from over: blacks avoided Duke, and poor whites, alienated by the Democratic party, rallied around his themes of "welfare reform" and so-called equal rights for all.

What we may be seeing in part is a movement protesting the relatively new black political efficacy. The historical precedent for the current period in Louisiana political history is Reconstruction, when black political and electoral participation was also high, although white groups soon reasserted their political power (Key, 1949). More recently, black voter registration and turnout has again been increasing, resulting in greater political power for blacks at all levels of government (Kilburn, 1990). New black political organizations such as the Southern Organization for Unified Leadership (SOUL) and the Community Organization for Urban Politics (COUP) have been very effective in increasing black voter turnout. In 1977, Ernest ("Dutch") Morial was elected the first black mayor of New Orleans, and he was re-elected to a second four-year term in 1981. He was succeeded by the two-term mayor Sidney Barthelemy, who is also black. In 1994, Marc Morial, Dutch's son, took over from Barthelemy. Many working-poor whites, threatened by the latest period of black political efficacy, are uniting to support candidates who challenge the present structure of government, which they perceive as racially biased against them.

This study finds that whites who supported Duke came from lower income brackets. Duke parishes had larger proportions of lower and working-class households, whereas non-Duke parishes had larger proportions of middle and upper income households. This is especially telling since blacks, who are disproportionately poor in Louisiana, make up a significantly larger percentage of the population in non-Duke parishes. However, it is doubtful that worsening economic conditions during the 1980s explain Duke's support, discrediting a popular hypothesis.

Another important finding of our study is that Duke broke up any temporary alliance that may have existed between the Cajun-black coalition and the poor white Baptist dirt farmer from North Louisiana. In all three elections, there was a relatively clean split between French-Catholic Acadiana and the Anglo-Saxon Protestant portion of the state comprising North Louisiana and the Florida parishes. Only two of the traditional Acadiana parishes cast a majority of their votes for Duke in the U.S. Senate race, whereas he did not capture a majority in a single Acadian parish in the gubernatorial runoff. An important reason for this north-south split may not only be the purported greater tolerance of outgroups in Latin-Louisiana, but also the fact that Duke once headed an organization that was anti-Catholic as well as anti-black. Though South Louisiana may be losing its French language, there has been a reawakened pride in its distinct non–Anglo-Saxon cultural roots, countering Duke's subtle emphasis on the superiority of the WASP heritage.

Although attacks against such social programs as affirmative action and welfare are not new to Republican campaigns, Duke's political sentiments and white supremacist past go an extra step in linking the issue of race with the distribution of governmental resources. He unearthed an unexpected amount of resentment among poor white voters, who felt that they were being cheated by governmental programs that unfairly distributed their tax dollars to minorities. Consequently, it is difficult to differentiate the strong resentment against those receiving government assistance from racially motivated distrust. In much the same way that prohibition was used against the Irish Catholics (Carter, 1956), and for some the anti-busing rallying cry has been a code word for racism (Bass and DeVries, 1976), Duke's agenda of ending what he called welfare abuse has become a haven for those continuing the legacy of racial politics.

As strong as the predictors of race and education are of who voted for David Duke, the single strongest predictor remains Republican voting propensity of the parish. It was not just parishes with less educated whites that threw their support to Duke, but also those with less educated whites that voted for Republicans in the 1986 Senate and 1988 Presidential elections. In spite of the effort expended by the Republican party to distance itself from Duke, the fact remains that not only did Duke "feel more comfortable in the Republican party" (Magnuson, 1989: 29), but those Louisianians voting Republican apparently felt comfortable with him as well.

Moreover, Duke's message appealed to conservative Republicans across the United States. In a phone-in poll conducted the day before the gubernatorial runoff by the conservative national radio talk-show host Rush Limbaugh, 82 percent of the 10,000 callers claimed that they would vote for David Duke if they could vote in the Louisiana election. It was also reported that 47 percent of Duke's campaign contributions came from outside of Louisiana (Hevesi, 1991). In sum, the appeal of Duke's brand of ultraconservatism extends well beyond the borders of his state. President George Bush, fully aware of this, modified his campaign rhetoric to make himself more attractive to this bloc of voters. During his 1992 State of the Union address, for example, he emphasized that welfare recipients needed to work for their checks, and "refrain from having children out-of-wedlock." This classic David Duke line was a centerpiece of Duke's appeal to disaffected white voters. Bush's adoption of this plea was not coincidental—although Duke has faded from the national scene, his message continues to be highly attractive to conservative voters.

5
David Duke and the Electoral Politics of Racial Threat

Michael W. Giles
Melanie Buckner

THE ELECTORAL POLITICS OF RACIAL THREAT

The politics of the South were long considered simply the politics of race. This position was most clearly articulated by V. O. Key (1949) in *Southern Politics:* "In its grand outlines the politics of the South revolves around the position of the Negro.... The hard core of the political South...is made up of those counties and sections of the southern states in which Negroes constitute a substantial proportion of the population. In these [black-belt] areas a real problem of politics . . . is the maintenance of control by a white minority" (p. 5).

Key's assertion that the racial tenor of southern politics varied with the concentration of blacks in the local context was substantiated by numerous studies focusing on the politics of this region in the 1950s and 1960s (for example, Price, 1957; Keech, 1971). Examinations of the presidential campaign of segregationist George Wallace in 1968 in particular provided strong support for the Key hypothesis (Lipset and Rabb, 1969; Crespi, 1971; Schoenberger and Segal, 1971; Wasserman and Segal, 1973; Black and Black, 1973; Wrinkle and Polinard, 1973; Wright, 1977). Residents in counties with higher concentrations of blacks were consistently found to give greater support to the Wallace candidacy.

Since Wallace's presidential bid in 1968, the political landscape of the South has been transformed. As a result of the Civil Rights Act of 1965, increasing numbers of southern blacks registered to vote and entered the Democratic party, which was seen as the champion of civil rights at the national level. With the growth of Republican and independent identification among southern whites in the 1970s and 1980s, the black vote has become an essential component of the electoral coalition of many successful Democratic candidates in the region (Petrocik, 1987). As a result, the openly race-baiting, segregationist campaigns of the earlier era have disappeared. Even George Wallace publicly repented his earlier segregationist position and successfully pursued black support in his 1982 campaign for the governorship of Alabama.

Studies of southern politics in this new era have largely ignored the possible contextual effects of black concentration on the political behavior of whites (for a notable exception see Prysby, 1989a). Although, given the racial polarization of the parties, race is recognized as an important aspect of the "new" southern politics, the role of racial hostility has been de-emphasized. Bullock and Campbell (1984), for example, conclude that the voting behavior exhibited by both blacks and whites in Atlanta municipal elections is better conceived of as "racial" than "racist." Racial backlash has even been discounted as a factor in the decline of support for the Democratic party among southern whites (Beck, 1977; Wolfinger and Arseneau, 1978; Wolfinger and Hagan, 1985; Stanley, 1987; Stanley and Castle, 1988; for a contrary view, see Lamis, 1988). Stanley and Castle (1988: 247), for example, argue that the general disaffection of southern whites toward the policies comprising the Great Society was more important in loosening Democratic loyalties than was racial animosity. Studies of partisan change among southern party activists in the 1980s have gone so far as simply to ignore the possible role of racial hostility (Nesbit, 1988).

Black and Black (1987: 39-40) have convincingly documented the decreased importance in the 1980s of the black-belt counties which Key saw as setting the tenor of southern politics in the earlier era. But has the linkage noted by Key between the political behavior of southern whites and the racial concentration in the surrounding context been extinguished in the "new" South? Or, has this linkage only been obscured by the absence of candidates with sufficient racist appeal to make the linkage evident? With Democratic candidates dependent on biracial coalitions and with only a few Republican candidates, such as North Carlina Senator Jesse Helms, willing to appeal openly to racist sentiment, there may simply have been few opportunities for whites "threatened" by higher black concentrations to express their fears through the ballot. The present study examines this possibility first by examining the campaigns of David Duke for the U.S. Senate in 1990 and the governorship of Louisiana in 1991, and second by examining the linkage between racial threat and support for George Bush among Louisiana voters in 1988.

Duke's bona fides as a racial conservative are exceptional for a statewide candidate for national office. He had formerly been associated with the Ku Klux Klan and the American Nazi Party, and had led the National Association for the Advancement of White People. As might be expected, his 1990 campaign for the Senate was characterized by extreme social conservatism openly opposing affirmative action and social welfare programs. At rallies he complained about welfare recipients "having children faster than they can raise your taxes to pay for them" and spoke of a woman who said, "Mr. Duke, I don't know if we're ever going to have another white Miss America in this country" (*New York Times*, October 1, 1990, A18). Because of his extremism, Duke was shunned by the national and state Republican parties. However, in spite of being outspent three to one and having both the Democratic and Republican parties against him, Duke received 44 percent of the total vote and almost 60 percent of the white vote on election day.

To some extent Duke's support reflected a sense of alienation from government among voters. In the words of Joseph Thibodeaux, a sixty-nine-year-old federal worker: "I don't believe in cross burning: I've never seen one . . . [but] . . . It's time for a change. I'd like to clear them all out—from ward constable to president. The government is in favor of rich people and minorities—not me" (*Washington Post*, October 8, 1990, A1). But the appeal of Duke to simple racism cannot be denied. As Grenes Neyaski, a college-aged Duke supporter, asserted: "The blacks are just taking everything. They're taking everything from us and the white race is going down the tubes. Its about time someone spoke up for white people" (*New York Times*, October 5, 1990, A1). Thus, Duke's candidacy provides an exceptionally clear parallel to the southern segregationist candidates of the previous era. Indeed, these quotations could have easily been attributed to supporters of Wallace's 1968 presidential campaign. If electoral support for Duke is unrelated to racial concentrations in the surrounding context, then we can be fairly confident in concluding that the dynamic which V. O. Key saw as defining southern politics has truly been extinguished.

If, on the other hand, a linkage between racial threat and support for Duke is found, then the question remains as to the generalizability of this linkage. Is this dynamic only operative when it is openly cultivated by candidates like David Duke or Jesse Helms? Or can it be invoked by the less explicit appeals of more mainstream candidates? Given the prominent position that the Willie Horton incident played in the Republican's presidential strategy in 1988 and the widespread belief that this strategy was characterized by racial undertones, support for Bush in that election also provides an opportunity to examine this question.

DATA

The variables in this study are measured at the parish level. Since Key's threat hypothesis is inherently contextual, this raises the possibility of an ecological fallacy. Even if a relationship between black concentration and support for Duke and/or Bush exists at the parish level, this does not ensure that individual white voters are responding to the racial context. The fact that earlier research has documented a linkage between racial concentration at the contextual level and individual level perceptions of threat (Giles and Evans, 1986), intolerance (Giles, 1977; Fossett and Kiecolt, 1989), and support for racist candidates (Wright, 1977) lessens concerns about ecological inference in the present case. Nevertheless, caution should be exercised when using aggregate data to infer individual-level relationships.

Because black districts did not vote for Duke, the percentage of the total vote that he received is negatively linked to the level of black concentration in a parish. Simply stated, the greater the extent to which the electorate of a parish is made up of blacks, the smaller the pool of potential support for Duke (see chapter 4). The focus of the present study is, thus, not on the percentage of the total vote received by Duke, but rather the percentage of white voters attracted to his candidacy. No information is available on the level of white turnout in this election, but because Louisiana does maintain voter registration records by race, the vote for Duke as a percentage of the total number of white registered voters in each parish is used as the measure of his support among whites. Similarly, support for Bush is measured as the vote for him as a percentage of the total number of white registered voters in each parish. While a few black voters may have inadvertently voted for Duke and a small percentage of blacks undoubtedly supported Bush, the number of such voters is assumed to be small and not systematically distributed across the parishes in such a way as to affect the test of the hypotheses.

Racial concentration is measured as the percentage of all registered voters classified as black. Although previous studies have employed the percentage of the population that is black as an indicator, the registration measure seems preferable. Racial concentration within the pool of registered voters is a more direct measure of threat to white political dominance than is population racial balance (Prysby, 1989: 308). By any means, the two indicators are so closely correlated that the choice of one over the other makes no difference empirically.[1]

Previous studies also have typically employed the county or its equivalent (parish, for example) as the appropriate contextual unit. However, Fossett and Keicolt (1989) argue that urban residents are responsive to the racial balance of the entire urban context rather than to that of the particular subcomponent in which they reside. Fossett and Keicolt's analysis of the impact of racial context on white racial attitudes provides strong support for this position. Following their example, for parishes outside of standard metropolitan statistical areas (SMSAs) black concentration is measured as the percentage of registered voters who are classified as black. Within SMSAs a single measure of black concentration is calculated by combining information on total voter registration and black voter registration across the constituent parishes. This overall measure is then assigned to each constituent parish.[2]

Although the impact of racial concentration on white support for Duke and for Bush is the principal focus of this study, the effects of additional variables thought to influence racial voting in general or support for the Duke candidacy in particular are examined. Numerous studies have linked social status negatively to racist attitudes and behavior (including Hyman and Sheatsley, 1964; Condran, 1979; Glenn and Weaver, 1981). This may reflect the higher levels of education and accompanying broader world view and tolerance of diversity associated with higher status. Alternatively, it may simply indicate that higher status whites are less likely to compete directly with blacks for jobs and other social goods. To capture both of these aspects, two indicators of status are included in the analysis: the percentage of the white parish population with at least a high school degree and the white median income in the parish.[3]

Urbanism has also been associated with greater tolerance in racial affairs (Black, 1973; Abrahamson, 1980). This variable is measured as the percentage of the population in a parish residing in urban areeas.[4]

The different socialization experiences of various southern age cohorts has been recognized as an important factor in the changing political contours of the region (Beck, 1977). Accordingly, we expect that an "old" South candidate like Duke would receive greater support where the population was socialized into the earlier style of southern politics. This variable is measured as the percentage of a parish's white population reaching voting age after 1961. The selection of any break point in the socialization process is, of course, somewhat arbitrary. However, given the central position of the 1964 presidential election in debates over southern realignment and the role of the passage of the Voting Rights Act of 1965 as a key step in transforming the region's politics, this distinction employed by previous scholars appears to be a reasonable one (Stanley, 1988: 71; Petrocik, 1987: 350).

Along similar lines, we expect persons socialized outside of the region to be less supportive of an "old" South candidate. This variable is measured as the percentage of the parish's white population born outside of the South. With the prolonged crisis in the oil industry in Louisiana, to some extent support for Duke may reflect a protest vote against economic hard times. To examine this explanation, information was collected on the percentage of the white population unemployed in each parish.

Results

The effects of black concentration among registered voters and the control variables on white support for Duke are presented in table 5.1. Consistent with the Key hypothesis, white mobilization for Duke in all three elections is positively and significantly associated with the black concentration among registered voters. The regression coefficients for white mobilization on black concentration indicate that an

Table 5.1
Regression[a] of White Mobilization for Duke and Bush on Black Registration and the Control Variables

	DUKE 1990 Senate	DUKE 1991 Primary	DUKE 1991 Runoff	BUSH 1988
%Black Registered	.390** (.065)	.291*** (.073)	.340*** (.085)	.178** (.068)
Median White Income	-.00002* (.00001)	-.00003** (.00001)	-.00005*** (.00001)	-.00002+ (.00001)
% Whites with H.S. Educ.	.003+ (.002)	.004* (.002)	.007*** (.002)	.009*** (.002)
% Unemployed Whites	.584 (.883)	1.103 (.989)	1.294 (1.153)	-1.708 (1.030)
% Urban	-.0007* (.003)	-.0008* (.0004)	-.0009* (.0004)	-.0000 (.0004)
% White In-migration	-.536** (.202)	-.654** (.226)	-.772** (.264)	-.103 (.232)
% White Young	-.136 (.132)	-.210 (.147)	-.463** (.172)	-.652*** (.157)
Intercept	.451	.459	.645	.524
R^2	.652	.617	.653	.618
R^2adj.	.608	.568	.609	.570

[a] Unstandardized regression coefficients with standard errors in parentheses.
+p<.10 *p<.05 **p<.01 ***p<.001

Table 5.2
Correlation Matrix among Dependent and Independent Variables

	WMOB	%BLACK	MWINC	%H.S. ED.	%WUNEMP	%URBAN	%INMIGR	%YOUNG
White Mobilization	1.000	.580**	-.367**	-.267*	.102	-.448**	-.431**	-.468*
%Black Registered		1.000	.162	.163	-.118	-.029	-.084	-.116
Median White Income			1.000	.700**	-.279*	.670**	.418**	.444*
% Whites with H.S. Education				1.000	-.054	.593**	.739**	.501*
% Whites Unemployed					1.000	-.168	.071	-.321
% Urban						1.000	.399**	.433*
% In-migration							1.000	.454*
% Young								1.000

* $p=.05$ ** $p=.01$

increase of 10 percent in the racial concentration of a parish on average will raise the percent of registered whites voting for Duke by approximately 3 percent (the 1991 gubernatorial primary) to 4 percent (the 1990 Senate race). Stated differently, if 50 percent of the registered voters in a parish are black, then the percentage of registered white voters supporting Duke in the 1991 primary would be 15 percent higher and in the 1990 Senate race would be 20 percent higher than in a parish without any black registered voters.

Although the effects of black concentration are as expected, the pattern for the control variables is less clear (table 5.2). As expected, median income, percent urban, in-migration, and youth are negatively related to white mobilization for Duke. However, the effect of the percentage of young voters is statistically significant only in the 1991 runoff. Also as expected, the percentage of unemployed voters is positively linked to support for Duke, but its effects are not statistically significant. Contrary to expectations, taking into account the effects of the other variables, the percentage of whites with a high school education is positively linked to the percentage of whites voting for Duke; further, this relationship is statistically significant in the two 1991 elections.

These anomalies result principally from multicollinearity among the independent variables. The zero-order correlations between white support for Duke and the control variables are all in the predicted direction (analysis not shown). In brief, parishes that have high median incomes also tend to have higher levels of education, to be more urban, to experience greater in-migration, and to have a younger population. Because the relative effects of each of these variables are not a principal concern of the present study, no attempt will be made to disentangle these relationships.

Given the consistent support for the operation of the threat hypothesis in the elections involving Duke, a clearly racist candidate, the question remains as to whether this linkage is operative in an election where the appeals to race are less overt, as in the 1988 presidential election. This relationship is also examined in table 5.1. Consistent with Key's hypothesis, support for Bush is positively and significantly associated with the level of black concentration among registered voters. As might be expected given the more subtle nature of the racial appeal, the effect of racial threat on white mobilization for Bush is less than that for Duke. An increase of 10 percent in the racial concentration of a parish on average is predicted to increase the percent of registered whites voting for Bush by slightly less that 2 percent. Thus, a parish in which 50 percent of the registered voters are black is predicted to have a 10 percent higher support level for Bush among white voters than a parish without any black registered voters.

Discussion

The threat to white political hegemony embodied in higher black concentrations was the central defining element of southern politics studied by V. O. Key. The implementation of the Voting Rights Act of 1965 and years of black mobilization efforts drastically altered the political topography of the region. Studies of the politics of the transformed South have deemphasized the role of racial hostility and have largely ignored the potential effects of black concentration. The present study hypothesized that the linkage between black concentration and white racial hostility, specifically the willingness to vote for a racist candidate, remains operative in the South but has lacked frequent opportunities for expression. An analysis of support for Duke in his 1990 Louisiana senatorial campaign and his 1991 campaign for governor provide strong support for this hypothesis. Despite controls for urbanism, social status, levels of unemployment, in-migration, and age, support for Duke was found to be linked positively to the racial concentration in the local context. Moreover, this analysis has indicated that the effect of racial threat is not limited to candidates with openly racist appeal. An examination of white support for Bush in 1988 indicates that racial threat also remains operative for candidates whose appeals to race are more subtly cast.

Although this analysis supports the continued potential for racial threat in the "transformed" South, this finding must be placed in perspective. These findings can be read several ways. On the upside, given the electoral empowerment of blacks, a strategy designed to take advantage of the dynamic of racial threat must mobilize an overwhelming majority of white voters to be successful. For example, if 25 percent of an electorate is black, a racist candidate must mobilize almost 70 percent of the white voters to obtain an overall majority. This can happen only if a large percentage of the white electorate resides in close proximity to a large concentration of blacks. In fact, throughout this century the number of southern whites living in this context has actually been declining (Black and Black, 1987:42). In Louisiana, in 1990 only about 15 percent of white voters were registered in parishes where the concentration of blacks exceeded 30 percent. The difficulty of following a racist strategy under such conditions is evidenced by the ultimate failure of the Duke campaign in 1990 and his subsequent failure in the gubernatorial race in 1991. Moreover, the negative effects of income, education, urbanism, in-migration and younger age cohorts on white support for Duke suggests that the current social and economic trends in the region also undermine the effectiveness of racist campaigns.

The downside of the findings of this chapter is the linkage between racial threat and support for Bush. While the effect is relatively small, an increment of 2 percent of the white vote can be crucial to the outcome of a competitive election. Thus, while racial threat may no longer play the defining role in southern politics ascribed to it by V. O. Key, and while openly racist candidacies may have become an anachronism, we can still expect the race card to continue to play an important, and at times crucial, role in southern elections.

6
The Candidacy of David Duke as a Stimulus to Minority Voting

◤

Charles S. Bullock III
Ronald Keith Gaddie
John C. Kuzenski

Lamenting the low level of turnout has become a postscript to many American elections. Participation in presidential elections has drifted downward since the 1960 Kennedy-Nixon contest. Off-year elections for Congress and state officers typically attract even fewer voters than do presidential elections. Municipal and local contests generate participation rates comparable to classroom attendance on the afternoon before the Thanksgiving vacation.

The surge in voting in the 1991 Louisiana gubernatorial election countered these patterns. This election, which offered choices that dissatisfied many voters, nonetheless found 79 percent of the registrants at the polls. This chapter examines turnout in the 1991 Edwards-Duke election from two perspectives. First, we compare participation rates by race in this election with other recent contests in Louisiana, Georgia, and South Carolina. Our objective is to explore the Edwards-Duke turnout vis-à-vis other elections involving David Duke and elections featuring black candidates for high office. Although this study is not comprehensive in scope, we hope to shed light on some of the conditions thought to affect turnout levels. Second, we use change in turnout between the 1991 Louisiana gubernatorial primary and the general runoff election as a dependent variable. In this part of the analysis we present models designed to explain parish-level variations in changes in black and white turnout between the two elections.

Background

The Edwards-Duke showdown came in the context of Louisiana's unique hybrid electoral system. As a result of Edwards's first gubernatorial campaign in 1971, he induced the state legislature to change Louisiana's primary election law (see chapter 1). Frequently, under this electoral system, both finalists are Democrats, although when David Duke won a special election to the Louisiana legislature he faced another Republican in the runoff.[1] Statewide runoffs have often resembled general elections in other states, in that a Democrat and a Republican compete.

Competitors for the 1991 gubernatorial nomination included incumbent Buddy Roemer, elected as a Democrat but recently converted to the GOP. A strong second candidate was three-time governor Edwin Edwards, who was on the rebound after acquittals in two corruption trials. David Duke was continuing a statewide effort that had netted him 44 percent of the vote against Democratic Senator Bennett Johnston in 1990. A fourth figure with some visibility was Republican U.S. Representative Clyde Holloway, whose district was soon to disappear, since Louisiana lost one seat in reapportionment due to lack of population growth in the 1980s. No black was among the leading candidates; so the "black candidate" explanation for black turnout would predict relatively lower levels of black participation.[2]

Widespread voter distaste for the two runoff contenders also pointed toward lower turnout. Edwards had enjoyed three flamboyant terms in office in which he made light of his reputation as a frequent and skilled visitor to casinos and the boudoir. Four years earlier, Edwards's past had caught up with him as his "laissez les bon temps rouler" motto seemed sadly at odds with the economic suffering in the Oil Patch. In 1987, Edwards trailed Roemer by five percentage points and, in recognition of the "incumbent loses" myth associated with runoff elections, pulled out of the runoff rather than risk massive rejection.[3]

Duke's unsavory association with the Ku Klux Klan and other extremist groups is well known (see chapter 1, or Rickey, 1992).

Although many Louisianans of both parties and races saw him as a throwback to a time they would rather forget, Duke nevertheless held a legislative seat from a New Orleans suburb. In 1990, he overcame vocal opposition—even from his own party leadership—to capture almost 60 percent of the white vote against an eighteen-year incumbent senator.

Previous Research

Many scholars have examined characteristics of voters and how these characteristics correlate with turnout. The general findings have been that better educated and more affluent voters participate at higher rates (Nie, Verba, and Petrocik, 1979; Wolfinger and Rosenstone, 1980).

Black political participation traditionally lagged behind that of whites, particularly in the South. Of course, for many years, most southern blacks were disfranchised through literacy tests, good character tests, and the "white primary" (Key, 1949; Rodgers and Bullock, 1972; Stanley, 1987). Some research has attributed much of the lingering disparity in black and white turnout to generally lower levels of income and affluence among black than white adults. Wolfinger and Rosenstone (1980) suggest that the enfranchisement of millions of poor blacks and whites in the South may have reduced the strong relationships between race, education, region, and turnout. Their study of turnout in the 1972 presidential election found little support for a distinct racial component. Rather, the authors discovered that education, age, and registration laws depressed voter turnout.[4]

Abramson and Claggett (1986; 1989; 1991), in contrast, offer evidence of a significant race-based difference in voting. Vote-validation studies reveal that, while educational and regional controls decrease the difference in turnout by race, black participation remains significantly below that of whites. Age-based differences help account for lower levels of black participation but do not eliminate all of the racial elements (Abramson and Claggett, 1989). Abramson and Claggett challenge studies based on self-reported turnout where racial differences are almost nonexistent. False reports of voting are higher among groups with lower turnouts, with black voters significantly more likely to overreport voting (Anderson and Silver, 1986).

The socioeconomic factors among blacks that may impede voting can be accounted for in such surveys. A factor often associated with higher levels of black turnout has been the campaign of an attractive black candidate. Although socioeconomic status had ceased to affect black turnout in Chicago by the latter half of the 1970s, the election of Harold Washington in 1983 was accompanied by exceptionally high black registration and turnout. At the time of Washington's first election, average registration in black wards was almost 85 percent, 13 points higher than in white wards. Further, about 75 percent of the registered blacks voted regardless of income level (Preston, 1987).

The black-candidate hypothesis was also supported in Atlanta, where black turnout was five points higher than white turnout in 1973, when Maynard Jackson became the first black mayor of a major southern city (Bullock, 1984: 241–42). The election of Dutch Morial as the first black mayor of New Orleans saw black turnout creep to within two percentage points of white turnout (Perry and Stokes, 1987), and when Wilson Goode was elected mayor of Philadelphia, black and white turnout was almost identical (Ransom, 1987: 270–75). Jesse Jackson evoked such enthusiasm in 1988 that blacks often participated in presidential primaries at higher rates than did whites (Norrander, 1989; Tate, 1991).

Having a black candidate near or at the top of the ticket, while often a stimulus, does not guarantee high rates of voting among blacks. In 1991, Richard Daley was elected mayor of Chicago by defeating black candidates in both the Democratic primary and the general election. Neither of Daley's black opponents could mobilize voters at rates comparable to those enjoyed by Harold Washington, and black participation trailed that of whites (Wilkerson, 1991).

The Closeness of Elections

Public choice theory offers an alternative perspective on voting to that found in the literature on socioeconomic characteristics. Although there is a baseline for participation that may be attributable to a sense of civic duty or the continuation of a ritual that will motivate some individuals to vote even if they care little about the outcome, small increases of participation above that level will indicate the presence of voters for whom the benefits of participation outweigh the costs (Downs, 1957). People may go to the polls because of interest in the outcome, because of the anticipation that the contest will be sufficiently close to make their votes effective or even decisive, or because of special interest in a candidate (Downs, 1957; Buchanan, 1975; Brennan and Buchanan, 1984). A perception that the candidates are radically different or that the stakes associated with the election outcome are high may encourage some people, who would otherwise stay at home, to vote.

When a narrow margin of victory is anticipated, more voters may go to the polls. Voting could be stimulated because of the greater interest produced by a competitive match-up or because the uncertainty surrounding the outcome of a close election increases the likelihood that one's vote could make a difference. In the past, pollsters had difficulty predicting the Duke vote (see chapter 3). After underestimating his support, pollsters hypothesized that Duke's background dissuaded some of his supporters from acknowledging their intentions. Consequently, polls prior to the 1991 runoff experimented with new techniques to tap the hidden Duke vote. Polls in the weeks between the two elections showed Edwards leading by margins of 6 to 10 percentage points (Bridges, 1991), although immediately after the primary, one pollster projected a Duke win (*Baton Rouge Morning Advocate*, 1991).

As the election drew closer, surveys generally showed Edwards's margin of support growing. The near unanimous opposition to Duke by the media, the leadership of both parties, and the business community, coupled with efforts to mobilize black participation, seemed to propel Edwards forward. The final Mason-Dixon survey for WAFB-TV in Baton Rouge proved to be accurate as it predicted a 20-point Edwards victory. If voters believed these polls, the incentive offered by the expectation of a close contest would have been diminished. Although the final poll accurately foretold Edwards's landslide victory, it would have been reasonable for voters to discount the magnitude of the spread in light of the underreporting of Duke's strength in previous elections. A Mason-Dixon survey released on the eve of the primary had shown Duke running third.

Types of Elections

The 1991 Edwards-Duke faceoff resembled a general election in that the opponents represented different parties. This election also had something of a runoff quality, however; if a candidate had polled a majority in the initial balloting, the second election would have been unnecessary.

Typically, there is less participation in runoffs than in first primaries (Foster, 1985; Wright, 1989). In the most extensive study of runoff elections, Bullock and Johnson (1992) found that, from 1970 until the mid-1980s, gubernatorial runoffs attracted 91.7 percent as many voters as the initial primary, and only a third of all gubernatorial runoffs had a larger number of votes cast than the preceding primary. In off-off-year elections, such as the 1991 Louisiana election, runoffs (gubernatorial and other elections are included) averaged 93.7 percent as many voters as the first primary. Wright (1989) reported that in gubernatorial runoffs between 1956 and 1984, turnout fell by 5 percentage points on average. This drop in turnout was far less than in runoffs for other offices.

If the Louisiana election is viewed as a runoff, then the prediction from the general pattern would be for the total votes cast to fall below the figure tallied in the initial primary. If, however, the matchup is treated as a general election, we would expect participation to rise above the initial round. Wright (1989) observed a 6-percentage-point surge in turnout in Louisiana runoffs; however, only one of his cases occurred after the 1975 change in electoral format.

Potential Black Influence

In addition to features surrounding the election that might account for turnout differences when compared with other elections, we will examine possible correlates of turnout variation among parishes in the 1991 runoff. One factor that may promote turnout among both blacks and whites is the potential for black political influence. Historically whites have felt threatened where blacks were numerous (Key, 1949), and this fear may have encouraged additional whites to vote in the 1991 runoff. Giles and Buckner (see chapter 5) found that in 1990, the Duke vote as a percentage of white registrants was greatest in heavily black parishes. Concentrations of blacks in the population did not, of course, change during the four weeks between the two elections. There was, however, a massive effort to increase black voter registration. Duke supporters in parishes experiencing higher black voter registration may have been more motivated to vote in the second election in order to offset these increases. Although Stanley (1987) finds that attitudes among white voters, especially compared to nonvoters, have been generally positive toward blacks, a countermobilization may have occurred among voters attracted to Duke's message.

If the black voter registration efforts paid dividends, then black turnout should rise more in parishes in which black registration increased most. Research on the turnout of recent registrants in other contexts, however, has not always found registration drives to be wholly successful. Registrants who enroll at the behest of others may vote at lower rates than those who sign up because of an internally generated desire (Hamilton, 1977; Vedlitz, 1985). We explore whether changes in black voter registration encourage higher turnout in the decisive election.

OTHER VARIABLES

As a measure of socioeconomic status, we use median education, which Wolfinger and Rosenstone (1980) and Abney (1974) found to be a particularly useful predictor of turnout. Our expectation is that turnout increases more in parishes in which the population is better educated.

Urbanization is another potential correlate of turnout. Tate (1991) finds urbanization to be related to black voting. Voters in urban parishes may show greater inter-election turnout increases because of ease of mobilizing an urban population. Moreover, to the extent that a residue of the racism which prevented black voting in the past persists, it is more likely to be found in rural communities. In the model for change in black turnout, we include a dichotomous variable which assigns a value of 1 to the central city parishes. Duke forces, in seeking to get white voters to the polls, may have concentrated on the suburban parishes such as the one that sent Duke to the state legislature. We examine a dummy variable that scores urban but non-central city parishes with a 1 to test whether suburban location is associated with changes in white turnout.

The voting pattern of a parish in the primary may condition turnout in the runoff. Because Roemer was the one candidate who carried some parishes but was not participating in the final showdown, his supporters, who cast 27 percent of the votes in the first primary, could potentially determine the outcome. Given the flaws in both of the surviving candidates, Roemer supporters may have chosen to abstain in the runoff. If that was the case, then Roemer support in the first primary may be negatively associated with vote change in the runoff. On the other hand, because of their potentially decisive nature, Roemer parishes may have attracted greater attention from both the Duke and the Edwards camps in the runoff, which might have resulted in greater increases in turnout between the two elections.

Edwards was the favored candidate among blacks in the initial primary, winning an estimated 84 percent of the black vote. It seems reasonable to expect that black turnout may have increased more in parishes in which Edwards did better in the primary. Alternatively, blacks living in parishes won by Duke in the first round may have felt an added impetus to go to the polls in the second election to counter the votes of their white neighbors.

Duke was the leading candidate among white voters in the first primary and in the runoff captured a majority of the white vote. Therefore, the increase in white turnout may have been associated with strength shown by Duke in the initial primary.

DATA

The data include turnout figures by race for both rounds of the 1991 gubernatorial election and the 1990 Johnston-Duke U.S. Senate election. In addition, parish-level data have been gathered for congressional elections involving biracial contests. Specifically, these include the 1986 and 1988 primaries and runoffs in Louisiana's Eighth Congressional District. Since 1988, Louisiana has kept turnout records by race. For earlier years, estimates of black and white turnout have been generated using ecological regression.

For comparative purposes, precinct-level data were used to estimate black and white participation rates in the 1990 Georgia gubernatorial primary and runoff, in which former Atlanta mayor and Congressman

Andrew Young sought to become Georgia's first black governor. In addition, data have been gathered for the 1990 South Carolina gubernatorial campaign in which a black state senator, Theo Mitchell, was the Democratic nominee. Also from South Carolina are election returns from the two attempts by James Clyburn, who is black, to be elected secretary of state. Two recent all-white general elections are included for Georgia and South Carolina.

FINDINGS

Edwards-Duke in a Comparative Context

Official turnout figures by race maintained by the Louisiana secretary of state indicate that 65 percent of the registered blacks voted in the first primary in 1991 along with three-quarters of the whites. Table 6.1 further shows that in the second election, black turnout rose to 78 percent while white turnout went to 79 percent. In addition, turnout for both blacks and whites in the 1991 runoff exceeded that in the Senate election in the previous year and that for biracial contests in the Eighth Congressional District.[5]

Black turnout in the 1991 primary was comparable to that in the previous year, but above that in the 1986 and 1988 Eighth District primaries. For both blacks and whites, contests involving David Duke have been accompanied by higher turnout than black-white elections—a pattern that holds for both primaries and runoffs. Although Louisiana turnout generally exceeds that in Georgia and South Carolina, the participation rates in the Edwards-Duke showdown were exceptional. The high black participation in the 1991 runoff does not fit a "black candidate" explanation for turnout variation.

In Georgia, black turnout in the 1990 gubernatorial primary is estimated at just under 45 percent, while approximately 39 percent of the whites participated in the Democratic primary. Another 118,118 voters participated in the Republican primary, where the great bulk of those voting were white. Assuming that 95 percent of the voters in the GOP primary were white, then the total turnout among whites would be about 43 percent. In the runoff, 47.5 percent of the blacks turned out to give overwhelming support to the Young candidacy, while whites had a turnout rate of 34 percent.[6] More whites voted in the two most recent general elections, but the rates lagged behind

Table 6.1
Registered Voter Turnout in Selected Elections in Louisiana, Georgia, and South Carolina

	Blacks	Whites	Total
Louisiana			
1986 Primary[a] (Eighth Cong. District only)	56.9%	60.6%	58.2%
1986 Runoff[a] (Eighth Cong. District only)	69.2	64.8	65.6
1988 Primary[a] (Eighth Cong. District only)	47.7	42.9	43.5
1988 Runoff[a] (Eighth Cong. District only)	71.9	74.2	73.7
1990 Primary[b]	63.6	70.4	68.5
1991 Primary[b]	65.3	75.7	72.1
1991 Runoff[b]	78.1	79.0	78.9
Georgia			
1988 General	48.9	66.4	61.7
1990 Primary[a]	44.6	43.1	43.4
1990 Runoff[a]	47.5	33.9	35.5
1990 General	38.2	53.9	52.3
South Carolina			
1978 Primary[a]	52.2	45.2	46.5
1986 Primary[a]	39.7	32.0	33.2
1986 General	53.8	61.6	59.1
1988 General	63.6	75.9	72.0
1990 Primary[a]	29.3	23.9	25.3
1990 General[a]	52.0	61.1	58.3

[a]Biracial election
[b]Contest involving David Duke

those for Duke contests in Louisiana. Black general election turnout in Georgia trailed white voting and was far below the black anti-Duke turnout in Louisiana.

South Carolina, like Louisiana, maintains turnout records by race. Figures for recent statewide black-white contests show lower levels of participation than in Louisiana. Approximately 52 percent of South Carolina's registered blacks voted in 1978, when James Clyburn lost a bid to become secretary of state. Approximately the same level of black turnout occurred in the 1990 general election, when Senator Theo Mitchell failed to halt the re-election bid of Republican Governor Carroll Campbell. Black turnout in 1986 when Clyburn made a second attempt to become secretary of state was about 40 percent, 10 points higher than the black turnout in the 1990 primary.[7] In contrast to the black-candidate hypothesis, the highest black turnout came in the 1986 and 1988 general elections, the two contests in which no black ran statewide.

South Carolina whites vote at lower rates than blacks in primaries, but are more active in general elections. While primary figures include both Democratic and Republican primaries, white interest at this stage may lag behind that of blacks because most whites identify with the Republican party, which has fewer primary contests than the more established Democrats.

Turnout levels in the Louisiana Duke elections for both blacks and whites exceed those in South Carolina and Georgia, except for the 1988 South Carolina general election, which has rates similar to Louisiana's 1990 and 1991 primaries. A factor that may account for the higher rates of participation in Louisiana is that it holds elections on Saturday, while elections in the other two states occur during the week.

Despite inter-state variations, intra-state racial turnout patterns for Georgia and South Carolina, as well as those prior to the 1991 gubernatorial runoff in Louisiana, conform to some features of the expected pattern. With one exception (the 1990 South Carolina general election), black turnout in black-white contests approximates or surpasses that of whites. In contrast, whites turn out at higher rates than blacks in elections having no black candidate. In the first two statewide elections involving David Duke (1990 Senate election and the 1991 gubernatorial primary) and in other all-white elections, white turnout eclipsed black participation levels. Thus, the nearly identical levels of black and white turnout in the 1991 runoff are exceptional not simply because they are the highest (see table 6.1), but also because there was no black candidate to attract black voters.

Increasing turnout between Louisiana's two 1991 elections accords with the notion that the second contest was seen as a general election and not as a runoff, and it matches the pattern for the two rounds of Eighth Congressional District elections in which a white Republican male defeated a black Democratic female. The nearly equal turnout rates in the Edwards-Duke contest are at variance with not only other all-white elections but also earlier contests involving David Duke. What accounts for this extraordinary level of mobilization?

Concern about the electoral outcome—perhaps a better characterization would be "fear"—may be the explanation. Why would anxiety over the outcome be greater in the Edwards-Duke faceoff than in Duke's two previous statewide campaigns? Perhaps fear that Duke might actually win was more widespread. His showing in the 1990 Senate election shocked most Louisianans, since polls had shown him running 20 to 25 percentage points behind the incumbent. Based on the 1990 results, prospective voters might have taken Duke more seriously in the 1991 primary and voted in higher numbers, but even here, the threat was less real than in the two-man contest. Preprimary polls showed no one with a majority and Duke getting only about a quarter of the vote, so marginal voters could await the second election before deciding whether the benefits of voting exceeded costs. The reality of a possible Duke win was driven home in a massive effort to mobilize opposition. The extent to which opposition to the less-than-perfect Edwards subsided is captured by the bumper sticker "Vote for the Crook. It's Important."

Change in Turnout

Black turnout in the second election exceeded that in the first election in sixty-two of Louisiana's sixty-four parishes, with white turnout rising in fifty-one parishes. Black turnout increased by more than ten points in thirty-seven parishes and by five to ten points in nineteen parishes. Only one urban parish had less than a 10 percentage point surge in black turnout. In all seven Roemer parishes, black turnout rose at least ten points. White turnout was unchanged or dropped in twelve parishes and increased by less than five points in forty-five parishes. White turnout increased by more than five points in only seven parishes, all but two of which are in the New Orleans media market.

There was no relationship between the Duke vote in the first primary and change in black turnout ($r=.03$). Black turnout increased notably where Roemer ran well ($r=.47$), but was inversely related to Edwards's performance in the first primary ($r=-.38$). Increased black participation correlated most strongly with change in black registration ($r=.55$). A massive effort was undertaken to enroll unregistered blacks to vote against Duke, and reportedly it added more than 25,000 votes in the two days available. There was some tendency for black turnout to increase more in heavily urban areas ($r=.26$) and where median black education was higher ($r=.26$).

Correlates with change in white participation were often weak. Changing white participation had a positive relationship with the Duke vote in the first primary ($r=.10$) and a negative relationship with initial Edwards support ($r=-.37$). The strongest correlates of change in white participation were changes in white registration ($r=.59$) and suburbanization ($r=.46$).

A Multivariate Analysis

A three-variable model is presented to explain change in black turnout. The strongest predictor of black turnout change is the increase in black voter registration between the two elections. Each additional percentage point of black voter registration is associated with an increase in black turnout of almost six-tenths of one percent. Black turnout is also associated with the support for Roemer in the first primary but was no greater in the central city parishes, as is shown in table 6.2. In a multivariate model that substituted Duke support in the first primary for Roemer support, the coefficient for the Duke term was not significant. The adjusted R-square indicates that a third of the variance can be explained by the three independent variables in table 6.2.

Change in black voter registration is also the strongest predictor of increased white turnout. For each percentage point increase in black registration, white turnout increased by almost one-half a percentage

Table 6.2
Models for Change in Black and White Turnout

Variable	Coefficient	Beta	T-Test
Black Turnout Change			
Intercept	.051		
Black registration change	.583	.422	3.580
Roemer support	.159	.300	1.972
Urban	.006	.051	.371
R^2 =	.36		
Adjusted R^2 =	.33		
White Turnout Change			
Intercept	.005		
Black registration change	.462	.451	4.354
Duke support	.063	.166	1.672
Suburban	.024	.338	3.251
R^2 =	.42		
Adjusted R^2 =	.39		

point. White turnout also increased in parishes in which Duke ran well in the first primary, and the Duke variable meets the .05 level of significance for a one-tailed test. (Five of seven parishes in which white turnout rose by more than five points supported Duke in the first primary.) The third predictor in table 6.2 is a dummy variable for suburban parishes, where white turnout increased two percent more than elsewhere. The model accounts for 39 percent of the variance.

Other possible configurations were attempted for the two models in table 6.2. Because of shared variance, none of these alternatives increased the overall explanatory power of the models and, instead, resulted in fewer statistically significant predictors.

CONCLUSION

Elections from Louisiana, Georgia, and South Carolina show that the turnout in the Duke-Edwards election was exceptionally high for both blacks and whites. Although Louisiana elections often attract higher turnout than do those in the other states studied, the figures from October 1991 were unprecedented. Apparently the excitement surrounding the controversial candidates coupled with a fear (or hope) that David Duke might actually win stimulated almost 80 percent of both races' registrants to go to the polls. These figures exceed turnout in contests that involved black candidates. With a candidate whose racist past is as visible as Duke's and who demonstrated sufficient appeal to become credible (Duke is estimated to have received the support of 55 percent of the whites who voted in the runoff), black turnout surpassed even the rates achieved when black candidates faced whites in contests for statewide or congressional office.

This research does not pretend to resolve the controversy over whether race continues to be a significant independent predictor of turnout. Our results show, however, that an element other than the presence of a black candidate can stimulate black voting. Except for the 1986 South Carolina general election, the black vote trails white turnout in the Duke contests by less than in other all-white elections. We do not know whether the racial turnout disparity in the first two Duke contests is attributable wholly to socioeconomic differences between blacks and whites. Socioeconomic status, however, was not a factor in the decisive contest. Because black voting equaled white turnout in only one Duke election, an extensive, highly publicized effort may be necessary to achieve parity. It may be that the publicity and efforts surrounding the Edwards-Duke faceoff are comparable to the election of Harold Washington and other black mayors cited earlier.

Increased turnout is strongly correlated with an increase in black voter registration. Parishes in which black registration rose most tend to be those in which black as well as white turnout increased substantially. Because the increase in turnout far outstrips the 25,000 additional black registrants, something broader than mobilization of the newly registered occurred. These same factors—organization, information, concern about the outcome—that added blacks to the registration lists prompted not only a share of the new registrants but also spurred some previous registrants who sat out the primary to vote in the second election.

The relationship between change in black registration and higher white turnout may be due to a countermobilization stimulated by high visibility efforts in the black community to sign up new registrants and turn out that vote. Notwithstanding some evidence of a white countermobilization, the percentage increase in white turnout is less than half that for blacks. That the black increase outstripped the white increase may indicate the great motivating influence of fear.

White turnout increased most in parishes carried by Duke in the first primary. The average increase in these parishes was 4.4 percentage points compared with a 3.1 percentage point rise in the parishes Edwards carried in the first primary and a 1.8 percentage point increase in white turnout in the Roemer parishes. The growth in turnout in parishes which Duke led may have initially resulted from heightened efforts by his partisans or from a countereffort by his opponents. Duke's share of the vote rose in all but two parishes; however, he lost 12 parishes in which he was primary leader but won only one parish where he did not lead in the primary.

Black turnout increased most in the Roemer parishes. This may reflect a successful effort to attract Roemer supporters to the Edwards camp. Granted, Roemer got relatively little black support (perhaps 10 to 12 percent); so the impact on blacks may have been indirect (Walsh, 1991). That is, if the two remaining candidates concentrated on the Roemer parishes, blacks living there may have been made more aware of the competitive nature of the campaign, and this awareness may have stimulated greater black turnout.

PART III

The Aftermath

7
Race and the Republican Resurgence in the South: Success in Black and White?

T. Wayne Parent

The day after running third in the 1991 Louisiana gubernatorial race, the newly converted Republican Governor Charles ("Buddy") Roemer blamed his defeat and the political power of David Duke on Ronald Reagan and the racial message of national Republican campaigns (*Times-Picayune*, October 21, 1991). Democratic critics of Republican tactics felt vindicated.[1] This new Republican had, in the emotion of defeat, stated what Democrats saw as an obvious and searing criticism of Republicanism. Roemer's new Republican colleagues were appalled: the would-be Republican star said publicly what many Democrats had been screaming since 1980: Republicans were winning in the South because of appeals to race and racism (the argument serves as the premise for the widespread criticism of George Bush's Willie Horton campaign ad in 1988). Is the active encouragement of racial divisiveness a fair explanation of Republican success in the South and the nation generally? Or is this simply a bitter reaction to the success of Republicans in winning the confidence of the working class? Elements of both of these compelling explanations can be found in the scholarly literature.

It is difficult to argue that race has not had a profound impact on Southern politics. Blacks are a significant proportion of both the urban and (unlike in the remainder of the country) the rural populations in the South and have historically been the objects of severe overt legal discrimination. As such, blacks have been the subject and object of political discourse in the South throughout its history. A contemporary watershed in black-white relations in the South coincides with the emergence of a two-party South. The current era of Southern politics is usually demarcated as beginning in the early 1960s, or, more specifically, in 1965, with the passage of the Voting Rights Act. With a stroke of the pen, Lyndon Johnson effectively signed into law an act of the U.S. government that allowed roughly one-fourth of the southern population to participate actively in a government with which they had uniform, fervent disagreements. Southern politics had been dramatically redefined.

Immediately after the Voting Rights Act, black people were registering and voting in unprecedented numbers and many white people were supporting candidates who opposed continued black progress. The degree to which white opposition to the black agenda continues to galvanize the white electorate in the South and the degree to which that support is associated with the concomitant rise of the Republican party in the South delineates the scholarly controversy.

In *The Vital South* (1992), Earl and Merle Black define the roots of the white revolt in the form of southern support for Republican presidential candidate Barry Goldwater in the 1964 election by noting that "Precinct returns in the Deep South cities confirmed the strength of Goldwater among *all strata* of the white community" (p. 156, emphasis added). They go on to stress the importance of the break between the Republican appeal of Eisenhower (1952–1956) and Nixon (1960), on the one hand, and Goldwater's 1964 run: "Goldwater retained enormous support among the so-called better sort of whites in these cities, but to this base he added tremendous support from lower-middle-class and blue-collar whites" (p. 156). The racial appeal of Goldwater is not lost on most analysts, journalists, politicians, or Black and Black. They conclude:

These lower-status and less-affluent whites in the Deep South had bent the traditional backbone of the Democratic party in presidential contests, but they were highly aroused in the 1960s by such practitioners of racial politics as Alabama's George Wallace and Georgia's Lester Maddox. Goldwater won them convincingly and, in so doing, broke the back of the Democratic party among Deep South whites. (p. 156)

The central point must be underscored: traditional Republican strength among upper-middle and upper income whites was expanded significantly to include lower-middle and lower income whites as a result of the overt and covert racial appeals of the Republican candidates. Black and Black's point, that at least part of the reason for the Republican revitalization in the South was a white segregationist appeal, is fairly noncontroversial.

The scholarly and political controversy begins in earnest when subsequent conclusions are drawn. Are racially based appeals the fundamental explanatory element in the southern Republican resurgence? Do racial appeals remain vital to Republican success in the South? Has race consequently even become fundamental to Republican success nationally? The remainder of the chapter is devoted to exploring these controversies.

THE FORMATION OF THE NEW REPUBLICAN COALITION

Positive white response to Republican opposition to the black agenda may not have been the only galvanizing effect of the civil rights movement on Republican party fortunes in the South. V. O. Key (1949) argued that the primary barrier to a two-party system in the South was the tight control of rural conservatives, who, through disfranchisement of blacks and whites and malapportionment of state legislatures, allowed the South to be dominated by a Democratic party that was controlled by a single power elite (see also Bass and DeVries, 1976). After the Voting Rights Act of 1965 forced party elites to break down participatory barriers to blacks and poorer whites, the two-party system could emerge and thus benefit both disfranchised classes. Republicans would inherit the traditional Whig constituency of business leaders and professionals, while Democrats would embrace poor and working-class whites and blacks. Therefore, Key and subsequent scholars argue that the beginnings of the two-party system were created by both the white backlash to the civil rights movement and by the removal of barriers to black and white participation in the elite-dominated system.

Although few dispute the importance of the Goldwater coalition in forming an integral part of the second party in the contemporary

South, many point to other concurrent forces that formed the Republican base. The rapid growth of industrialization in the South led to an influx of white-collar immigrants from states where they already had firm ties to the Republican party. The increased number of young southern professionals and business people resulting from the economic growth were also open to the Republican message of economic conservatism. When these people were added to the newly converted Goldwater Republicans, a critical mass began to develop. The Goldwater, race-based Republicans alone could not have caused such a rapid rise in second party fortunes. Bruce Schulman (1991) notes the importance of transplanted "businessmen, professionals, and skilled worked who filled the new positions in defense firms and research laboratories" and contributed to the election of Republicans like "ex-Hoosier Mack Mattingly [who] became Georgia's first Republican U.S. Senator since Reconstruction" (pp. 214–15). He also points out that young white suburbanites were registering and voting Republican in much greater numbers than their older counterparts.

Although this class-based political party definition is accepted by many scholars, there are two reasons for dissent. The first is that race is the single underlying factor that dictates party cleavages in the contemporary South. Republican strength continues to be based primarily on the perception that the party opposes the black agenda. The other, more subtle argument focuses on the importance of social issues, with race as part of that broad set of issues. The latter argument is more likely to be found in the more prominent, longer works on the subject and will be discussed first. The centrality-of-race argument has widespread support, especially among the purveyors of conventional wisdom and, perhaps not insignificantly, in some of the studies carried out by this author and therefore bears discussion as well.

Despite the changes dictated by the Voting Rights Act, Key's original prediction that the two-party South would look much like the New Deal alliance appears to have been discredited in the decade immediately following the act's passage. Indeed, poorer citizens of both races were confronted with equally important additional socioeconomic trends. William Havard, in 1972, argued that blacks and poor whites were not obvious beneficiaries of the new two-party system and that "The Whig mentality certainly survives . . . the growth of the new urban—or suburban—Republicanism in the South" (p. 25). The conclusions of two of the most often cited works on the topic, Alexander Lamis's *Two-Party South* and Earl and Merle Black's *Politics and Society in the South* are telling: although these works are often at odds, there is agreement that the two-party system in the South continues to leave the middle and upper-middle classes firmly in control of both parties. Indeed, as Harold Stanley (1987) concludes, the Voting Rights Act did little to stimulate white voter mobilization.

Broadly defined social issues—not economic class—lead many analysts to point to the relative insignificance of class in the new coalitions forming the two parties in the South, and, therefore, the absence of a place for lower-income whites in the two-party system. These "Reagan Democrats" vote Democratic in state and local elections for economic reasons and Republican in national elections for reasons based on social issues. Indeed, as one southern U.S. Senator once confidentially told this author, "If a Democrat remains conservative on abortion and gun control, it's easy to win as a Democrat—it's the social issues that get the Democratic presidential candidates in trouble in the South" (anonymous interview not for attribution, September, 1988).

Most social scientists, like Earl and Merle Black, find evidence for the importance of social issues essentially in analysis of voting behavior. Christopher Lasch (1991) provides a strong theoretical case for this position in *The True and Only Heaven: Progress and Its Critics*. His insightful discussion of a "cultural class war" is worth repeating here:

From the wrong side of the tracks, the dominant culture looked quite different from the way it looked from the inside. Its concern for creativity and self-expression looked self-indulgent. Its concern for the quality of human life seemed to imply a belief that life has to be carefully hoarded and preserved, protected from danger and risk, prolonged as long as possible. Its permissive style of child rearing and marital negotiation conveyed weakness more than sympathetic understanding, a desire to avoid confrontations that might release angry emotions. Its eagerness to criticize everything seemed to bespeak a refusal to accept any constraints on human freedom, an attitude doubly objectionable in those who enjoyed so much freedom to begin with. The habit of criticism, from a lower-middle-class point of view, appeared to invite people to be endlessly demanding of life, to expect more of life than anyone had a right to expect. (p. 493)

Thus the white working class opposition to the Democratic party in the South beginning in the 1960s was not a response to calls for racial equality—it was a response to the Democratic general social agenda.

While the argument that broadly defined social issues provides the best characterization of the southern Republican coalition is widely accepted, some scholars point to a predominantly racial argument. The case for a primarily racial explanation is muddied by the difficulty in supplying attitudinal evidence. Racial responses are not socially acceptable and are difficult to elicit. The problem is well illustrated by the "racial slippage" phenomenon in polls assessing support for black candidates. Examples of black candidates faring much more poorly at the voting booth than in survey results, especially when compared to their white colleagues, are numerous: Tom Bradley and Douglas Wilder in their races for governor of California and Virginia, respectively, and David Dinkins's races for mayor of New York City are among the most prominent cases. In addition, underpolling support of candidates like David Duke, who are marked as racists, illustrates the same point. The social unacceptableness of racial motivations for opinions and behavior inhibits any precise understanding of the effects of racial attitudes on partisanship. Therefore, behavioral evidence must provide the principal support for such a case.

The Duke candidacies in 1990 and 1991 provide an opportunity to examine the lingering suspicion that race plays a significant role in Republican appeal in the South, despite the inability of attitudinal studies to test reliably for it. Yet other behavioral evidence for racially motivated voting in the South abounds. Black candidates almost always lose in majority white districts. In recent years this trend has abated only slightly. This fact is not lost on strategists for campaigns against black candidates or (more relevant to this argument) against candidates associated with the black agenda. In the South, those candidates associated with the black community are almost always Democrats. If Duke's appeal is presumed to be primarily racial (a debated but credible assumption), then Duke support can be used as a surrogate for white racial voting. The studies in this book and others (see Parent et al., 1992) demonstrate a clear Republican voting pattern among Duke votes. Because of such evidence, the case for continued racially motivated Republican voting in the South warrants serious consideration.

The character of the emerging Republican coalition in the South is therefore the subject of some disagreement. After the initial jump-start of the opposition to civil rights legislation in the South, the Republican party may have simply captured its economically defined base that already existed elsewhere in the country. It may have created a coalition not found in other parts of the country—a coalition where racial issues and/or other sociocultural issues define its appeal. Is the two-party South now simply a reflection of the economic cleavages that define the party system in the remainder of the country, or is the two-party system in the South based on new racial and social issues that came to prominence in the 1960s? A third option is also worth considering: that the racial and social issues that led to the emergence of a two-party South also led to a redefinition of the two-party system nationally. We may not have witnessed the nationalization of southern politics but a "southernization" of American politics.

RACE AND NATIONAL REPUBLICAN SUCCESS

Several interpretations of American electoral politics begin with the assumption that Southern politics at the presidential level has long been nationalized and that the diversions, such as the Dixiecrats and the Wallace phenomena, are simply exceptions to the rule. These broad works emphasize the core explanations for the changes in political fortunes of the two parties that do not depend on regional eccentricities. The purely economic explanation of Kevin Phillips in *The Politics of Rich and Poor* (1991) relegates racial and social issues to a secondary place in American electoral politics. The generational theory offered by Arthur Schlesinger in *Cycles of American History* (1990) points to broad patterns of support for public and private enterprise. Even Herbert McCloskey and John Zaller, who discuss tolerance at length in *The American Ethos* (1988), view the tension between capitalism and democracy as the essential element in changes in support for the Democrats and the Republicans. These and similar grand works allow for idiosyncracies like racial and social issues, but view them as details in a much larger picture. Yet racial and social issues may have a significant or even determining role in races during times of political transition, like the 1988 Bush-Dukakis presidential race, but generally cycles of change are dependent on broader currents. The Clinton victory in 1992 underscores the importance of such economically defined trends.

Others suggest that the social issues that figured so prominently in the Republican successes in the South fundamentally changed party politics nationally. The working-class Democratic coalition in the South was shaken first by racial issues, then by other social issues. This same transformation in party cleavages began to reverberate nationally. Debate continues on whether this was the beginning of a classic party realignment, but many argue convincingly that the same social issues that tore the Democratic coalition apart in the 1960s in the South began to eat away at the Democratic coalition across the nation.

Christopher Lasch's cultural class war implies that the cleavage along the racial issue was part of a larger cultural cleavage. The Democratic party sought to address racial issues through policies that were out of touch with working-class southerners and working-class Americans in general. The way in which Democrats wished to solve the race problem downplayed the importance of personal responsibility and was perceived as patronizing. This general policy perspective—not the desire to provide a solution to racial prejudice—turned off the middle and working classes. Therefore, the new party cleavages are based to some extent on racial issues, but only as symptoms of a much larger new partisan cultural cleavage.

Another view of the national redefinition of party alignments as an outgrowth of the dynamic that occurred in the South in the 1960s puts race squarely on the fault line with other fundamental issues. In *Chain Reaction* (1991), Thomas and Mary Edsall explain how the issues of race, civil rights, and taxes were used by the Republicans to forge a presidential majority in the past thirty years. Their interpretation differs from Lasch's cultural explanation:

The Republican party, in developing a populist stance around the issues of race and taxes, has partially resolved one of the central problems facing a political party seeking to build a conservative majority: how to persuade, working and lower-middle-class to join in an alliance with business interests and the affluent. Opposition to busing, to affirmative action, to quotas, and to housing integration have given a segment of the traditionally Democratic white electorate ideological common ground with business and the affluent shared opposition to the federal regulatory apparatus. Shared opposition to taxes provides affluent and working-class voters—adversaries in the pre–civil rights era—with a common ground in the fight to restrict the growth of the coercive, redistributive state. Under the banner of a conservative "egalitarianism," the political right can maintain the loyalty of its low-income supporters by calling for an end to "reverse discrimination" while simultaneously maintaining the loyalty of the richest citizens by shaping to their advantage government policies that provide them with the greatest economic benefit. (pp. 13–14)

As race interacts with other issues, it has become a powerful national conservative and Republican force.

Finally, Edward Carmines and James Stimson (1989) place racial issues at the fulcrum of national party and ideological redefinition. In *Issue Evolution: Race and the Transformation of American Politics* they analyze congressional voting patterns, attitudes of opinion leaders, and public attitudes from approximately 1950 until the early 1980s. They conclude: "Over the last half-century racial issues have transformed American politics" (p. 185). The Democratic party is the party of racial liberalism and gone are Republican racial liberals who were so instrumental in passing key civil rights legislation. Racial politics in the South was instrumental: "We have seen the issue develop from a regional concern into a national issue, from partisan obscurity to a fundamental division between the parties, from being unconnected to mass political beliefs to being at the core of mass identification" (p. 185). The analysis presented in this study provides strong evidence for a centrality-of-race thesis.

Conclusion

Did racial politics play a crucial role in the Republican resurgence in the South? Almost all analysts agree that it did. Does it play an enduring role in Republican appeal in the South? Scholars disagree on the form and degree to which race continues to define the two-party system in the South and nationally. Will it play a role in the future? That answer depends on whether it is nurtured by our political leadership.

Gunnar Myrdal (1944) and Alexis de Tocqueville (1955) recognized long ago that to some extent racism permeates all of American culture. Racism continues to exist to some degree in America, in David Duke's state legislative district in Metairie, in the state of Louisiana, in the states of the Old Confederacy, and throughout the United States. Candidates like Duke will overtly, and other candidates will more subtly, kindle that racism for their own political gains. Candidates have won elections by addressing legitimate problems in distinctly racist terms. Such candidates should recognize the long-term social costs of such short-term thinking.

8
The Downfall of David Duke?
Duke, Republicans, and the Structure of Elections in Louisiana

◤

Ronald F. King
Douglas D. Rose
Matthew Crozat

March 10, 1992—Super Tuesday—was a critical day for David Duke, presidential candidate. In October, he had defeated incumbent Charles ("Buddy") Roemer to qualify for the runoff in the Louisiana gubernatorial race. The media immediately focused upon this formerly avowed racist, now running as a Republican, and made his a household name across America. In November, Duke had lost the runoff election but obtained 56 percent of the white vote. Seeking to capitalize on his achievement, he soon announced his candidacy for the 1992 Republican nomination for president.

Duke had little chance of winning, but he hoped to garner 20 to 25 percent of the vote, especially in the South (Bridges, 1992a). This would ensure his legitimacy at the Republican convention and possibly allow him to dictate the agenda regarding platform debates. However, as the primaries approached, Duke's campaign showed little momentum and raised little money. If Duke was to keep his candidacy alive, he would have to prove his support in Louisiana and surrounding states on March 10.

David Duke's performance on Super Tuesday fell well short of his prophecy. He received only 8.9 percent of the vote in his home state and 10.6 percent in neighboring Mississippi, but no more than 3.1 percent elsewhere. The press wasted no time in heralding the death knell.

Duke had gone from his greatest victory to resounding defeat in just six months. Commentators happily announced that the Duke phenomenon had been a temporary aberration to mainstream American politics, that the threat he posed had been repelled almost as soon as voters fully understood the meaning of his message, and that Duke himself "has slouched home to the fringe" from which he had emerged (Meacham, 1992). Patrick Buchanan, who now occupied the position Duke had coveted as the protest candidate on the Republican far-right, proudly proclaimed, "I just finished interring the political career of David Duke in a bayou in Louisiana" (Bridges, 1992b).

Reality is often more complex than appearance. Election outcomes can shift over time because voters change their minds in assessing the virtues of a given candidate. Outcomes can also shift because, while keeping the same individual assessment, voters confront a different field of candidates from which to choose, affecting relative weightings. Outcomes can also shift depending upon the election rules that determine who can vote and what is defined as winning. It is possible that voters in Louisiana had changed their minds about David Duke between October of 1991 and March 1992. The complication in comparing the October 1991 gubernatorial primary and the November 1991 runoff is that the field of candidates differed. In the October 1991 gubernatorial primary and the March 1992 presidential primary, the election rules were dissimilar and the pool of eligible voters differed.

This chapter uses weighted ecological correlation to estimate the support for David Duke among Republican voters in Louisiana, looking for changes between the October 1991 gubernatorial primary and the March 1992 presidential primary. Its main finding, surprisingly, is that Duke did not lose support between the two elections because there was almost nothing to lose. Few registered Republicans had voted for him in October, and few again voted for him in March. Dramatic stories of Duke's political death in the Louisiana Republican presidential primary were based upon a faulty inference. This chapter uses the differences in voting rules and candidate choices across elections to explain why the faulty inference occurred. Offering the appropriate comparisons, it provides a more accurate portrayal of the character of Duke's support, especially among registered Republicans. Based on the findings, we speculate about party allegiance and Duke's political future in Louisiana.

Two Primaries: Different Headlines, Same Result

Our central hypothesis is that one cannot infer rejection from Duke's vastly different electoral results in Louisiana statewide primary elections. Our claim is that, contrary to the popular headlines, essentially nothing changed. Testing depends upon the right comparison, performed methodologically in the right way. The March 1992 presidential primary was open to registered Republicans only, whereas the October 1991 gubernatorial primary was open to all registered voters. Under Louisiana law, voters are eligible to cast ballots in ordinary primaries regardless of party affiliation, all certified candidates are listed on the ballot, and the top two vote-getters then face each other in a runoff election unless one of them obtained a majority in the primary (see chapter 1). These rules did not apply in the presidential contest.

There are no available exit polls for the gubernatorial primary. Voters in the presidential primary were asked how they had voted in the November 1991 gubernatorial runoff, but not how they had voted in the October primary. Thus it is necessary to estimate Duke's Republican support in October 1991 in order to compare it to March 1992. This estimation is critical, for only by a comparison of roughly similar voters in roughly similar elections can we assess whether Duke gained or lost ground. Because only registered Republicans were eligible to vote in the presidential primary when Duke ostensibly suffered defeat, we must for the sake of comparability statistically isolate the registered Republicans and assess how they voted in the October gubernatorial primary when Duke won a spot in the runoff. Conclusions based on anything less are unsound and possibly misleading.

This study uses precinct-level data from the Louisiana Department of Elections and the State Archives of the Secretary of State's Office. Our data base consists of 3,708 of the 3,927 election precincts in the state. We deleted those precincts with suspect results, for example, where the sum of the votes cast exceeds the total number of individuals who signed in to vote.[1] There are no observable patterns to the deleted precincts, and thus the deletions should not bias the statistical results.

The statistical technique employed is weighted ecological correlation. Our goal is to assess the behavior of individual Louisiana voters, yet our data are for Louisiana election precincts. Ecological correlation, when correctly designed and specified, allows one to make the proper individual-level inferences from aggregate data. Estimation efficiency depends on the manner of grouping and the assumption that the within-group variation does not change systematically with the between-group variation across precincts (Johnston, 1972; Erbring, 1989).

In this study, the dependent variables are candidate votes, operationalized as each candidate's vote in a precinct as a share of the total number of individuals who signed in to vote on election day in that precinct, weighted by the precinct's number of voter sign-ins. As a substitute for individual-level data, we treat the candidate scores in each precinct as if they reflected the division of preferences for each voter within the precinct (that is, rather than candidate A receiving the vote of x percent of the sign-ins in precinct i, we assume that A receives x percent of the vote from each sign-in in i; the net outcome is the same). Because each individual in a precinct is given the same score, we then count each precinct as many times as there are eligible individuals in it. In essence, therefore, we are counting each individual only once. Weighting precinct vote by sign-ins as a computational shortcut achieves this result without in any way affecting the estimate. The operation gives unbiased regression coefficients that reflect the behavior of individual voters.

The independent variables in this analysis are race and party, which are recorded in the Louisiana voter registration data and are reported by precinct for the individuals signing in to vote on a given election day. Again, each variable is operationalized as the share of individuals per precinct who signed in to vote belonging to that particular group relative to the total number of individuals who signed-in, weighted by the precinct's total number of sign-ins. In the full model, each major candidate receives his own equation, which regresses his vote share against all the logically possible descriptive categories minus one to ensure appropriate degrees of freedom.

The main descriptive categories in the study are white Democrats, white Republicans, and white others. Empirically, because of the relatively small number of black Republicans and independents in Louisiana, we combined all nonwhite voters into a single category. Because, theoretically, very few nonwhites supported Duke, we used that category for the constant in our parameter estimates. The combined result from the set of equations for an election should equal 100 percent of the vote. The actual results sum to less than 100 percent because of minor candidates, absentee voters who are not counted in the precinct totals, and precinct sign-ins who did not vote in the election contest under study.

The October 1991 gubernatorial primary contained three notable Republican candidates—Buddy Roemer, the incumbent governor who had recently switched his party affiliation; Clyde Holloway, a conservative Congressman endorsed by the state Republican party; and David Duke. It also contained Democrat Edwin Edwards, a three-term former governor, and a host of minor candidates. Tables 8.1a and 8.1b represent a way of understanding the voting results. Edwards and Duke made the runoff. Roemer was defeated in his bid for reelection, and Holloway never became an effective challenger.

Because of the open primary and the lack of exit poll data, ecological correlation is used to estimate the distribution of voters, by race and party, among the various candidates. Because the estimates are based on precinct totals, the technique can generate seemingly implausible results even when validly applied; sometimes members of a group appear to support a given candidate more than unanimously or less than never. Nevertheless, our overall results suggest clear and straightforward conclusions.

Edwin Edwards received an enormous percentage of the votes cast by nonwhites, especially blacks. These votes were absolutely essential to Edwards's success in the primary, constituting nearly two-thirds of his total share. Edwards received slightly less than a third of the vote by white Democrats, an even smaller share of the vote of white others, and approximately no votes (statistically negative) from white Republicans.

Buddy Roemer received only a small percentage of the vote by nonwhites, white others, and white Democrats. He was the overwhelming choice of white Republicans. Statistically, the estimated coefficient is greater than 1.0, implying that in more heavily Republican precincts Roemer received the votes of white Democrats to a greater extent than otherwise, leading to the impression of Republicans casting more than 100 percent of their votes for him. White Republicans supplied Roemer with nearly three-quarters of his total vote. This is

Table 8.1
October 1991 Gubernatorial Primary

8.1A: Parameter Estimates

	Constant (Nonwhite)	White Democrat	White Other	White Republican
Duke	.010986*	.486942*	.785792*	-.056462*
Roemer	.066804*	.001070	.184060*	1.007877*
Holloway	.006429*	.072002*	-.003364	.038746*
Edwards	.841152*	-.578455*	-.663812*	-1.030276*
Total	.925372*	-.018442*	.302675*	-.040115*

* $p < .01$

8.1B: Allocation of Voters (percentage of sign-ins)

	Nonwhite	White Democrat	White Other	White Republican		Estimated Total	Actual Total
Duke	.28%	25.77	4.83	-.77	=	30.11%	30.19%
Roemer	1.68	3.51	1.52	18.22	=	24.94	24.90
Holloway	.16	4.06	.02	.77	=	5.01	5.03
Edwards	21.21	13.60	1.07	-3.21	=	32.68	32.47
						92.74	92.59

Notes: Allocation based on $(a+b_i)x_i$, where x_i = percentage of total sign-ins per group.

Actual total is less than 100% because of:
    1.09% of sign-ins who did not vote in the gubernatorial primary;
    0.62% of sign-ins who voted for other candidates in the gubernatorial primary;
    3.71% of sign-ins who voted by absentee ballot for one of the four major candidates in the gubernatorial primary. Absentee ballots were not included in the precinct-level data.

especially remarkable given his recent conversion to the Republican party and his failure to secure the official party endorsement.

Clyde Holloway, although the official Republican candidate, received only a tiny share of the votes cast by white Republicans and received a slightly higher share of the vote cast by white Democrats. Given the greater number of Democrats in the state, this constituted about four-fifths of Holloway's total. Holloway was identified with conservative positions on school integration and abortion. Party allegiance and social conservatism diverge for certain Louisiana voters.

As expected, David Duke received almost no support among non-whites. He garnered about two-thirds of the votes by white others, which constituted about a sixth of his total. He garnered more than half of the votes by white Democrats, which constituted almost all the remainder of Duke's count. It is important that, by our estimate, Duke received no votes in the October gubernatorial primary from white Republicans. Statistically, the estimate is even slightly negative, implying that the sort of Democrats and independents living in heavily Republican districts voted for Duke less than the norm for their group, by a small margin.[2] A critical inference here is that in October 1991, when the voters registered by the Louisiana Department of Elections as Republicans had a choice that included three very different Republican candidates for governor, almost none of them voted for David Duke.

A parallel analysis was run for the March 1992 Republican presidential primary. This was a closed primary, in which only registered Republicans were entitled to vote. The field included three prominent candidates—George Bush, the incumbent seeking reelection; Patrick Buchanan, seeking the conservative protest vote and running with the endorsement of the state Republican party chairman; and David Duke. There are some rather obvious parallels to the Republican field in the October 1991 gubernatorial primary. Bush was more established as a mainstream Republican than Roemer, Buchanan as the conservative challenger was more visible than Holloway, and there was no Democrat in the race. Yet the general character of the choices presented to Republican voters was sufficiently alike to warrant comparison (see tables 8.2a and 8.2b)

It was in a sense superfluous to estimate the matrix of ecological correlations for this primary. Ostensibly, no Democrats or others could vote in the Republican presidential contest. We ran the equations, first, to insure that the model performs as expected and to insure strict complementarity between our results for the October and March primaries. Second and more important, we ran the equations because an exit poll reveals that 2 percent of those who voted in the March Republican presidential primary identified themselves as Democrats, and another 15 percent identified themselves as independents or others. Some of this could be explained by the difference between official registration and self-perception. But some could have been caused by individuals voting in the "wrong" election. Certain Louisiana precincts are notably lax in their enforcement of election laws. Thus we suspect that our multiparty estimate gives a more accurate picture of the allocation of voters by group than it would have if we had simply made inferences about the behavior of Republican voters from the raw vote totals.

The election result, of course, was that Bush soundly defeated Buchanan who soundly defeated Duke, by the ratio of approximately 7:3:1. As expected, white Democrats and white others were only a small part of the total vote. As expected, Bush and Buchanan both received the overwhelming percentage of their support from white Republicans. Yet, curiously, Duke's results were significantly affected by the votes of white Democrats. Duke received by far the greatest share of such votes, and they appear to have contributed somewhat more to his total than the votes from white Republicans. Even in a closed Republican primary, white Democrats continued to help Duke. Without them, he would have lost twice as badly to Bush and Buchanan, by the even greater ratio of 15:6:1.

In March 1992, when voters who were registered as Republicans in the state of Louisiana had a choice for president that included three very different Republicans, few of them voted for Duke. This replicates the result for the gubernatorial primary of October 1991. Nothing changed. There was no dramatic shift in preferences. The popular story, carried in all the national media, was grossly misleading.

Missing Duke's Shifting Support: Different Choices and Rules

The media, seeking instant explanation for a specific electoral out-

Table 8.2
March 1992 Presidential Primary

8.2A: Parameter Estimates

	Constant (Nonwhite)	White Democrat	White Other	White Republican
Duke	.001443*	.021648*	-.065533*	.042755*
Bush	.006481*	-.035404*	.033721	.665921*
Buchanan	.003493*	-.001255	-.034073*	.263012*
Total	.011417*	-.015012*	-.065886*	.971688*

*$p < .01$

8.2B: Allocation of Voters (percentage of sign-ins)

	Nonwhite	White Democrat	White Other	White Republican		Estimated Total	Actual Total
Duke	0.04%	1.15	-0.15	1.02	=	2.05%	2.05%
Bush	0.16	-1.43	0.10	15.50	=	14.32	14.34
Buchanan	0.09	0.11	-0.07	6.14	=	6.27	6.25
						22.64	22.64

Notes: Allocation based on $(a+b_i)x_i$, where x_i = percentage of total sign-ins per group.

Actual total is less than 100% because of:
    9.85% of sign-ins who did not vote in the presidential primary;
    66.70% of sign-ins who voted in the Democratic primary;
    0.50% of sign-ins who voted for other candidates in the Republican primary;
    0.31% of sign-ins who voted by absentee ballot for one of the three major candidates in the Republican primary. Absentee ballots were not included in the precinct-level data.

come, have come to rely heavily upon exit poll data. In the case of Louisiana on Super Tuesday, the main poll was taken by Voter Research and Surveys, formed in 1990 as a cooperative arrangement among ABC, CBS, CNN, and NBC News to collect and tabulate exit poll results. Voter Research and Surveys supplied the detailed data for the television commentary on election night and for newspaper stories, for example, in the *New York Times* and the New Orleans *Times-Picayune* the following day.

The most striking aspect of the Voter Research and Surveys exit poll for Super Tuesday is the dominance of a single national-level story and the relative ignorance of Louisiana politics. The national-level story concerned the so-called protest vote resulting from Republican frustrations with President Bush. Of the 35 percent of voters in the Louisiana Republican primary who disapproved of Bush's performance as president, 64 percent said they voted for Buchanan and another 18 percent voted for Duke. The key issue was the economy. Three-quarters of Louisiana Republican voters considered the economy to be less than good. The more negative the voter's assessment of the economy, the lower the degree of support for Bush. This was especially true of those who believed that their own financial situation had worsened over the previous four years and those who said that someone in their household was unemployed. Yet it was Buchanan far more than Duke who attracted these individuals, by a ratio of approximately 2:1. By contrast, voters who valued experience and decided more on a candidate's character than his specific ideas strongly backed President Bush. The exit poll, therefore, was a story of significant although minority Republican disaffection, which benefited Duke somewhat but Buchanan much more. David Duke apparently was not a principal protest candidate, even in his home state.

Regarding Louisiana politics, the exit poll asked Republicans how they had voted in the November 1991 gubernatorial runoff—but not how they had voted in the October gubernatorial primary (table 8.3). This is surprising because the runoff pitted a Republican (Duke) against a Democrat (Edwards), whereas the October primary, like the March presidential primary, contained Duke and two other prominent Republicans.

Of the 46 percent of March 1992 Republican voters who said they had voted for Edwards in the runoff, and of the 12 percent who had not

Table 8.3
Exit Poll
How Voters in the 1992 Republican Presidential Primary
Voted in the 1991 Gubernatorial Runoff

	All Respondents	Buchanan Supporters	Bush Supporters	Duke Supporters
Duke	(39%)	36%	41%	23%
Edwards	(46%)	21%	77%	1%
Did Not Vote	(12%)	26%	72%	1%
	(97%)			

Source: Voter Research and Surveys.

voted in the runoff, virtually none cast their presidential ballot for Duke. Moreover, of the 39 percent of 1992 Republican voters who said they had voted for Duke in the runoff, less than one-quarter voted for him now. A larger share went to Buchanan, and an even larger share went to Bush. The ostensible conclusion is that Duke could no longer hold on to his own supporters. To the extent that there was a protest vote, it went to Buchanan almost unanimously among those who had not formerly backed Duke and quite strongly even among those who had formerly backed Duke. Duke, it was inferred, was losing ground. He was thus declared defeated and there was almost no media coverage of the man or his campaign afterward.

Yet the popular interpretation emphasizing Duke's decline depends on the critical assumption that the registered Republicans who voted for Duke in the November runoff were, in some sense, Duke loyalists who then deserted him in March. This interpretation involves a misunderstanding of voter preferences in open primary-runoff elections in general, and of the 1991 gubernatorial contest in particular.

As a rule, open primary-runoff elections require a certain sophistication from voters (Bullock and Johnson, 1992). Sometimes one's most preferred candidate has little chance of making the runoff; sometimes one's least preferred candidate has an excellent chance. The extensive field in the primary gives voters the opportunity to express a clear first choice; the fact that voters have only two options in the runoff can produce a different outcome than the primary. Therefore, analysts must attend to the structure of the election contest before interpreting the results. This is especially critical for understanding the electoral fortunes of David Duke. He was the first choice of virtually no Louisiana Republicans in statewide contests involving other Republican candidates, although he was the preference of a significant share of them in a runoff against a mainstream Democrat. The March 1992 exit poll, by inquiring about November but not October preferences, could not have shown this, leading to mistaken conclusions.

For the October 1991 gubernatorial primary, Duke's voters can be considered loyalists. In addition to Duke, the three notable candidates in the race were a conservative Republican with the endorsement of the state party, a three-time former Democratic governor with an unsavory reputation, and the reform-minded incumbent who had recently switched his party identification. Both partisans and issue ideologues apparently had viable alternatives. Under these conditions, we have shown, virtually no nonwhites and virtually no white Republicans opted for Duke. His support came primarily from white non-Republicans, especially Democrats with less education (according to exit polls, he traditionally does best among high school graduates or those with some college) and the middle class (doing best among those earning between $15,000 and $50,000 per year).

In the November runoff against Edwards, Duke significantly added to his total from Republicans. According to the Voter Research and Surveys' exit poll, both Duke and Edwards held their base of voters from the primary. Holloway's voters divided 50:50 between Edwards and Duke, while Roemer's divided 75:25. Self-identified Democrats split 73:27 Edwards over Duke, but the poll does not distinguish white from black voters. Self-identified Republicans divided 44:56, giving Duke a majority. Because of the larger number of Democrats in the state, Democrats and Republicans contributed just about equally to Duke's November total vote (see table 8.4).

Ecological correlation using weighted precinct data gives a similar finding. In the runoff, Edwards did even better than before in the precincts where previously he had been strong (parameter estimates greater than 1.0); Duke did likewise. Far more of Roemer's October voters went to Edwards than to Duke. A sizable portion of Holloway's voters did not turn out in the runoff; the majority of those who did vote preferred Duke.[3]

Nevertheless, given the distinction between primary and runoff

Table 8.4
Exit Poll
How Voters in the November 1991 Gubernatorial Runoff
Voted in the October Primary for Governor

	All Respondents	Edwards Supporters	Duke Supporters
Duke	(26%)	6%	94%
Edwards	(32%)	94%	6%
Holloway	(5%)	50%	50%
Roemer	(26%)	75%	25%
Other	(1%)	—	—
Did Not Vote	(10%)	61%	39%
	(100%)		

Source: Voter Research and Surveys.

supporters, it cannot be inferred that those who voted for Duke against Edwards had become Duke loyalists. Instead, these were people who had favored Holloway or Roemer and then had the hard choice to make, "between the crook and the Nazi." It is important that 31 percent of all voters—37 percent of Edwards's and 22 percent of Duke's—explicitly said that they were voting for the lesser of two evils. For most Republicans who voted for Duke in the runoff, he was a second choice—perhaps a very reluctant second choice indeed.

The March 1992 presidential primary again gave Louisiana's registered Republicans a chance to express their preferences. Other than Duke, the viable alternatives included the incumbent president and a conservative challenger endorsed by the state party chairman. As in the previous first-choice contest, Duke fared poorly. A sizable percentage of the voters who had favored him in the runoff apparently left Duke's column once the primary format allowed them to express a preference for a different kind of Republican.

What, therefore, can properly be inferred from the evidence? The Super Tuesday Louisiana presidential primary certainly represented a chance for advancement missed by David Duke. From the October primary to the November gubernatorial runoff, Duke's vote total increased from 485,000 to 671,000, although this was a lower proportion of the vote than he expected because of the exceptionally high turnout. Similarly, relative to his 1990 race for the U.S. Senate against Bennett Johnston, Duke gained 10 percent in total votes but declined in percentage (44 percent versus 39 percent). There was a possibility that Duke could have capitalized on the opportunity, turning those who found him merely not the worst choice in November into first-choice supporters in March. Among this group were approximately half of all registered Republicans who had voted. Moreover, voters in November were asked by the Voter Research and Surveys exit poll to consider Duke as a possible presidential candidate. Only 16 percent of Duke's voters in the runoff (unlike 92 percent of Edwards's) said that they would not consider supporting him for president.

Yet Duke could not transform those who in November considered him only not worst into voters who in March would make him their first choice. He could not expand his core popularity among registered Republicans, despite the fact that a good percentage of them had at least once consciously pulled the lever on behalf of a former professed Nazi and ex-Grand Wizard of the Ku Klux Klan. The lesson of the March primary vote is not that Duke lost support, because he never had it to lose, at least among Republicans voting in a primary election with other Republicans on the ballot. Instead, Duke could not gain significant primary election support from those who had preferred him to Edwards in the runoff, and thus who might conceivably have been thought eligible for conversion. In this sense, it is a story of what did not happen.

More than this, however, is required in order to proclaim Duke's Louisiana political defeat. The March 1992 Republican presidential results give no indication about defections of Duke's core primary election voters, who previously had advanced him in place of the incumbent governor. Few registered Republicans had ever been among this group. Similarly, the March 1992 results give no indication about defections for Duke's runoff voters, who previously had made him a threat to win the governor's race. There were registered Republicans here, but the electorate in March was looking among rival Republican candidates, not comparing Duke to a mainstream Democrat. It is inappropriate to infer from this evidence that Duke would necessarily fail to be among the top two finishers in an open primary or would perform much worse than before in a competitive runoff. The character of an election—who can vote and what choices are available—should never be ignored when interpreting the outcome.

REPUBLICANISM AND DUKE IN LOUISIANA'S FUTURE

Only four months after Duke won 55 percent of the white vote in his failed but celebrated governor's bid, Louisianians have turned their backs on their homegrown, blow-dried, onetime Ku Klux Klan wizard as if he were a drunken Saturday night fling they can hardly remember and hope to forget.
—Mary T. Schmich, *Chicago Tribune,* March 9, 1992

Thanks to a good number of factors—the good sense of voters, the resilience of the American social compact, a Buchanan campaign that co-opted Duke's message—the Duke campaign is in a state of collapse.
—Jack Wardlaw, New Orleans *Times-Picayune,* March 15, 1992

The supreme moment in Duke's life, primary night in Louisiana, standing victorious before the jammed bank of microphones, was replaced on Super Tuesday by a few people loitering around his Metairie office. CNN stopped by, but to record his obituary.
—Julie Reed, *New York Review of Books,* April 9, 1992

In a host of commentaries, the Louisiana Republican presidential primary of March 10, 1992, was taken in large part as a referendum on the political career of David Duke. His rise or fall was to be read in the results. Implicit in such accounts is a view that the vote of Louisiana registered Republicans was critical for Duke and that changes in that vote could be used to assess his fortunes. There was a large degree of naiveté in many of these commentaries. Duke's percentage of the vote on Super Tuesday was simply compared to Duke's percentages in previous state-wide contests without recognition of the differences in the eligible population and the voting rules. Some commentators might not have been aware that ordinary primaries in Louisiana are open to all voters and all candidates. Others failed to make the distinction between primaries and runoffs. This chapter has drawn attention to the importance of making the correct comparisons and careful inferences.

It is interesting to see what Duke himself believed about these matters. He was interviewed by Matthew Crozat three months after Super

Tuesday and many weeks after he had officially dropped out of the presidential contest. Duke had taken his poor performance in the Louisiana primary hard, but he had few prepackaged answers when asked to explain it. Unlike in previous campaigns, Duke said, he failed to generate momentum, partly because of his portrayal by the media and partly because of a conscious campaign of harassment orchestrated by the White House. He dismissed any possibility that he could not become a viable candidate at the national level but said that his late start put him at a disadvantage. Moreover, Duke argued, he did not have the money to compensate for these disadvantages. Buchanan "spent a couple of hundred thousand dollars here," he told Crozat resentfully. "I didn't spend a dime. He campaigned extensively here, I . . . [had] one meeting here. And he still didn't beat me that decisively. . . . Considering the dollars expended, I got forty times the votes he did."

Yet behind these weak rationalizations Duke expressed a sense that his base of support differed from that of other Republican candidates. Of course, he viewed this as one of his greatest strengths. Asked whether he and Buchanan had been competing largely for the same voters, Duke responded:

Many of the same voters, yes. But I think that I had a much stronger base among conservative Democrats. Conservative Democrats were not voting for Buchanan, but many conservative Democrats voted for me in Louisiana. . . . I got much more of the cross-over vote. Buchanan got almost purely Republican votes. About half of my votes in the governor's race or more were Democrats. And that difference could have been a new dynamic in the presidential primaries if the momentum would have been there.

Duke apparently recognized that a significant amount of his support came from white Democrats. Yet he, like the political commentators, probably did not realize the extent to which the core of his support came from that group, nor the decisive impact the exclusion of that group from the March 1992 Republican primary had upon the outcome.

Very few of Louisiana's registered Republicans voted for David Duke in the primaries in October 1991 or March 1992. Duke's share of their ballots in the November runoff was not overwhelming, especially given that the opponent was a supposedly corrupt and highly partisan former Democratic governor, nor did those who did vote for Duke in the runoff become his loyalists. In fact, according to the March 1992 exit poll, among the approximately one-quarter of Republican voters who said that party mattered, 48 percent backed Bush and 47 percent backed Buchanan. Strong partisans chose either the incumbent president or the designated protest candidate and treated Duke as an outsider.

Of those loyalists who formed the core of Duke's electoral support, only a small minority had an explicit affiliation with the Republican party. The jury is still out on whether the South is in the throes of some fundamental partisan realignment (Bass and DeVries, 1977; Greenhaw, 1982; Black and Black, 1987; Lamis, 1988). Yet we cannot conclude, as do Wayne Parent et al. (1992), that "the Duke vote was simply part of what has become the normal . . . Republican vote in the South." Duke's rise to prominence was not within the domain of ordinary and acceptable party politics (Rose, 1992). Nor did his vote reflect customary party allegiance, based upon the association of general partisan sympathies with support for a given party candidate. We recognize that party registration must be distinguished from party self-identification, which must be distinguished from regular party voting behavior, and that the open primary–runoff form of Louisiana elections reduces the need for consistency. Yet it does not appear that partisan Republican feeling induced the loyalists to vote for Duke, but rather that Duke led them to vote for a Republican. To the extent that the Louisiana Republican party wishes to attract and annex more firmly the Duke loyalists, it has to make greater overtures to both the man and his divisive issue agenda. In our opinion, this is a dangerous strategy to pursue.

The salience of David Duke's campaign for electoral respectability, the deep emotions it raised, and the enormous attention it received lead us to another speculation concerning Duke's future political career. For those worried about the continued viability of a candidate with such a virulent past and such extremist views, there are some grounds for optimism in the fact he could not expand his first-choice support among registered Republicans from October 1991 to March 1992. However, there are equally good reasons to be less than sanguine. There is no objective evidence from the March 1992 primary that Duke lost his core of supporters (who were not registered Republicans), or that many registered Republicans would be less likely to vote for Duke as a lesser-of-the-evils candidate in a two-person race against a conventional Democrat. According to the November exit poll, 91 percent of those who voted for Duke for Senator over Bennett Johnston also voted for him in the runoff over Edwards. It is not hard to assume that those who once found Duke an acceptable second choice would be able to find him an acceptable second choice again and again.

From the electoral evidence, one cannot rule out the possibility of a replay of the 1991 gubernatorial contest. If Duke can retain sufficient first-choice core support (mostly from white Democrats) to make the runoff, and if he can retain sufficient second-choice support (including a sizable block from registered Republicans) to make a serious challenge, he could remain a statewide force in Louisiana. In this scenario, Duke's opponents would be compelled to generate intensity and turnout similar to 1991, and likewise to rally behind a candidate capable of attracting black Democrats while alienating fewer white Republicans and independents.

There are signs that Duke has, in fact, been losing support. According to a poll taken for the *Times-Picayune*, if the October gubernatorial primary were restaged in June 1992, only 11 percent of respondents would choose Duke as opposed to 30 percent for Roemer, 31 percent for Edwards, and 10 percent for Holloway (Renwick, 1992). Although Duke's supporters have usually been more evident in the election results than in the public opinion polls, 11 percent is less than he was polling in fall 1991. According to Lance Hill of the Louisiana Coalition Against Racism and Nazism, since his November defeat, Duke's ideologically conservative backers increasingly drifted into more mainstream Republicanism while the extremists largely abandoned their compromise with electoral politics and returned to the fringe, leaving Duke somewhat isolated between them. Most white Louisiana voters still believe that Duke had the right message, but they now have many more doubts about the messenger (see Epilogue).

Ironically, Duke's statewide Louisiana election contests did not apodictically proclaim defeat. Yet the misperception of these outcomes has hurt Duke considerably. Increasingly, he has come to be viewed as a perennial candidate and a loser, without a stable occupation but with a frightening and controversial past. Moreover, interpretation in politics often functions as a self-fulfilling prophecy. Thus the belief that Duke has been rejected by Louisiana voters has resulted in further reducing his base of support and weakening his chances for a reversal in electoral fortune. Although Duke's opponents stand prepared to fight again, they hope for the persistence of negative perceptions announcing failure and retreat. In the long run, the role of such perceptions might well become a critical part of the story and the social science regarding the political career of David Duke.

9
The White Knight Fades to Black: David Duke in the 1992 Presidential Campaign

◢

Euel Elliott
Gregory S. Thielemann

Few political movements of the twentieth century have resulted in as much concern and public division as the rise of David Duke to national prominence at the end of the 1980s. To some, his candidacies for the U.S. Senate, governor of Louisiana, and president of the United States heralded a dramatic and needed change in the political landscape, while to others his candidacies signaled a frightening attempt to turn back time and reverse the trends toward equality and civil rights in the United States. In both scenarios, the Duke phenomenon presents an interesting case study for political theorists to explore.

In electoral politics, success is judged by the number of votes a candidate receives. The ultimate success is fifty percent plus one and thus electoral victory, but for Duke success was often found in defeat, as when he exceeded expectations in his race for the U.S. Senate and received a significant bloc of votes in his gubernatorial contest. Because he was never the favorite, the expectations for his campaign were initially quite low, and thus considerably easier to obtain. Even as he launched his presidential bid, success did not depend on defeating George Bush, but rather in making a strong enough showing to force the Republican establishment—that had worked so hard behind the scenes to defeat him in his races for the U.S. Senate and governorship of Louisiana—to take him seriously. In the end, he failed to achieve even these lower standards of success, as he quietly disappeared from the political landscape he had so desperately hoped to reshape.

If David Duke did, in fact, change the contemporary electoral scene, the impact on his own political career was short-lived. Early fears that a Duke presidential candidacy might be "an embarrassment to the President" (Cook, 1991) were quickly dispelled when Duke's Super Tuesday total in the Louisiana Republican primary was a paltry 9 percent, a distant third behind President Bush and conservative columnist Patrick Buchanan. Why did this rising star of Louisiana politics, who garnered impressive percentages against a powerful incumbent U.S. senator and a former governor, fade so quickly in the 1992 Republican presidential contest? In this analysis we find three primary reasons: he never gained momentum, he never raised the funds necessary to compete, and, most important, he failed to understand the variation in the constituencies to which he was attempting to appeal and, thus, failed to adapt to these new demands.

Momentum and Presidential Nominations

In the last decade, a formidable literature has emerged that addresses the dynamics of presidential nomination campaigns and sheds light on Duke's poor primary season showing. Prominent among the findings of this research (Patterson, 1980; Aldrich, 1981; Orren and Polsby, 1987; Gurian, 1986, 1991; Asher, 1992; Bartels, 1988; Crotty and Jackson, 1985) are the dramatic increase in importance of primaries since the late 1960s and the change in candidate behavior which underscores the direct primary's importance. In addition to delegate selection, the primaries and caucuses, particularly the early ones, shape the race by winnowing down the list of potential candidates. Although neither Iowa nor New Hampshire offer much electoral clout in November, they hold disproportionate influence in the primaries by initially handicapping the field of contenders. Candidates who run well in these early contests can expect more media attention and more money from potential contributors who often want to be reassured of a candidate's viability before writing their checks. In this way, the early primaries have been known to create momentum on which candidates may build in later primaries.

In the wake of the McGovern-Fraser reforms of the late 1960s (see Polsby and Wildavsky, 1988; Cook, 1989), presidential delegate selection in the United States has moved increasingly away from the use of party caucuses and toward direct primaries.[1] Candidates emphasize delegate-rich primary states, since delegates are by definition necessary to obtain nomination (Polsby and Wildavsky, 1988; Asher, 1992). However, the emerging role of the media has been of particular importance in influencing election outcomes, especially its substantial coverage of early presidential primaries (Polsby and Wildavsky, 1988; Orren and Polsby, 1987; Gurian, 1986, 1988, 1991). The combination of heavy media coverage of early primaries and the importance of early victories to candidates has been recognized as a dynamic in presidential nomination campaigns called momentum.

According to the concept of political momentum, a candidacy "moves" in a positive direction, boosted by previous success, and continues to attain electoral success. Similarly, a candidacy loses momentum when the rate of success declines or the candidate fails to meet expectations. Gurian (1986) has been most successful in developing a quantified measure of momentum. In his model of presidential nomination campaign spending, momentum is measured by an interaction of media coverage and the temporal position in the sequence of primaries. Gurian finds that momentum and the number of delegates to be won in a state contribute to candidate spending. However, differences in candidates' allocation strategies vary according to whether or not they are established candidates or long-shot candidates prior to the primary. Long-shot candidates are those who were supported by less than 10 percent of the party in pre–Iowa caucus polls and have won no more than one primary. Candidates who exceed these thresholds are considered established candidates. According to Gurian's findings, substantial differences exist between the allocation strategies of long-shot and established candidates. Long-shot candidates place substantial financial emphasis on momentum: they need to strike early with lots of publicity. Conversely, established candidates emphasize delegate-rich contests over media-rich contests, although both variables are significant predictors of established candidate expenditures. These differences reflect long-shot candidates' need to establish credibility and viability, thereby winning primaries, to become established candidates.

In 1988, party leaders in the South made a conscious effort to reduce the importance of the early primaries and caucuses by holding a regional primary that became known as Super Tuesday. The theory was that, by grouping the southern primaries together, the region could be assured of boosting support for a favorite son, or, in the case of the Democrats, a more moderate candidate. The idea was sound in theory, as the region could steal momentum away from the earlier contests and give it to a candidate whose ideology more closely resembled their own. Against this backdrop, Al Gore introduced his "southern strategy" during the 1988 Democratic primaries, for he avoided committing major resources in Iowa or New Hampshire and instead concentrated on key southern states. Although Gore received a significant number of southern votes, so did Michael Dukakis and Jesse Jackson. Because Gore was not the clear winner (placing second to Jackson), Super Tuesday failed to generate momentum for a favorite son, or even for the moderate wing of the Democratic party. Gore raised the expectations with his southern strategy and then failed to meet them.

In 1992, David Duke's campaign strategy took a similar course, as he also avoided the Iowa caucuses and the New Hampshire primary by deciding to start in the South. Duke's strategy paralleled Gore's in many ways and, in fact, might have made more sense for Duke than Gore. Duke had virtually no national credentials on which he could run, unless one counts his selection as Grand Dragon of the Ku Klux Klan. Although he was a Louisiana legislator, this did not afford him the same prominence that Senator Gore had achieved four years earlier. In addition, because many of Duke's policy positions were tailored to the underlying racial tensions of Louisiana and the South, his campaign had no chance in places like Iowa and New Hampshire. Indeed, a strong argument could be made that an active Duke candidacy would not have found the early northern contests at all hospitable where—it could be argued—there was not the potent combination of economic discontent and racial anxieties present in the South, given the small black populations in those states.

As Gore discovered in 1988, concentrating on Super Tuesday is extremely risky and raises the stakes of the southern primaries. Following this strategy, a candidate must meet or even exceed expectations in the South in order to be taken seriously in subsequent contests.

When Duke, like Gore, did not accomplish this, his candidacy was doomed.

Duke's southern strategy, even though it failed, offered him his best hope. Ironically, his campaign would hinge on following a strategy of Jesse Jackson's 1984 and 1988 Democratic presidential bids. Jackson had foregone the usual approach of constructing an elaborate campaign organization in the various primary states as he entered the race (at least in 1988) relatively late and did not create an elaborate campaign network. Jackson relied upon name recognition in the black community and black churches as a surrogate for more traditional organizational structures. Similarly, Duke entered the 1992 campaign without first establishing the kind of state-level political networks usually seen in presidential nomination contests. This may have at least been partially due to the fact that, like Jackson, virtually no one in local and state party organizations joined in the effort. And, like Jackson, Duke relied on what he surely viewed as a ready-made constituency—a "silent majority" he hoped—that would serve as the core of his support, just as Jackson relied on a foundation of black support in the region.

Duke did not even file for the New Hampshire primary, making him the only one of sixty-eight presidential hopefuls not to run in the first primary event. As a long shot, Duke acted contrary to the conventions of presidential nomination campaigns. Duke removed himself from the electoral spotlight, and his national media exposure consequently declined.

During his gubernatorial campaign of October-November 1991, Duke was the subject of more than 125 articles in major national newspapers, and his candidacy and history were feature topics on national television and radio news broadcasts.[2] Of course, not all of this coverage was favorable, and Duke often came off looking like a reactionary or a dishonest alternative to anyone else. In December, Duke's presidential campaign generated thirty-eight articles in national newspapers and speculation on television and radio broadcasts of the impact of a Duke presidential campaign on GOP fortunes in the South. However, the balance of the publicity Duke received after announcing his candidacy related to efforts elsewhere among the states of the South, including Georgia, South Carolina, and Florida, to keep Duke off the ballot (see table 9.1) or reported Duke's decision to forego early nonsouthern primaries in New Hampshire, Colorado, and Maryland. Indeed, following a January court ruling that supported the exclusion of Duke from the first southern primary in Georgia, national press coverage of David Duke's candidacy decreased markedly.

Thus, Duke's demise may be at least partially attributed to faulty timing. By forgoing entry into the early contests, he forfeited the possibility of valuable media exposure. Duke's failure suggests that name recognition and notoriety alone are no substitute for the kind of media coverage that can be generated in early contests.

Perhaps the most important result of Duke's failure to compete in the early primaries was that it allowed right-wing columnist Patrick Buchanan to assume the role of a viable protest candidate, even though Buchanan announced his candidacy only ten weeks prior to New Hampshire. Buchanan tapped into the vein of discontent with George Bush and reaped a bonanza of media attention after attaining nearly 40 percent of the vote in the first primary in the nation. This media attention was invaluable in Buchanan's effort to articulate issue positions that were remarkably similar to Duke's. Buchanan had become the spokesman for the silent majority on which Duke was counting, and the fact that his past did not include membership in anything more controversial than the Nixon White House allowed him to become a viable alternative to Duke.

By the time the southern primaries got underway, Buchanan's role as a protest candidate for disaffected conservatives was solidified. On NBC's December 14 "Today" show, Buchanan lashed out at Duke, stating, "I am going to confront Mr. Duke, and we'll let the people in the South and the nation decide who is the authentic conservative and who is the bogus one" (Cook, 1991). Following his impressive New Hampshire showing, Buchanan carried his campaign into the South and procured a southern pedigree by visiting the gravesite of his Confederate forefathers in Mississippi. With considerable care, Buchanan outflanked the Duke campaign by offering the same message from a different messenger.

With Duke off the ballot in the March 3 Georgia primary, Buchanan attracted large numbers of disaffected Peach State voters and nearly matched his New Hampshire performance in the first southern primary. By choice, Duke did not appear on the ballot in the other two March 3 primaries—Colorado and Maryland—again leaving the Bush protest vote to find another home with Buchanan. By the March 7 South Carolina primary, Duke had obtained little recent national media exposure as a presidential candidate, and he relied on a half-hour television advertisement on election eve to introduce himself to the Palmetto State electorate.

Duke forces hoped for success in South Carolina, where racial politics have traditionally played a more prominent role than in any other southern state, save Mississippi. Mississippi and South Carolina, states with large black populations, were the most intolerant of steps toward racial equality (Key, 1949). This trend continued through the 1960s, as these states were among the most violently opposed to civil rights. Even today, these states contain large blocks of the black belt (counties whose history is tied to the rich black soil and with large black populations), which tend to produce extremely conservative white voters (Black and Black, 1987:9–12). Only Mississippi and South Carolina had more black citizens than Louisiana among southern states, and Duke's strategists had to believe that his now notorious past would not be held against him in the birthplace of the Confederacy. Duke garnered a paltry 7 percent of the South Carolina primary vote, while Buchanan took over 24 percent (table 9.1).

On March 10, Super Tuesday was no kinder to David Duke. Denied access to the Florida ballot, Duke failed to surpass Buchanan in any southern state, which solidified Buchanan's role as the protest candidate and made Duke obsolete. Duke's best performance, in Mississippi, was 11 percent, and he obtained only 9 percent in his home state, Louisiana. In both Tennessee and Texas, Duke barely twitched the meter with 3 percent of the vote. By March 11, the southern body politic had made quite clear the lack of enthusiasm for David Duke, and one observer of southern politics noted, "David Duke is dead . . . and the South can take credit for burying him" (Wyman, 1992b). Duke's campaign, broke and beaten, limped through March to the April 11 Wisconsin primary, before Duke withdrew on April 22 (Cook, 1992a). The failure of David Duke is seen in table 9.1, which examines his results. In three primaries (Texas, Mississippi, and Maryland), primaries for other offices were held simultaneously, thereby limiting the potential pool of protest voters to those who were also willing to vote in the Republican down ballot elections.

In retrospect, David Duke confronted massive credibility problems

Table 9.1
David Duke's Performance in the 1992 Presidential Primary Season

Date	Primary	Type of Primary	Duke's Performance
February 18	New Hampshire	Open	Did not file
March 3	Colorado	Open	Did not file
	Georgia	Open	Denied ballot position
	Maryland	Closed	Did not file
March 7	South Carolina	Open	7%, third place
March 10	Florida	Closed	Denied ballot position
	Louisiana	Closed	9%, third place
	Massachusetts	Open	2%, fourth place
	Mississippi	Open	11%, third place
	Rhode Island	Open	2%, fourth place
	Oklahoma	Closed	3%, fourth place
	Texas	Open	3%, third place
	Tennessee	Open	3%, third place
March 17	Michigan	Open	3%, fourth place
	Illinois	Open	Not on ballot
March 24	Connecticut	Closed	2%, fourth place
April 7	Kansas	Closed	2%, fourth place
	Minnesota	Closed	Not on ballot
April 11	Wisconsin	Closed	3%, third place

as a presidential candidate, even within the South. Duke was unable to translate his 67 percent name recognition among the national electorate after his gubernatorial campaign into positive support for the presidential contest (Cook, 1991). In early February, a poll of likely southern voters by the Atlanta *Journal-Constitution* showed that "Southern voters don't like David Duke, but they're looking for someone who talks like him" (Wyman, 1992a). Only 10 percent of respondents had a favorable opinion of Duke, whereas 67 percent held an unfavorable opinion of the former Klansman. The extent to which Duke struck a chord of dissatisfaction is reflected by the 36 percent of respondents who stated that he was "saying something that needs to be said" in the presidential campaign.

Buchanan seriously undermined Duke's ability to capitalize on dissent. Evoking similar themes to Duke both before and after entering the presidential race, Buchanan's name recognition was as high as Duke's, yet he did not carry the negative baggage of a past like Duke's, which one observer described as being "more than you can carry on a 747" (Cook, 1991). Buchanan went to great lengths to establish himself as a viable conservative alternative while also discrediting Duke. Pat Buchanan, on the fading crest of his New Hampshire momentum, purloined the symbols of Duke's infamy and wrapped them in his greater legitimacy.

Credibility Gap: Money and Patrick Buchanan

In presidential primary politics, momentum means money. By allowing Patrick Buchanan to become the protest candidate of choice in the early primaries, Duke's political fortunes never recovered. By the time the campaigns headed south, Duke was seriously low on cash and unable to respond to Buchanan's attacks. The economics of Duke's campaign clearly contributed to the non-competitiveness of his candidacy. The early 1992 Federal Election Commission filings showed Duke—who projected a campaign war chest of $10-15 million dollars—with insufficient funds to file for matching fund support. Duke had only $58,000, including $50,000 transferred from his failed Louisiana gubernatorial bid; by the end of his campaign on April 22, he had raised only $140,000, and he had never tried to qualify for federal matching funds. By comparison, George Bush had qualified for over $4.2 million in matching funds and Buchanan had qualified for over $1 million at the time of the initial filing in January.

Duke's inability to raise the really big dollars is evident by examining the campaign receipts from his 1991 gubernatorial bid. Duke raised his $1.7 million gubernatorial war chest from over 20,000 individuals, an average of just over $80 per contribution. Edwards, meanwhile, raised over $4 million from approximately 4000 contributors. While federal campaign laws which govern matching presidential funds call for candidates to demonstrate broad, grassroots type support ($5,000 in 20 states, made up of contributions of $250 or less), Duke was unable to raise sufficient funds to qualify. Apparently, the goodwill of David Duke's small-dollar benefactors ended with his loss to

Edwin Edwards, and Duke continued to be shut out from large-dollar contributors (Cook, 1992a, 1992b).

Duke's only hope was to show well enough in the South to generate media attention, and hopefully financing. His failure to run well in his home region assured his demise as a potentially viable candidate and thus as a fund-raiser. The all-or-nothing southern strategy had failed again. Ultimately, Duke's failure lies with his inability to attract sufficient votes to win elections, but as is usually the case in primaries, when the votes do not come the money does not either.

The Constituency Difference

Perhaps the most important reason Duke failed is found in the fact that the constituencies in which he was running were very different (see chapter 8). Similarly, Duke's vote-getting ability was influenced by the nature of the electoral systems in which he ran. The unique electoral structures of Louisiana politics, particularly the open (nonpartisan) primary (see chapter 1), contributed to Duke's strong senatorial and gubernatorial candidacies. When they were absent in presidential primaries, Duke was at a disadvantage from the start. This system was ideally suited for Duke, as his bloc of protest voters was large enough to guarantee him a slot in the runoff. These voters were able to cast protest votes for Duke, with some assurance that they could send a message in the first round of balloting and not be stuck with the messenger after the runoff. In particular, the Louisiana open primary system facilitated the Duke candidacies of 1990 and 1991 by allowing him to assume the label of Republican while also being able to draw support from non-GOP voters in both the initial primary and runoff. Because voters could vote for the Republican Duke while also supporting Democrats for other offices on the ballot in the initial primary, Duke was able to tailor a message to which a large constituency might respond.

The evidence indicates that Duke's strategy succeeded in bringing a segment of Louisiana voters under the GOP's "big tent," where many felt they had belonged for years anyway. The profile of the Duke voter (Sadow, 1992) and of the typical Duke parish (see chapter 4) indicate that this type of voter—poor, white, less educated, possibly unemployed—would support Duke and turn out to vote for him (chapter 6).

In gaining their support, Duke penetrated a portion of the southern electorate that the GOP had unsuccessfully pursued in down-ticket races for years (Murphy and Gulliver, 1971).

This open primary system is markedly different from the system of partisan presidential primaries. In the presidential contests, voters tend to be rank-and-file party members rather than protest voters. For southern Republican party members, whose primary electorate differed substantially from the profile of the Louisiana voters who supported David Duke in 1990 and 1991, the Duke campaign presented special problems that made his candidacy unappealing, in particular as another alternative was present in Buchanan.

Although some might argue that Duke was an isolated enigma, a careful analysis of the GOP's strategy in the South suggests otherwise. Since Goldwater's strategy of "hunting where the ducks are" in 1964, Republicans have made inroads in the region by offering staunch opposition to big government and all the trappings that come with it. In this way, opposition to big government meant opposition to civil rights and any number of redistributive programs whose minority participation had drawn the ire of white southerners. In that way, opposition to government intervention became a more acceptable way for southern whites to oppose blacks (see Carmines and Stimson, 1980: 78-91). The GOP as a whole has used these symbolic "easy" issues to build support among white southerners. Ironically, Duke's down ticket success in using this strategy was not considered a blessing by mainstream Republicans who had been using this approach unsuccessfully for years. However, it was Duke's past, not his message, that was a constant source of irritation to southern Republicans.

Unfortunately for Duke, the profile of the GOP voter in southern presidential primaries did not resemble that of the typical Duke voter in 1990 or 1991. In Louisiana, the closed presidential primary system effectively shut many previous Duke voters out of the GOP primary. Voters who had supported Duke would need to change party registration prior to the presidential primary, an additional step that many lower-income individuals might be less inclined to take (Wolfinger and Rosenstone, 1980; Nagler, 1991). In such open primary states as Texas and Mississippi, party presidential primaries occurred concurrently with party primaries for down-ticket offices: potential Duke voters had to decide whether supporting Duke was sufficiently important to forego voting in the Democratic congressional primaries. In spite of the record turnout for GOP primaries in most southern states (Wyman, 1992b), the influx of new GOP voters showed little inclination to support the former legislator from Metairie.

David Duke withdrew from the GOP presidential nomination campaign on April 22, 1992. Cumulatively, he won less than 2 percent of the GOP primary vote and failed to net a single delegate. When asked about the possibility of a third-party candidacy, Duke ruled out any further role in 1992 presidential politics: "At this point, I've gone as far as I can go. I know my role in this presidential election in over" (Cook, 1992a).

Conclusion

The preceding discussion has documented and analyzed three primary reasons behind the collapse of David Duke's presidential bid. A variety of sources contributed to Duke's failure, but the principal reasons were a refusal to adapt to a different constituency, an inability to develop any type of positive campaign momentum, and the resulting failure to raise adequate amounts of campaign funds. In the end, candidates lose because they do not win enough votes to meet or exceed expectations. In this case, David Duke's campaign was not able to attract the discontented voters in both parties who had supported him throughout the 1991 primary season. Early voter disaffection manifested itself in support for Patrick Buchanan, which resulted in the void being filled before the campaign reached the South. Once in the region, Buchanan's skillful maneuvers made Duke's candidacy obsolete. This, coupled with Duke's resource problems, ensured the failure of Duke's campaign.

In retrospect, serious questions exist about the viability of a Duke candidacy. Certainly, had Buchanan not entered the nomination contest, Duke could then have served as the lightning rod, attracting disaffected Republicans. With Buchanan, Duke was pushed to the far right of the ideological spectrum. One could imagine Duke trying, perhaps successfully to some extent, to portray himself as nothing more than a Reaganite conservative, occupying a large territory on the right. Moreover, the absence of Buchanan on the ballot would have meant that the loss of momentum suffered by Duke from not entering the early contests would not have occurred. This would have given Duke an opportunity in his home South, but if the strategy failed for Gore, it would have failed for Duke. In any case, it is difficult to imagine conservative Republican partisans contributing heavily to Duke. Even given these advantages, it would have been virtually impossible for Duke to deny President Bush the nomination, or, given the winner-take-all rule in Republican primary states, even to amass a respectable number of delegates. The net effect would have been to divide the party between social moderates and conservatives, with possibly disastrous electoral consequences for the Republicans.

The shortcomings of Duke's campaign, however, may point to a more fundamental flaw: Duke himself. Thomas Edsall noted that David Duke may not have been up to the struggle before him. Edsall observed significant changes in David Duke from the end of his gubernatorial campaign to his declaration for president a month later. Duke "looked like a winner" following his gubernatorial defeat, and appeared to be a real threat to George Bush in the South and elsewhere. However, by December, when Duke declared for his intention to challenge the president, Edsall stated that Duke appeared "overwhelmed" by the spectacle of running for president. The fire and power of the night of November 16 had disappeared, replaced by the whimper of Duke's kick-off for the presidency.

One question still remains: Could David Duke have run an independent presidential campaign? He could have, but it probably would have been an under-financed failure. Third-party candidacies are virtually assured of failure as a result of the financing advantage enjoyed by the major parties. Additional problems like petition drives, filing fees, and the need to attract media attention would have troubled Duke in an attempt to get on the November ballot. In addition, the candidacy of Ross Perot, although aimed at a different audience, would have reduced the news coverage of a Duke campaign. When the media concentrated on independents, Perot would have received the coverage because Duke would have been relegated to the second tier of obscure protest candidates. For David Duke, who was poor in resources, the same problems of financial support, negative images, and competition for the support of discontented voters would have hindered an independent candidacy much as they did his bid for the GOP nomination.

10

EPILOGUE

Throughout his political fortunes in Louisiana, to both friend and foe, David Duke has never been so much a *person* as an *event*. To supporters, he is a messenger of white establishment resentment toward the notion, however correct or skewed, that the social reformist agenda of the 1960s and 1970s has become counterproductive. To his detractors, Duke represents the potential destruction of institutions that have finally brought a peace, albeit an uneasy one, between white and black residents of the post–Civil War South.

Duke himself objects to having the theme of his political ambitions considered as racially based. Indeed, he mustered that very objection during his gubernatorial campaign by trumpeting an endorsement from James Meredith, the first African-American to register at the University of Mississippi. But at its root, racial issues are exactly what drew the line between him and other candidates. In this respect, Duke is not fundamentally different from many other political figures—black and white—who continue to seek office in modern southern politics. These issues came to the fore and fueled his rise, however, because of Duke's explicit connections to white supremacist groups. "White backlash" voters saw him as the most attention-getting expression of their disdain for the political system; he was the biggest gun they had to make their point. Local media assisted in fomenting the Duke phenomenon by constantly searching for more and more sensational headlines, a trend quickly picked up by the national media. As a headline-grabber, Duke was then taken seriously by even more media who regarded him as a freakish phenomenon, by borderline conservatives looking for a viable candidate, and by pollsters seeking to advance their own reputations. Duke's successes thus snowballed.

Climbing the political ladder, however, also means becoming a clearer target, and this is precisely what happened to David Duke in the 1991 gubernatorial race. Those who once thought little of Duke as a serious contender soon replaced apathy with concern and, as this volume repeatedly notes, mobilized their counteroffensive in time to stop him. Duke's failure in the 1992 presidential election was largely a result of being overtaken by better-recognized and better-financed interests without Duke's unfavorable public relations baggage, most notably Patrick Buchanan, who stepped in to take his place as the electable spokesman for "the movement." By the time of the 1994 congressional elections, Duke's monopoly on legitimizing open opposition to mainstream positions on racially charged political issues had been completely shattered by candidates for a variety of offices in almost every state in the union. The tactic proved remarkably effective for right-wing candidates, as the results of that election demonstrate.

And what of David Duke's future? As this book goes to press, he is, in the classic manner of Louisiana politics, officially an unofficial candidate for governor in 1995. Yet he has not been drawing nearly the same media attention this election season and probably will not draw nearly the same number of votes, for several reasons. (1) The field of candidates numbers almost twenty, many of whom—including former Governor Buddy Roemer—have painted themselves with various shades available to the rock-ribbed conservative brush. (2) Anti-Duke voters are reminding themselves of 1991, guarding against a Duke surge in the polls. (3) News reporters have taken a "been there, done that" approach to the sensationalism of the 1991 election and do not have the antics of retiring Governor Edwin Edwards against which to play Duke's maneuvers. (4) And Duke himself has not come up with particularly innovative or unique answers to the state's most serious problems—unemployment, crime, and legalized gambling. For all of these reasons and a handful more, David Duke is simply old news.

This evaluation is not meant to proclaim that Duke will never again meet with political success nor to indicate that his impact will be permanently minimal. To succeed, however, he must radically reinvent himself and find another popular political wave to ride. A cursory view of current Louisiana politics suggests a belying stability and relative calm. It is well to note, however, that political waves are as unpredictable as the Gulf's, and David Duke is as practiced at reinvention as any American politician in the last fifty years.

Notes
References
Contributors
Index

NOTES

CHAPTER 1

1. The nonpartisan primary has also been referred to as an "open" or a "blanket" primary. There are certain problems with these alternative terms. While certainly open from a partisan perspective, the use of the term *open primary* too easily confuses nonpartisan elections with traditional open primaries, in which candidates are separated by party but crossover and independent voting are allowed. The term *blanket primary* is repeatedly misused in many general politics textbooks and national newspaper articles. Blanket primaries, currently used only by the states of Washington and Alaska, are those in which all candidates, regardless of party, are placed on the same ballot for a given office. This is where that system's similarities with nonpartisan elections end, for in blanket primaries, results by party are kept separate, whereas in nonpartisan elections they are not. As a native Louisianian, I favor the term *nonpartisan*, as it is most often used, in my experience, by in-state politicians and observers of Louisiana politics. Use of the term "nonpartisan" raises some questions, since the traditional understanding is that party identification is *not* allowed in such elections, whereas Louisiana's system is substantially more laissez-faire. Effectively, however, a nonpartisan ballot is precisely what it uses.

2. Runoff primaries are necessary when a state's election law requires a majority (50 percent plus one vote) to determine a winner (see Bullock and Johnson, 1992).

3. It is possible that a given candidate may face the same number of elections in a nonpartisan primary as in a partisan one; the minimum number of battles under a partisan majority system would be two (one primary and one general election), which would also be the case if the candidate made a runoff under the nonpartisan system. However, the general perception in Louisiana is that the nonpartisan system reduces the number and cost of elections in the state, despite this scenario and Charles Hadley's (1985) finding to the contrary.

4. This is a verbatim, albeit awkward, accounting of Edwards's statement; see Lamis (1988). The problem occurrred again in my interviews with state party leaders, later in this essay. I have chosen to use their exact words whenever possible, however, and to interpolate or paraphrase only where it is required for purposes of clarity or flow. Spoken words are rarely as reflective or smooth as written ones; nevertheless, the interview technique is a remarkable way of receiving candid opinion and ideas from those in the know.

5. Although the Democratic endorsement mechanism per se has not faced a serious

legal challenge, this is not to say that the nonpartisan primary system has had similarly smooth sailing. The original bill was rejected by the U.S. Department of Justice as part of that agency's obligatory Voting Rights Act preclearance review. State legislators subsequently rewrote the legislation to conform to Justice's standards, resubmitted it, and won federal approval for it in time for Edwards's 1975 gubernatorial bid. Hadley (1985) notes, in addition, that the perception of a "discriminatory effect" in the nonpartisan system against the Democratic party is more prevalent among white party members than black.

6. It is most likely that Duke, having decided to run for a Louisiana House seat from the strongly Republican Eighty-first Legislative District in and around Metairie, chose a Republican affiliation as a matter of convenience. Only Duke knows for certain if his newfound affiliation was calculated for maximum future political effect, or if he figured out after the fact that racial issues were in vogue with many of the new rural, lower socioeconomic status white southern voters attracted to Republican candidates. For the purposes of this essay the distinction is not a critical one.

7. I use the term antiregimist here in deference to McCloskey and Zaller's (1984) excellent definition and exposition in *The American Ethos*; a suitable synonym might be "populist," if a proper distinction is made between traditional populists of the Old South (such as the Long machine in Louisiana), which was comparatively free of race-baiting, and the anti-black populism later encouraged and supported by elements of the Bourbon elite. For a more complete discussion of these differences, see Goldfield (1990).

8. In Louisiana, voting registrants mark their preferred party affiliation in a space on the application. This seems to be primarily for record-keeping purposes, as party, under the nonpartisan system, is virtually meaningless in state and local elections. Traditionally, the state has recognized and kept records for the categories "Democratic," "Republican" and "other," the latter being a catch-all that includes independent voters; if the party affiliation space is left blank, the voter is considered "other." In 1992, the Louisiana Department of Elections also began keeping party registration records for United We Stand America, Ross Perot's organization, as it qualified for consideration as a recognized party under state law by virtue of the percentage of vote it captured in the 1992 presidential election. Despite the existence of a "Republican wing of the state Democratic party," in Brady's words, Democratic registration has remained remarkably stable over the past half-decade; currently, 71 percent of Louisiana voters are registered as such, compared with 19 percent for Republicans and 10 percent for "others." Louisiana has traditionally been a consistently Democratic state (Key, 1984; Heard, 1952); the lack of noticeable movement from Democratic into Republican ranks may also pay tribute to the relative meaninglessness of party labels in a nonpartisan primary state. Presumably, affiliation would matter in Louisiana only during presidential contests, which still operate under traditional closed-primary rules.

9. For why Louisiana and Georgia are good states to use for such comparative purposes, see Kuzenski (1994). Technically, Louisiana has an interesting system of off-off-year state elections; the Louisiana legislative races actually occurred within 1987.

10. This issue speaks to another nagging point for the Louisiana Republican party; namely, that against two seemingly unbeatable Democrats, Senator J. Bennett Johnston and Governor Edwin Edwards, Duke is the only Republican who has seriously chal-

lenged them in the recent past. Given the reactions of the party and its candidates to him, however—including one prominent Republican's withdrawal from the Senate race and subsequent endorsement of Johnston, and national censure of Duke by Ronald Reagan and George Bush—it seems that Duke's type of success is one with which the Louisiana GOP does not wish to be affiliated. The comments of state Republican committee member Elizabeth Rickey (1990) seem to bear this out.

11. According to selected stories from the Baton Rouge *Morning Advocate* during the period immediately after Roemer's switch to the Republican party, there was some speculation that the deciding factor in his deliberations was a promise that he would be endorsed and presented to state Republicans as the gubernatorial standard bearer. These rumors are rendered less important by the fact that Holloway's distaste for Roemer and Duke's maverick positioning all but guaranteed Roemer the opposition he ultimately faced, promises or not.

As with Duke's 1990 bid for the U.S. Senate, in which he faced incumbent J. Bennett Johnston, Republican leaders themselves cut the party's throat in the gubernatorial race to effect a Duke loss. Republican standard bearer Ben Bagert withdrew from the election so as not to split anti-Duke votes and urged his supporters to vote for Democrat Johnston. In the 1991 gubernatorial race, the state GOP rebuked David Duke (as President Bush had done), and vanquished incumbent Roemer endorsed Edwin Edwards in the runoff election. This latter point was ironic given the vehemence with which Roemer and Edwards attempted to broadside each other during the campaign.

This point brings up profound questions regarding coalescing behavior, or how defeated primary candidates' voters vote (if at all) in the runoff election. There appear to be a number of crucial factors; Bullock and Johnson (1992) provide a good foundation for an understanding of electoral myths surrounding the runoff.

12. In 1975, perhaps smelling defeat as the result of adoption of the nonpartisan primary or because the party had not developed to the point where it could regularly run serious candidates for such high office, the Louisiana Republican party had no candidates for governor. In 1979, with Edwards constitutionally prohibited from seeking a third term, Republican David C. Treen won the primary and then defeated Democratic Public Service Commissioner Louis Lambert in a runoff. In 1983, incumbent Treen faced his old nemesis, Edwards, for yet a third time (and lost), and he was the only Republican in that race. In 1987, Republican Congressman Bob Livingston ran third to then-Democrat Roemer and Edwards, in that order; this would have set up a Democrat-versus-Democrat runoff election had Edwards not bowed out of the race. In 1991, three Republicans were on the ticket—Roemer, Holloway and Duke.

13. The "Republican bloc vote" refers to a coalition that, while made up primarily of traditional Republican identifiers, almost always includes a significant number of conservative Democratic or "other" party registrants.

14. There is a certain amount of prophecy in Brady's words; at the time of this interview, the 1991 gubernatorial race was only beginning to get underway and the slate of candidates had not been determined. Duke had run against incumbent Senator J. Bennett Johnston the year before, but GOP favorite Ben Bagert withdrew from that race and endorsed Democrat Johnston, claiming that he did not want to contribute to a potential Duke victory by splitting the vote that would otherwise go to Johnston. Duke ran a

close race for that seat, but Johnston was reelected—thanks largely, as in the 1991 governor's race, to a coalition of traditional Democratic and vehemently anti-Duke Republican and independent voters.

15. See chapter 9 for a discussion of the momentum theory of elections. Although developed as a paradigm for presidential races, it fits Duke's campaigns remarkably well.

CHAPTER 2

None

CHAPTER 3

1. In an interview during the spring of 1990, Duke told me of his plans for the Senate and the presidency. I asked him why he was not considering a run for the House. With total seriousness he replied, "I can become a congressman any time I want."

2. One could build on this model and test some of Howell's interesting hypotheses about the composition of the Duke vote. Howell reports standard errors based on assumptions of random sampling, that is the standard error of a proportion. This is optimistic (i.e., type I error–prone) for telephone samples, and the margin of error needs better calibration based on the actual sampling design.

CHAPTER 4

None

CHAPTER 5

1. The correlation between percentage of black registered voters in 1990 in a parish and the percentage of the population that was black by the 1990 census is .964. Hence, the results of the analysis would be essentially the same regardless of the choice of indicator.

2. In 1980 there were seven SMSAs in Louisiana. However, only four of these included multiple parishes and are affected by this measurement approach. The SMSAs and their constituent parishes are: Alexandria (Grant and Rapides); Baton Rouge (Ascension, East Baton Rouge, Livingston, and West Baton Rouge); New Orleans (Jefferson, Orleans, St. Bernard, and St. Tammany); Shreveport (Bossier, Caddo, and Webster).

3. Census data except for urbanism are for whites only. Age and racial composition data were available from the 1990 census at the time of this writing. All other census data from 1980.

4. Census data on urbanism are available only for the total population. While data on whites only would have been preferable and consistent with measurement of the other variables, we do not believe that the analysis is biased by the use of this indicator. Bias would only occur if within parishes there was a differential urban/nonurban pattern for blacks and whites, e.g., whites tended disproportionately to dwell in the urban areas and blacks in the nonurban areas of a parish or vice-a-versa. Absent systematic differences, the percentage of the total population dwelling in urban areas is a reasonable estimate of the percentage of the white population residing in urban areas. To the extent that the two depart in a nonsystematic way, the reliability of our indica-

tor is reduced and we may underestimate the effects of urbanism.

CHAPTER 6

1. Duke beat John Treen, brother of former Republican Governor David Treen.

2. The "black candidate" explanation postulates that African-American turnout is stimulated by the presence of a black in the candidate field.

3. The "incumbent loses" myth holds that incumbents held below a majority invariably lose in a runoff. Bullock and Johnson (1992) report that incumbents who led in the initial primary win their runoffs 64.7 percent of the time while incumbents who trailed in the first primary overtake the leader in only 26.4 percent of the runoffs.

4. However, see Magler (1991) for an alternative perspective on the Wolfinger and Rosenstone hypothesis. Morris (1982) argues that continued low black turnout during the 1970s was a product of the enfranchisement of 18- to 20-year-olds.

5. Turnout figures from the Eighth Congressional District for the three Duke contests show blacks participating at lower levels than whites but with less disparity than statewide.

Election	Turnout		Total
	(Black)	(White)	
1990 Primary	70.1%	74.0%	72.5%
1991 Primary	70.4	77.6	75.4
1991 Runoff	79.5	79.7	79.7

6. There was no statewide Republican runoff.

7. South Carolina primary turnout figures are somewhat inflated. An individual who votes in the primary *or* the runoff (if there is one) is reported as having voted in the primary. Individuals who vote in both are counted only once. Even with the overreporting of primary participation, due to the inclusion of any voters who participated in the runoff but not the primary, the black turnout rates are far below those reported for Louisiana in table 6.1.

CHAPTER 7

1. This was not the first time an "establishment" Louisiana Republican had been hurt by the bitter connection between racial hatred and Republican politics. Republican Congressman Henson Moore lost the race for the U.S. Senate in 1986 to Democrat John Breaux when, days before the election, it was reported that there was a Republican effort to purge blacks from the voter rolls.

CHAPTER 8

1. Part of the problem derives from faulty data entry. Yet part of it derives from a far more perverse cause. Registration data in Louisiana is under the purview of the Department of Elections, but vote totals come from the Secretary of State's Office, and the two agencies cannot always agree on the precinct boundaries. Thus there are some districts with more votes cast than official registrants; there are some precincts with more registrants than votes cast; there are some election results for precincts that do not exist according to the Department of Elections. We offer no excuses for the peculiarities of

Louisiana record-keeping, and we have done our best to clean the available data.

2. The standard error of estimate for David Duke's vote among white Republicans is .01669. Using a 95 percent confidence interval, this implies that Duke's share of the white Republican October vote ranged from -1.2 percent to -7.9 percent, that his white Republican share of the total October vote ranged from -.2 percent to -1.3 percent. This range approaches but does not include zero, the minimum possible. The steep impact of Republican sign-ins results either from an overextrapolation of the Republican vote relative to Republican sign-ins per district or from a difference in the behavior of Democrats and independents contingent upon the number of Republicans per district. The latter seems most probable. Most Louisiana precincts have fewer than one-eighth Republican voters. Yet, as the proportion of Republicans increases, the Duke vote among whites decreases at a slightly faster rate. This does not appear to be based primarily upon changes in those precincts with low (5 percent) to moderate (25 percent) Republican share, casting doubt upon the extrapolation hypothesis. Rather, it appears due to changes in precincts with moderate (25 percent) to high (50 percent and above) Republican shares. The precincts with a greater proportion of Republicans are predominantly white, and thus the Democrats and Independents living in those precincts on first glance could be considered potential Duke voters. However, in survey and exit poll data, educated individuals were least likely to support Duke; educated Democrats and independents are more likely to live near Republicans. This suggests a probable explanation for our findings. White, non-Republican voters living in Republican neighborhoods would be less likely than other white, non-Republicans to support Duke. Hence, more Republicans in a precinct means fewer votes for Duke both because the Republicans do not support him and because, to a greater degree than otherwise predicted, their Democratic and Independent neighbors do not either.

3. Our ecological estimates for the November 1991 Gubernatorial runoff are:

	Constant	Holloway	Roemer	Duke	Total
Duke	.228268*	.371446*	.171342*	1.205895*	-.267516*
Edwards	230519*	-1.175550*	-.373777*	-1.490105*	1.102011*
Total	.458787*	-.804104*	-.202435*	-.284210*	.834495*

* $p < .01$

Thus the vote allocations (constant + total + candidate) are:

	Holloway	Roemer	Duke	Edwards
Duke	33.22%	13.21%	116.66%	-3.92%
Edwards	15.70	95.88	-15.76	133.25
Total	48.92	109.08	100.91	129.33
Non-voters	51.08	-9.08	-.91	-29.33

Chapter 9

1. Presently, thirty-four states, including every southern state except Virginia, use a primary to choose presidential delegates.

2. The major newspapers cited here are the *Washington Post, New York Times, Los Angeles Times, Wall Street Journal,* and *Christian Science Monitor.*

REFERENCES

Abney, F. Glenn. 1974. "Factors Related to Negro Voter Turnout in Mississippi." *Journal of Politics* 36: 1057–63.

Abrahamson, Mark. 1980. *Urban Sociology.* Englewood Cliffs, N.J.: Prentice-Hall.

Abramson, Paul, and William Claggett. 1986. "Race Related Differences in Self-Reported and Validated Turnout in 1984." *Journal of Politics* 48: 412–22.

———. 1989. "Race Related Differences in Self-Reported and Validated Turnout in 1986." *Journal of Politics* 51: 397–408.

———. 1991. "Racial Differences in Self-Reported and Validated Turnout in the 1988 Presidential Election." *Journal of Politics* 53: 186–97.

Anderson, Barbara A., and Brian D. Silver. 1986. "Measurement and Mis-Measurement of the Validity of the Self Reported Vote." *American Journal of Politics* 30: 771–85.

Asher, Herbert B. 1992. *Presidential Elections and American Politics,* 5th ed. Pacific Grove, Calif.: Brooks/Cole.

Baker, Riley. 1982. "Intergovernmental Relations." In *Louisiana Politics: Festival in a Labyrinth,* ed. James Bolner, 221–54. Baton Rouge: Louisiana State University Press.

Bartels, Larry M. 1988. *Presidential Primaries and the Dynamics of Public Choice.* Princeton: Princeton University Press.

Bass, Jack, and Walter DeVries. 1976. *The Transformation of Southern Politics.* New York: Basic Books.

Beck, Paul A. 1977. "Partisan Dealignment in the Postwar South." *American Political Science Review* 71: 477–96.

Berkley, G. E., and D. M. Fox. 1978. *Eighty-thousand Governments: The Politics of Subnational America.* Boston: Allyn and Bacon.

Bernick, E. Lee, and Charles W. Wiggins. 1983. "Legislative Norms in Eleven States." *Legislative Studies Quarterly* 8: 191–200.

Black, Earl. 1973. "The Militant Segregationist Vote in the Post-Brown South: A Comparative Analysis." *Social Science Quarterly* 54: 67–84.

Black, Earl, and Merle Black. 1973. "The Wallace Vote in Alabama: A Multiple Regression Analysis." *Journal of Politics* 35: 730–36.

———. 1987. *Politics and Society in the South.* Cambridge: Harvard Univeristy Press.

———. 1992. *The Vital South: How Presidents Are Elected.* Cambridge: Harvard University Press.

REFERENCES

Boyd, Richard W. 1989. "The Effects of Primaries and Statewide Races on Voter Turnout." *Journal of Politics* 51: 730–39.

Brady, James. 1990. Telephone interview with John C. Kuzenski, May 28, 1990.

Brennan, Geoffrey, and James M. Buchanan. 1984. "Voter Choice: Evaluating Political Alternatives." *American Behavioral Scientist* 28: 185–201.

Bridges, Tyler. 1990. "Bagert Quits to Keep Duke out of Runoff." (New Orleans) *Times Picayune*, October 5, 1990: 1A, 8A.

———. 1991. "Edwards Leads Duke in Three Polls: Duke Vote Hard to Tally." (New Orleans) *Times Picayune*, November 14, 1991: A1, A16.

———. 1992a. "Duke Flounders as His Campaign Fizzles in Texas." (New Orleans) *Times-Picayune*, February 29, 1992: A1.

———. 1992b. "Duke's Swift Ascent Matched by Fast Fall." (New Orleans) *Times-Picayune*, March 11, 1992: A1.

———. 1994. *The Rise of David Duke*. Oxford: University Press of Mississippi.

Browning, Rufus P., Dale Rogers Marshall, and David H. Tabb. 1984. *Protest is Not Enough*. Berkeley: University of California Press.

Bullock, Charles S. III. 1984. "Racial Crossover Voting and the Election of Black Officials." *Journal of Politics* 46: 238–51.

———. 1985. "Aftermath of the Voting Rights Act: Racial Voting Patterns in Atlanta-Area Elections." In *The Voting Rights Act: Consequences and Implications*, ed. Lorn Foster. New York: Praeger, 185–208.

———. 1990. "Turnout in Municipal Elections." *Policy Studies Review* 9: 539–49.

———. 1991. *The Georgia Political Almanac, 1991*. Decatur, Ga.: Cornerstone Publishing.

Bullock, Charles S. III, and Bruce A. Campbell. 1984. "Racist or Racial Voting in the 1981 Atlanta Municipal Elections." *Urban Affairs Quarterly* 20: 149–64.

Bullock, Charles S. III, Ronald Keith Gaddie, and John C. Kuzenski. 1987. "The Candidacy of David Duke as a Stimulus to Black Voting." Presented at the 1992 Annual Meeting of the Southwestern Political Science Association, Austin.

Bullock, Charles S. III, and Loch K. Johnson. 1992. *Runoff Elections in the United States*. Chapel Hill: University of North Carolina Press.

Caldas, Stephen J. 1992. "The Politics of Welfare Reform, Religion, Education, and Racism: Evidence from Three Southern Elections." *Southern Studies* 3: 1–14.

Caldas, Stephen J., and John Kilburn. 1987. "A Profile of Parishes Supporting David Duke." Presented at the 1987 Annual Meeting of the Southwestern Political Science Association, Austin, Tex.

Campbell, Angus, with Philip Converse, Warren Miller, and Albert Stokes. 1960. *The American Voter*. New York: John Wiley and Sons.

Campbell, David, and Joe R. Feagin. 1975. "Black Politics in the South: A Descriptive Analysis." *Journal of Politics* 37: 129–59.

Carmichael, Stokely, and Charles V. Hamilton. 1967. *Black Power*. New York: Vintage.

Carmines, Edward G., and James A. Stimson. 1980. "The Two Faces of Issue Voting." *American Political Science Review* 74: 78–91.

———. 1989. *Issue Evolution: Race and the Transformation of American Politics*. Princeton: Princeton University Press.

Carter, P. A. 1956. *The Decline and Revival of the Social Gospel*. Ithaca, N.Y.: Cornell University Press.

Combs, Michael, John R. Hibbing, and Susan Welch. 1984. "Black Constituents and Congressional Roll Call Votes." *Western Political Quarterly* 37: 424–34.

Condran, J. G. 1979. "Changes in Attitudes Toward Blacks, 1969–1977." *Public Opinion Quarterly* 43: 463–76.

Converse, Philip. 1964. "The Nature of Belief Systems in Mass Publics." *Ideology and Discontent*, 206–61. Ed. David E. Apter. New York: Free Press.

Cook, Rhodes. 1989. "The Nominating Process." In *The Elections of 1988*, ed. Michael Nelson. Washington, D.C.: Congressional Quarterly Press.

———. 1991. "In Wake of Louisiana Defeat Duke Eyes National Office." *Congressional Quarterly Weekly Report* 49: 3475–79.

———. 1992a. "Candidate Field Shapes Up As Primaries Approach." *Congressional Quarterly Weekly Report* 50: 28–29.

———. 1992b. "Duke Out of Race:'My Role is Over.'" *Congressional Quarterly Weekly Report* 50: 1086.

Cooper, C. 1990. "Duke, Johnston Fighting From Afar." (New Orleans) *Times Picayune*, October 5, 1990: 1A, 8A.

Crespi, Irving. 1971. "Structural Sources of the George Wallace Constituency." *Social Science Quarterly* 52: 115–32.

Crotty, William J., and John S. Jackson III. 1985. *Presidential Primaries and Nominations*. Washington, D.C.: Congressional Quarterly Press.

Crotty, William J., and Gary C. Jacobson. 1980. *American Parties in Decline*. Boston: Little, Brown.

Dalton, R. J. 1988. *Citizen Politics in Western Democracies*. Chatham, N.J.: Chatham House Publishers.

Davies, J. C. 1962. "Toward a Theory of Revolution." *American Sociological Review* 27: 5–19.

Dexter, Lewis Anthony. 1970. *Elite and Specialized Interviewing*. Evanston, Ill.: Northwestern University Press.

DiLeonardi, J. W., and P. A. Curtis. 1988. *What To Do When the Numbers Are In: A User's Guide to Statistical Data Analysis in the Human Services*. Chicago: Nelson-Hall.

Downs, Anthony. 1957. *An Economic Theory of Democracy*. New York: HarperCollins.

Duke Campaign Committee. 1991. Direct mail survey.

Edsall, Thomas. 1992. Address to the 1992 Citadel Symposium on Southern Politics, Charleston, S.C., March 6.

———, and Mary Edsall. 1991. *Chain Reaction: The Impact of Race, Rights, and Taxes on American Politics*. New York: Norton.

Erbring, Lutz. 1989. "Individuals Writ Large: An Epilogue to the 'Ecological Fallacy.'" *Political Analysis* 1: 235–69.

Faucheux, Ronald, 1992. *The Ringmaster*. Ann Arbor, Mich.: University Microfilms International.

Feld, S. L., and Bernard Grofman. 1988. "Ideological Consistency as a Collective Phe-

nomenon." *American Political Science Review* 82: 773–88.
Fossett, Mark, and K. Jill Kiecolt. 1989. "Relative Size of Minority Populations and White Racial Attitudes." *Social Science Quarterly* 70: 820–35.
Foster, Lorn. 1985. Prepared statement in *Voting Rights Act: Runoff Primaries and Registration Barriers*, Subcommittee on Civil and Constitutional Rights of the Committee on the Judiciary, U.S. House of Representatives, 98th Cong., 2d Sess. Washington, D.C.: U.S. Government Printing Office.
Gallup, George, Jr., and Frank Newport. 1991. "Blacks and Whites Differ on Civil Rights Progress." *Gallup Poll Monthly* (August 1991).
Giles, Michael W. 1977. "Percent Black and Racial Hostility: An Old Assumption Reexamined." *Social Science Quarterly* 58: 848–65.
Giles, Michael W., and Arthur Evans. 1985. "External Threat, Perceived Threat and Group Identity." *Social Science Quarterly* 66: 50–66.
———. 1986. "The Power Approach to Intergroup Hostility." *Journal of Conflict Resolution* 30: 469–86.
Glenn, Norval, and Charles Weaver. 1981. "Education Effects of Psychological Well-Being." *Public Opinion Quarterly* 45: 22–29.
Goldfield, David R. 1990. *Black, White and Southern*. Baton Rouge: Louisiana State University Press.
Gove, W. R., and M. Hughes. 1980. "Reexamining the Ecological Fallacy." *Social Forces* 58: 1157–77.
Grabb, E. G. 1979. "Working-Class Authoritarianism and Tolerance of Outgroups: A Reassessment." *Public Opinion Quarterly* 43: 36–47.
Greenhaw, Wayne. 1982. *Elephants in the Cottonfields*. New York: Macmillan.
Grofman, Bernard. 1992. "The Use of Ecological Regression to Estimate Racial Bloc Voting." Paper presented at the Conference on Spatial and Contextual Models of Political Behavior, State University of New York at Buffalo, October 1992.
Grosser, Paul E. 1982. "Political Parties." In *Louisiana Politics: Festival in a Labyrinth*, ed. James Bolner. Baton Rouge: Louisiana State University Press.
Gurian, Paul-Henri. 1986. "Resource Allocation Strategies in Presidential Nomination Campaigns." *American Journal of Political Science* 30: 802–21.
———. 1991. "Less Than Expected: An Analysis of Media Coverage of Super Tuesday 1988." *Social Science Quarterly* 72: 761–73.
Gurr, T. R. 1970. *Why Men Rebel*. Princeton: Princeton University Press.
Hadley, Charles D. 1985. "Support for the Return to Closed Primary Elections: Louisiana Party Professionals on the Open Elections System." *Southeastern Political Review* 13: 167–77.
Hamilton, Charles V. 1977. "Voter Registration Drives and Turnout: A Report on the Harlem Electorate." *Political Science Quarterly* 92: 43–46.
Hanushek, E. A., with J. E. Jackson and J. F. Kain. 1974. "Model Specification, Use of Aggregate Data, and the Ecological Fallacy." *Political Methodology* 1: 89–107.
Havard, William C. 1972. *The Changing Politics of the South*. Baton Rouge: Louisiana State University Press.
Hawley, Willis D. 1973. *Nonpartisan Elections and the Case for Party Politics*. New York: John Wiley and Sons.

Heard, Alexander. 1952. *A Two-Party South?* Chapel Hill: University of North Carolina Press.
Hebert, F. Ted, and Lelan E. McLemore. 1973. "Character and Structure of Legislative Norms: Operationalizing the Norm Concept in the Legislative Setting." *American Journal of Political Science* 17: 506–27.
Henry, Charles P. 1980. "Black-Chicano Coalitions: Possibilities and Problems." *Western Journal of Black Studies* 4: 202–32.
Herring, Mary. 1990. "Legislative Responsiveness to Black Constituents in Three Deep South States." *Journal of Politics* 52: 740–58.
Hevesi, D. 1991. "Duke Forgiven His Past by Out-of-State Donors." *New York Times*, November 15, 1991: A21.
Howell, Susan. 1990. *Quality of Life and Government Services in Orleans and Jefferson Parishes*. New Orleans: University of New Orleans Survey Research Center.
———. 1991. "Governor's Race Survey, October, 1991." New Orleans: University of New Orleans Survey Research Center.
Huckfeldt, Robert, and Carol Kohfeld. 1989. *Race and the Decline of Class in American Politics*. Chicago: University of Illinois Press.
Hyman, Herbert H., and Paul B. Sheatsley. 1964. "Attitudes Toward Desegregation." *Scientific American* 211: 16–23.
Johnston, J. 1972. *Econometric Methods*. 2d ed. New York: McGraw-Hill.
Kazee, Thomas A. 1983. "The Impact of Electoral Reform: 'Open Elections' and the Louisiana Party System." *Publius* 13: 131–39.
Keech, William R. 1968. *The Impact of Negro Voting: The Role of the Vote in the Quest for Equality*. Chicago: Rand McNally.
Key, V. O. Jr. 1949. *Southern Politics in State and Nation*. New York: Vintage. Reprint, 1984. Knoxville: University of Tennessee Press.
———. 1956. *Politics, Parties, and Pressure Groups*. New York: Thomas Y. Crowell.
Kilburn, John C., Jr. 1990. "Jesse Jackson, the Rainbow Coalition and the Black Vote." Paper presented at the 1990 Annual Meeting of the Mid-South Sociological Association, Hot Springs, Arkansas.
Kramer, G. H. 1971. "Short Term Fluctuations in U.S. Voting Behavior, 1896–1964." *American Political Science Review* 65: 131–43.
———. 1983. "The Ecological Fallacy Revisited." *American Political Science Review* 77: 92–111.
Kuzenski, John C. 1990. "The Nonpartisan Primary: A View From the State Legislature." Unpublished manuscript commissioned by anonymous private interest.
———. 1994. "Party Nomination Strategies in Partisan and Nonpartisan Primary Systems: The Cases of Georgia and Louisiana." Paper presented at the 1994 Citadel Symposium on Southern Politics, Charleston, South Carolina.
Lamis, Alexander P. 1988. *The Two-Party South*. New York: Oxford University Press.
Landry, D. M., and J. P. Parker. 1982. "Louisiana Political Culture." In *Louisiana Politics: Festival in a Labyrinth*, ed. James Bolner, 1–13. Baton Rouge: Louisiana State University Press. .
Lasch, Christopher. 1991. *The True and Only Heaven: Progress and Its Critics*. New York: Norton.

Lipset, Seymour M. 1981. *Political Man: The Social Bases of Politics*. Baltimore: Johns Hopkins University Press.

Lipset, Seymour M., and Earl Rabb. 1969. "The Wallace Whitelash." *Transaction* 7: 23–25.

Magler, Jonathan. 1991. "The Effect of Registration Laws and Education on U.S. Voter Turnout." *American Political Science Review* 85: 1393–1406.

Magnuson, E. 1989. "Kluk! Kluk! Kluk!." *Time*, March 29, 1989: 29.

Mahe, Edward, and Xandra Kayden. 1985. *The Party Goes On*. New York: Basic Books.

McCloskey, Herbert, and John Zaller. 1984. *The American Ethos: Public Attitudes Toward Capitalism and Democracy*. Cambridge: Harvard University Press.

McMahon, William B. 1992. "David Duke in the Legislature: 'A Mouth That's Different.'" In *The Emergence of David Duke and the Politics of Race*, ed. Douglas D. Rose. Chapel Hill: University of North Carolina Press.

Meacham, Jon. 1992. "Dukedumb: How a Lightweight Louisiana Racist Came to Spook a Nation." *Washington Monthly* 51 (July/August): 49-51.

Moreland, Robert, and T. Wayne Parent. 1991. "Continuity in the Southern Dilemma: Would Huck Finn Vote for David Duke?" Paper presented at the 1991 Annual Meeting of the Southern American Studies Association, Williamsburg, Va.

Murphy, Reg, and Hal Gulliver. 1971. *The Southern Strategy*. New York: Charles Scribner's Sons.

Myrdal, Gunner, with R. Sterner and A. Rose. 1944. *An American Dilemma*. New York: Harper & Row.

Nagler, Jonathan. 1991. "The Effects of Registration Laws and Education on U.S. Voter Turnout." *American Political Science Review* 85: 1393–1406.

Nauth, Zack. 1989. "Lawmakers: Duke Flunked Freshman Term." (New Orleans) *Times-Picayune*, July 16, 1989: B1.

Nesbit, Dorothy Davidson. 1988. "Changing Partisanship Among Southern Party Activists." *Journal of Politics* 50: 322–34.

Nie, Norman H., with Sidney Verba and John Petrocik. 1976. *The Changing American Voter*. Cambridge: Harvard University Press.

Norrander, Barbara. 1989. "Turnout in the 1988 Presidential Primaries." Paper presented at the 1989 Annual Meeting of the Midwest Political Science Association, Chicago.

———. 1992. *Super Tuesday: Regional Politics and Presidential Primaries*. Lexington: University of Kentucky Press.

Orren, Gary R., and Nelson W. Polsby. 1987. *Media and Momentum: The New Hampshire Primary and Nomination Politics*. Chatham, N.J.: Chatham House.

Parent, T. Wayne, with S. Caldas, J. Kilburn, and P. Petrakis. 1992. "An Ordinary Explanation of an Extraordinary Election: The 1991 Louisiana Vote." Paper presented at the 1992 Annual Meeting of the American Political Science Association, Chicago.

Parent, T. Wayne, with C. Jillson and R. Weber. 1987. "Voting Outcomes in the 1984 Democratic Party Primaries and Caucuses." *American Political Science Review* 81: 67–84.

Patterson, Thomas E. 1980. *The Mass Media Election*. New York: Praeger.

Perry, Huey L., and Albert Stokes. 1987. "Politics and Power in the Sunbelt." In *The*

New Black Politics. 2d ed. Ed. Michael B. Preston, Lenneal J. Henderson, Jr., and Paul Puryear, 222–55. New York: Longman.

Petrocik, John R. 1987. "Realignment: New Party Coalitions and the Nationalization of the South." *Journal of Politics* 49: 347–75.

Pinderhughes, Diane M. 1987. *Race and Ethnicity in Chicago Politics*. Urbana: University of Illinois Press.

Powell, Lawrence N. 1992. "Slouching toward Baton Rouge: The 1989 Legislative Election of David Duke." In *The Emergence of David Duke and the Politics of Race*, ed. Douglas D. Rose. Chapel Hill: University of North Carolina Press.

Preston, Michael B. 1987. "The Election of Harold Washington: An Examination of the SES Model in the 1983 Chicago Mayoral Election." In *The New Black Politics*. 2d ed. Ed. Michael B. Preston, Lenneal J. Henderson, Jr., and Paul Puryear, 139–71. New York: Longman.

Price, Hugh D. 1957. *The Negro and Southern Politics: A Chapter of Florida History*. New York: New York University Press.

Prysby, Charles L. 1989a. "Attitudes of Southern Democratic Party Activists Toward Jesse Jackson: The Effects of the Local Context." *Journal of Politics* 51: 305–18.

———. 1989b. "The Structure of Southern Electoral Behavior." *American Politics Quarterly* 17: 1630–80.

Raber, R., and B. Alpert. 1990. "Racial Issues Get New Focus." the (New Orleans) *Times-Picayune*, October 8, 1990: 1B, 3B.

Ransom, Bruce. 1987. "Black Independent Electoral Politics in Philadelphia and the Election of W. Wilson Goode." In *The New Black Politics*. 2d ed. Ed. Michael B. Preston, Lenneal J. Henderson, Jr., and Paul Puryear. New York: Longman.

Renwick, Edward F. 1992. "The 1992 Louisiana Gubernatorial Campaign." Presented at the 1992 Annual Meeting of the American Political Science Association, Chicago.

Rickey, Elizabeth A. 1990. "The Nazi and the Republicans." In *The Emergence of David Duke and the Politics of Race*, ed. Douglas D. Rose. Chapel Hill: University of North Carolina Press.

Robinson, W. S. 1950. "Ecological Correlations and the Behavior of Individuals." *American Sociological Review* 15: 351–57.

Rodgers, Harrell R. and Charles S. Bullock III. 1972. *Law and Social Change*. New York: McGraw-Hill.

"Roemer Says Reagan Paved Way for Duke." 1991. (New Orleans) *Times Picayune*. October 21, 1991: A8.

Rose, Douglas D. 1992a. "David Duke's U.S. Senate Campaign." In *The Emergence of David Duke and the Politics of Race*, ed. Dougals D. Rose, 156–96. Chapel Hill: University of North Carolina Press.

———, ed. 1992b. *The Emergence of David Duke and the Politics of Race*. Chapel Hill: University of North Carolina Press.

Rosenthal, Alan. 1981. *Legislative Life*. New York: Harper and Row.

Ross, P. J., with H. Bluestone and F. K. Hines. 1979. *Indicators of Social Well-Being for U.S. Counties*. Washington, D.C.: U.S. Department of Agriculture.

Sadow, Jeffrey D. 1992. "Racism or Resentment? The Duke Campaign Activist." Paper presented at the 1992 Annual Meeting of the American Political Science Association, Chicago.

Schlesinger, Arthur M., Jr. 1986. *The Cycles of American History.* Boston: Houghton-Mifflin.

Schoenberger, Robert A., and David R. Segal. 1971. "The Ecology of Dissent: The Southern Wallace Vote in 1968." *Midwest Journal of Political Science* 15: 583–86.

Schroeder, Charles. 1990. Telephone interview with John C. Kuzenski, May 18, 1990.

Schulman, Bruce J. 1991. *From Cotton Belt to Sunbelt: Federal Policy, Economic Development, and Transformation of the South, 1938–1980.* New York: Oxford University Press.

Smith, J. Owens, Mitchell F. Rice, and Woodrow Jones, Jr. 1987. *Blacks and American Government.* Dubuque, Iowa: Kendall/Hunt.

St. Raymond, James V. 1989. "Lawmaker Distances Himself from Duke's Beliefs." (New Orleans) *Times-Picayune*, March 16, 1989: B10.

Stanley, Harold W. 1987. *Voter Mobilization and the Politics of Race: The South and Universal Suffrage, 1952–1984.* New York: Praeger.

Stanley, Harold W., and David S. Castle. 1988. "Partisan Changes in the South: Making Sense of Scholarly Dissonance." In *The South's New Politics: Realignment and Dealignment*, ed. Robert H. Swansbrough and David M. Brodsky. Columbia: University of South Carolina Press.

Tate, Katherine. 1991. "Black Political Participation in the 1984 and 1988 Presidential Elections." *American Political Science Review* 85: 1159–76.

Theodoulou, Stella Z. 1985. *The Louisiana Republican Party, 1948–1984: The Building of a State Political Party.* Tulane Studies in Political Science. New Orleans: Tulane University.

Tocqueville, Alexis de. 1955. *Democracy in America.* New York: Vintage.

Vedlitz, Arnold. 1985. "Voter Registration Drives and Black Voting in the South." *Journal of Politics* 77: 643–51.

Wahlke, John C., et al. 1962. *The Legislative System: Explorations in Legislative Behavior.* New York: John Wiley.

Wasserman, Ira M., and David R. Segal. 1973. "Aggregation Effects in the Ecological Study of Presidential Voting." *American Journal of Political Science* 17: 177–81.

Wayne, Stephen J. 1992. *The Road to the White House 1992.* New York: St. Martin's Press.

Wildgen, John. 1982. "Voting Behavior in Gubernatorial Elections, in *Louisiana Politics: Festival in a Labyrinth.* Ed. James Bolner, 319–44. Baton Rouge: Louisiana State University Press.

Wilkerson, Isabel. 1991. "Daley is Easy Victor in Mayoral Primary." *New York Times*, February 27, 1991.

Williams, T. Harry. 1969. *Huey Long.* New York: Alfred A. Knopf.

Wilson, W. J. 1991. Studying Inner-City Social Dislocations: The Challenge of Public Agenda Research." *American Sociological Review* 56: 1–14.

Wolfinger, Raymond, and Michael Hagen. 1985. "Republican Prospects." *Public Opinion* 8: 8–13.

Wolfinger, Raymond, and Steven Rosenstone. 1980. *Who Votes?* New Haven: Yale University Press.

Wolfinger, Raymond, and Robert B. Arseneau. 1978. "Partisan Change in the South, 1952–1976." In *Political Parties: Development and Decay*, ed. L. Sandy Maisel and Joseph Cooper. Beverly Hills, Calif.: Sage.

Wright, Gerald C. 1976. "Linear Models for Evaluating Conditional Relationships." *American Journal of Political Science* 20: 349–73.

———. 1977. "Contextual Models of Electoral Behavior: The Southern Wallace Vote." *American Political Science Review* 71: 497–508.

Wright, James D. 1976. *The Dissent of the Governed: Alienation and Democracy in America*. New York: Academic Press.

Wright, Stephen G. 1989. "Voter Turnout in Runoff Elections." *Journal of Politics* 51: 385–96.

Wrinkle, Robert D., and Jerry L. Polinard. 1973. "Populism and Dissent: The Wallace Vote in Texas." *Social Science Quarterly* 54: 306–20.

Wyman, Hastings, Jr. 1992a. "Presidential Campaign Notes." *Southern Political Report*, February 11.

———. 1992b. "South Backs Clinton, Bush." *Southern Political Report*, March 17.

Zatarain, Michael. 1990. *David Duke: Evolution of a Klansman*. Gretna, La: Pelican.

LIST OF CONTRIBUTORS

WILLIAM ARP III
　Associate Professor of
　Political Science
　Southern University

KEITH BOECKELMAN
　Assistant Professor of
　Political Science
　Louisiana State University

MELANIE BUCKNER
　Graduate Student in
　Political Science
　Emory University

CHARLES S. BULLOCK III
　Richard B. Russell
　Professor of Political Science
　University of Georgia

STEPHEN J. CALDAS
　Assistant Professor
　Department of Educational
　Foundations and Leadership
　University of Southwestern Louisiana

MATTHEW CROZAT
　Graduate Student in Political Science
　Cornell University

EUEL ELLIOTT
　Associate Professor
　School of Social Science
　University of Texas at Dallas

RONALD KEITH GADDIE
　Research Assistant Professor of
　Environmental Health Sciences
　Tulane University

MICHAEL W. GILES
　Professor of Political Science and
　Fellow of the Carter Center
　Emory University

JOHN C. KUZENSKI
　Assistant Professor of
　Political Science
　Vanderbilt University and
　Southeastern Louisiana University

JOHN C. KILBURN
　Graduate Student in Sociology
　Louisiana State University

RONALD F. KING
　Associate Professor of
　Political Science
　Tulane University

T. WAYNE PARENT
　Associate Professor of
　Political Science
　Louisiana State University

DOUGLAS D. ROSE
　Associate Professor of
　Political Science
　Tulane University

LIST OF CONTRIBUTORS

BERNARD TERRADOT
   Graduate Student in
   Political Science
   Louisiana State University

GREGORY S. THIELEMANN
   Associate Professor
   School of Social Sciences
   University of Texas at Dallas

JOHN K. WILDGEN
   Freeport / McMoRan Professor
   College of Urban and Public Affairs
   University of New Orleans

INDEX

Abney, F. Glenn, 105
Abrahamson, Mark, 93
Abramson, Paul, R., 69, 101
Acadiana-black coalition, 66
Acadiana: caucus, 26; parishes, 68, 85
affirmative action, 12, 24–26, 63, 86, 90, 124
aggregate-level determinants of voting behavior, 57-60, 67–87, 91–98; education, 68, 77, 79–80, 82–83, 86, 93, 96, 170 n.2; income, 68–70, 78–80, 82, 96; race, 67–68, 77, 86; racial concentration, 91–94, 96–97; urbanization, 70, 78, 80, 93, 168 n.4; voting propensity, 70–71, 77, 80, 82–83, 86
Agnew, Spiro, 57
American Ethos (McCloskey and Zaller), 123, 166 n.7
American Nazi Party, 90
American Nazi, 20
anti-black, 66, 68, 86, 166 n.7
anti-Catholic, 66, 68, 86
anti-civil rights, 5, 23–24
anti-Semitism, 5, 59
Arp, William, III, xi

Bagert, Ben, 22, 50, 63, 68, 167 n.11
Baker, Riley, 70
Barthelemy, Sidney, 85
Morning Advocate (Baton Rouge), 103, 167 n.11
Benjamin, Judah P., 3
black caucus. *See* Louisiana Legislative Black Caucus
black constituencies, 23, 25–26, 33

Black, Earl, 8, 12-13, 16, 68, 88–89, 93, 98, 118–121, 143, 152
Black, Merle, 8, 12-13, 16, 68, 88–89, 98, 118–121, 143, 152
Boeckelman, Keith, xi
Bourbon Democrats, 9, 65, 166 n.7
Bradley, Tom, 122
Brady, James, 8, 21, 166 n.8, 167 n.14
Breaux, John, 66, 169 n.1b
Bridges, Tyler, 52
Browning, Rufus P., 28
Bruneau, Peppi, 47
Buchanan, Patrick, xv, defeat of, 134–137; and Duke, 140, 143, 147, 154, 160; as protest candidate, 128, 133, 151–152, 154, 156–157; support of, 134, 136
Buckner, Melanie, xiii, 104
Bucktown (New Orleans): 36–38, 44
Bullock, Charles S., III, xiii, 20, 89, 104,
Bush, George, 58, 60, 146–147, 167 n.10; and anti-Duke sentiment, 39, 44, 167 n.11; influenced by Duke campaign, 86–87; and protest vote, 136–137, 151–152; and race, 90–92, 96–98, 117, 123; support for, 92, 96–98, 136, 143, 154, 158
busing, 12, 86, 124

Cajun-black coalition, 66, 85
Caldas, Stephen J., xiii, 12, 15, 68–69, 83
Campbell, Bruce A., 89
Campbell, Carroll, 109
Campbell, David, 28
Camrines, Edward G., 125
candidates: black, 99–100, 102, 107,

109–110, 113, 122; dark-horse, 14–15, 20–21; established (experienced), 10, 16, 148; long shot (fringe), 15, 17, 148; protest, 69, 128, 136, 143, 151–152, 154, 158; racist, 43, 59, 91, 96–97; renegade, 10–13; uncontested, 14
Carter, Jimmy, 66
Chain Reaction (Edsall and Edsall), 124
Chicago Tribune, 141
Christian Science Monitor, 171 n.2
Citizen's Council, 5
Civil Rights Act, 9, 89
civil rights, 12, 24, 89, 124–125, 146, 152, 156; legislation, 23, 123, 125; movement, 5, 60, 70, 119; policy, 34; stance, 68, 147
Claggett, William, 101
Clinton, Bill, 58, 60, 66, 124
Clyburn, James, 107, 109
coalition politics (theory), 23, 28, 33
Community Organization for Urban Politics (COUP), 85
Condorcet winner, 20–21
Confederate Emancipation Proclamation, 3
constituency; black, 23, 25–26, 30, 33; heterogeneous, 36; "natural," xv; and pressure, 30. *See also,* Duke, David Ernest: and constituency
Converse, Philip, 70
crossover votes, 7, 10, 16, 142. *See also,* voting
Crozat, Matthew, 16, 141
Cycles of American History (Schlesinger), 123

Daley, Richard, 102
dark horse candidate. *See* candidates
Davies, J. C., 69
Davis, Jefferson, 3
Dinkins, David, 122
Dixiecrats, 21, 123
Donahue Show, 4
Donaldson, Sam, 39
Donelon, Jim, 47
dual-primary, 20. *See also,* primary system
Dukakis, Michael, 39, 44, 149
Duke, David Ernest: and anti-affirmative action, 26; as attention-seeker, xii, 30–32, 160; charisma of, 13, 55, 59; and constituency, xiii, xv, 33, 36, 59, 66–67, 147, 150, 155, 157; coalition, 15, 20; as Democrat, 11, 16; and early years, 5–6; failure (ineffectiveness) of, xiv–xv, 23, 25, 28, 31–33, 152, 157–158, 160; and funding, xv, 154–155, 157; and "hidden" vote, xii, 51–54, 56–58, 103; and Ku Klux Klan, 11, 20, 24, 53, 63, 68, 90, 100, 140, 149; as legislator, xi, xii, 23–26, 29–30, 36, 44, 47–49; and media, 20, 31, 33, 39, 150–152, 155, 158; message of, xi, 20, 23-34, 66, 70, 86–87, 90, 105, 117, 144, 151, 155–156, 159; and neo-Nazi organizations, 24, 33, 63, 68; and the nonpartisan primary, 13, 15; and parish politics, 36; as a phenomenon, xi, xiv, 6, 17, 35–36, 44, 128; as a political force, xi–xii, 13, 15; as populist, 66–67; and race, xi, 6, 11, 16, 20, 24–25, 29–31, 43, 57, 59–60, 63, 67–68, 126, 127, 159; rejected for public office, 11; as Republican, 12–13, 15, 18, 45, 47–49, 57, 63, 86, 127-128, 166 nn.6, 10; and source of support, xi, xiii–xiv, 11, 128-129, 133–145, 150, 154–155; as white supremacist, 4, 53, 63, 159; and 1988 Republican primary, 4, 15, 36–44; and 1990 Senatorial race, xiii, 15, 17, 22, 24, 44, 50–57, 66–68, 90, 94, 97, 109, 167 n.11; and 1991 gubernatorial race, xiii–xiv, 15, 17–18, 24, 44, 66–69, 90, 94, 97, 99, 103–104, 109-110, 131–133, 138, 150, 160, 167 nn. 12, 14; and 1992 Republican presidential primary, xiv–xv, 18, 67, 133–134, 139, 149–158, 160
Duke, David H., 5
Duke, Dorothy, 5
Duke, Maxine, 5

Edsall, Mary, 124
Edsall, Thomas, 124, 158
Edwards, Governor Edwin W., xii, 160, 165 n.4; and black turnout, 20, 66, 103, 106–107, 110, 113–114, 131; and corruption, 51, 57–78, 100, 110; as

Duke opponent, 18, 44, 52–59, 63, 67, 76, 99–100, 103–104, 106–107, 110, 113–114, 131, 136, 138–140, 144, 166 n.10; and funding, 154–155; and hidden vote, 48, 52, 54, 56–58; and Johnston, 50; and nonpartisan primary, 4, 7–8, 166; and Roemer, 22, 50–51, 100, 167 n.11; and Treen, 167 n.12; and Vitter, 48
Eisenhower, Dwight, D., 118
Elliott, Euel, xv
endorsement mechanism, 19, 165 n.5

far right, xv, 21, 157
Feagin, Joe R., 28
Federal Election Commission, 154
Fossett, Mark, 92
Free Speech Alley (LSU), 6

Gaddie, Ronald Keith, xiii
Gegenheimer, Jon, 41–42
gerrymander, 47
Giles, Michael W., xiii
Gill, James, 39
Goldwater Republicans, 120
Goldwater, Barry, 5–6, 57, 118–119, 156
Goode, Wilson, 102
Gore, Al, 149–150, 158
Great Society, xiii, 89
gubernatorial runoff elections: in Georgia, 107–109; in South Carolina, 107–109. *See also,* Duke, David Earnest: 1991 gubernatorial race; Louisiana gubernatorial election (1991)
Gurian, Paul-Henri, 148
Gurr, T. R., 69

Hadley, Charles, D., 15, 21–22, 165 n.3, 166 n.5
Hamilton, Charles V., 28
Hand, Skip, 47
Harvard, William C., 120
Hawley, Willis, 17
Helms, Jesse, 90–91
Herring, Mary, 29
Hibbing, John R., 25
Hill, Lance, 144
Holloway, Clyde, 18, 63, 100, 131–133, 138–139, 144, 167 nn.11–12, 170 n.3
Horton, Willie, 91, 117
Howell, Susan, 51–54, 57, 168 n.2a
ideologues, 70, 138
"incumbent protection act," 8
Issue evolution: Race and the Transformation of American Politics (Carmines and Stimson), 125

Jackson, Jesse, 60, 102, 149–150
Jackson, Maynard, 102
Jefferson Parish, 36, 38–39, 41, 43, 57
Jillson, C., 69
John F. Kennedy High School (New Orleans), 6
Johnson, Loch K., 104
Johnson, Lyndon B., 118
Johnston, J. Bennett: support of, 66–68, 167 n.10; vs. Duke, 17, 22, 106, 140, 144; win over Duke, 15, 24, 44, 50, 63, 64, 100, 166 n.10, 167 nn.11, 14
Journal-Constitution (Atlanta), 153

Kazee, Thomas A., 19–20
Kennedy, Ted, 67
Kennedy-Nixon contest, 99
Key, V. O., 8, 16, 85, 88–90, 94, 96–98, 104, 119–120, 152
Kilburn, John C., xiii, 84
King Cotton Democrat, 16
King, Martin Luther, Jr., 28
King, Ronald F., xiv, 16
Kramer, G. H., 64, 69
Ku Klux Klan, xi, 4, 6, 11, 20, 24, 53, 63–64, 68, 90, 100, 140–141, 148, 153
Kuzenski, John C., xi, xiii

Lake Pontchartrain, 38
Lambert, Louis, 19, 167 n.12
Lamis, Alexander P., 67, 120
Landry, D. M., 68
Lasch, Christopher, 121, 124
Lee, Harry, 39, 41–42, 44, 47
left-right continuum, 46–47
legislative norms, 23, 31–33
Liberal-Populist, 65
Limbaugh, Rush, 86
Lipset, Seymour M., 83
Livingston, Bob, 167 n.12

Long, Earl, 3
Long, Huey, 3, 29, 50, 65–66
Los Angeles Times, 171 n.2
Louisiana Coalition Against Racism and Nazism, 144
Louisiana Democratic State Central Committee (DSCC), 10
Louisiana Department of Registration and Elections, 25, 129, 133, 166 n.8, 169 n.1c
Louisiana Eighth Congressional District, 106–107, 110, 169 n.5
Louisiana gubernatorial election (1991), xiii, 24, 50, 63, 66–67, 70, 98, 99–100, 106, 117, 137, 144, 146, 150, 153–154, 158–160, 167 nn.11, 14; primary of 1991, 50, 63, 67–68, 72–75, 78, 81, 83–84, 96, 99, 128–129, 131, 133–134, 136, 138, 144; runoff of, 63, 65–69, 72–76, 78, 81, 83–86, 99, 104, 127–129, 136, 139, 170 n.3. *See also,* gubernatorial runoff elections
Louisiana House Bill 1623, 25
Louisiana House of Representatives, xi–xii, 24, 44–47; black members of, 45, 47
Louisiana Legislative Black Caucus, 24, 29–31, 45
Louisiana lottery, 3, 26
Louisiana Secretary of State, 71, 107, 129, 169 n.1c
Louisiana State Archives, 129
Louisiana State Legislature, xii, 4, 8, 67, 70, 82, 100, 105
Louisiana State University (LSU), 6
Loyola University, 52

Maddox, Lester, 118
Magler, Jonathan, 169 n.4
majority-rule runoff, 7. *See also,* dual-primary
Marshall, Dale Rogers, 28
Mason-Dixon Opinion Research, 52–53, 63, 103
mass media. *See* media
Mattingly, Mack, 120
McCloskey, Herbert, 123, 166 n.7
McGovern-Fraser reforms, 148
media, 3, 6; attention, 147–148, 151, 155, 158, 160; coverage, 148, 151, 158; and Duke, 17, 31–32, 34, 59, 63, 69, 82, 127, 137, 142, 155, 160; exploitation of, 39; exposure, 59, 150–152; local, 6, 159; as messenger, xv, 6, 23–24; and misleading stories, 134, 136; national, 20, 134, 159; and New Orleans market, 111; and opposition to Duke, 103; status, 20
Mein Kampf, 45
Meredith, James, 159
Michigan model of normal vote analysis, 64
Mitchell, Theo, 107, 109
Moore, Henson, 169 n.1b
Morial, Ernest "Dutch," 85, 102
Morial, Marc, 85
Myrdal, Gunner, 126

Napoleonic Code, 3
National Association for the Advancement of White People, 53, 60, 68, 90
National Socialist Liberation Front, 6
neo-Nazi organizations, 4, 20, 24, 63, 68, 90. *See also* American Nazi Party
New York Review of Books, 141
New York Times, 90, 136, 171 n.2
Neyaski, Grenes, 90
Nie, Norman H., 66
Nixon, Richard M, 99, 118, 150

Orleans Parish, 36

Parent, T. Wayne, xiv, 15, 67, 69, 71, 83, 143
Parker, J. P., 68
party identification (affiliation), xiii–xiv, 13, 16, 20, 128, 133–134, 143, 166 n.8
Perez, Leander, 5
Perot, Ross, 158, 166 n.8
Petrakis, P., 83–84
Petrocik, John, 66
Phillips, Kevin, 123
Pinderhughes, Diane M., 28
Plaquemines Parish, 5
political momentum, 148, 154, 157
Politics and Society in the South (Black and Black), 120
Politics of Rich and Poor (Phillips), 123

polling (pollsters): exit, 133–136; problems of, xii, 51–58; and gubernatorial primary (1991), xii, 51–57;
Powell, Lawrence N., 43–44, 57–58, 68, 70, 83
press. *See* media
primary system, 147, 165 nn.1, 3, 5, 166 n.8; blanket primary, 165 n.1; nonpartisan open primary, xi, 4, 6–7, 11, 13–18, 20–22, 131, 137, 140, 143, 155–156, 165 n.1; partisan-preferential, xiv, 7, 14, 133, 165 n.3
Prime Time Live, 39

questionnaire, 29, 31, 34
quotas, 124

race (racial issues), xiv, 5, 23, 28–30, 69, 84, 86, 89, 117–118, 149, 169 n.1b
race-baiting, 11, 48, 89, 166 n.7
racial threat, 88–98
racism (racists), xv, 16,35, 43, 50, 52, 57–58, 67–68, 90, 105; and Republican rise, xiv, 12, 43, 117–126, 127
Reagan and Bush administrations, xii, 35, 43–44, 57
Reagan Democrats, 121
Reagan, Ronald, xiv, 13, 39, 117, 167 n.10
Renwick, Ed, 52–54, 144
Republicanism in the South, xiv
Rickey, Elizabeth A., 45, 100, 167 n.10
right-wing, 6, 151, 160
Robinson, W. S., 64, 84
Rockwell, George Lincoln, 6
roll call votes, 36, 45–47, 57
Roemer, Charles "Buddy", xiv; and behavior in office, 50, and Bush, 133; and defeat, 52, 117, 127, 131; and Duke, 18, 44, 59, 63, 138–139, 144, 160; and Edwards, 22, 50–51, 100; and the 1991 gubernatorial nomination, 100; and Holloway, 20, 167 nn. 11–12, 170 n.3 ; and party switching, 47, 50, 117, 131, 167 n.11; and support, 106, 111, 114, 131
Rose, Douglas, D., xiv, 16–17
Rosenstone, Steven, 105, 169 n.4
runoff elections, 7–8, 10, 14, 17–22, 51–52, 68, 104, 142, 155, 165 nn.2–3,
167 nn.11–12, 169 nn.3, 5, 7, 170 n.3

Schlesinger, Arthur M., 123
Schmich, Mary T., 141
Schroeder, Charles, 9
Schulman, Bruce J., 120
social welfare programs, 29, 90
Southern Organization for Unified Leadership (SOUL), 85
Southern Politics (Key), 88
Stanley, Harold W., 89, 105, 121
State-Times (Baton Rouge), 4, 7
statistical analysis; aggregate-level data analysis, 64, 67–71, 84; individual-level data analysis, 64, 84
"Stealth Duke vote," xi, 12. *See also* Duke, David Ernest: and "hidden" vote
Stewart, Jimmy, 42
Stimson, James A., 125

Tabb, David H., 28
Tate, Katherine, 105
Terradot, Bernard, xi
Theodoulou, Stella Z., 20
Thibodeaux, Joseph, 90
Thielemann, Gergory S., xv
Times-Picayune (New Orleans), 24, 31, 39, 45, 52, 57, 117, 136, 141, 144
Tocqueville, Alexis de, 126
Treen, David C., 7, 10, 19, 38–39, 44, 59, 68, 167 n.12
Treen, John, 169 n.1
True and Only Heaven: Progress and Its Critics (Lasch), 121
Two-Party South (Lamis), 67, 120

U.S. Census Bureau, 71
U.S. Department of Justice, 9, 166 n.5
ultraconservative, 20, 86
University of New Orleans Poll, 51–52, 54

Verba, Sidney, 66
Vital South (Black and Black), 118
Vitter, David, 47–48
vote-splitting phenomenon, 15
voter: mobilization, xiii; "qualifications tests," 9, 101; protest, 69, 136–137

Voter Research and Surveys, 136, 138, 140
voter turnout, 99-114; and age, 101; and education, 101, 105; and "fear," 110, 113–114; and race, 101, 107, 110-111, 113; and region, 101; and registration, 104–105, 111–113; and socioeconomic status, 101–102, 105, 113, and urbanization, 105
voting: blocs, 8, 10, 15, 19, 35, 47, 146, 155, 167 n.13; of blacks, xiv; rights, 12; rules, 127-128, 141; and "white backlash," xiii, 12, 23, 159; of "white" Democrats, xiv, 4, 8, 45, 130–134, 142, 144; of "white" Republicans, 110, 130–131, 133–134, 138, 144, 170 n.2
Voting Rights Act, 9–11, 23–24, 93, 96, 118–121, 166 n.5

Wall Street Journal, 171 n.2

Wallace, George, 43–44, 88–90, 118, 123
Wardlaw, Jack, 141
Washington Post, 90, 171 n.2
Washington, Harold, 102, 113
Weber, R., 69
Welch, Susan, 25
Whig, 119-120
White Citizen's Council. *See* Citizen's Council
White Power (Rockwell), 6
white supremacist, 4–5, 53, 86
Wilder, Douglas, 122
Wildgen, John K., xii
Wolfinger, Raymond, 100, 105, 169 n.4
Wright, James D., 69

Young, Andrew, 107

Zaller, John, 123, 166 n.7
Zatarain, Michael, 5

DAVID DUKE AND THE POLITICS OF RACE IN THE SOUTH

was composed electronically using
Trump Medieval types, with
display types in Bauer Bodoni.
The book was printed on acid-free, recycled
Glatfelter Natural paper, with 80-pound colored endsheets,
Smyth sewn, and bound over 88-point binder's boards
in Holliston Kingston cloth, with dust jackets printed in three colors
by Rose Printing Co., Inc.
Book and jacket designs are the work of Gary Gore.
Published by Vanderbilt University Press
Nashville, Tennessee 37235